MULTIPERSPECTIVE STUDIES O.
THEORY AND APPLICATION
—SELECTED PROCEEDINGS OF THE 8TH INTERNATIONAL FREE LINGUISTICS CONFERENCE

语言的多维视角研究：
理论与实践
——第八届国际跨学科语言学大会论文选集

主　编：赖良涛
副主编：阿玛·马哈布（澳）　王品
Edited by Liangtao Lai, Ahmar Mahboob and Pin Wang

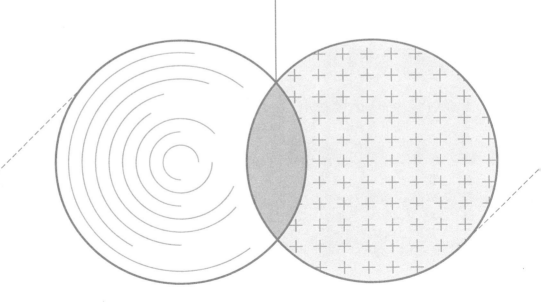

外语教学与研究出版社
FOREIGN LANGUAGE TEACHING AND RESEARCH PRESS
北京 BEIJING

图书在版编目（CIP）数据

  语言的多维视角研究 ：理论与实践 ：第八届国际跨学科语言学大会论文选集 ：英文 ／
赖良涛主编. —— 北京 ：外语教学与研究出版社，2016.7
  ISBN 978-7-5135-7851-6

  Ⅰ．①语…　Ⅱ．①赖…　Ⅲ．①语言学－国际学术会议－文集－英文　Ⅳ．①H0-53

  中国版本图书馆 CIP 数据核字（2016）第 177997 号

出 版 人　蔡剑峰
责任编辑　李婉婧
封面设计　彩奇风
出版发行　外语教学与研究出版社
社　　址　北京市西三环北路 19 号（100089）
网　　址　http://www.fltrp.com
印　　刷　北京九州迅驰传媒文化有限公司
开　　本　787×1092　1/16
印　　张　18.75
版　　次　2016 年 7 月第 1 版 2016 年 7 月第 1 次印刷
书　　号　ISBN 978-7-5135-7851-6
定　　价　59.90 元

购书咨询：（010）88819926　电子邮箱：club@fltrp.com
外研书店：https://waiyants.tmall.com
凡印刷、装订质量问题，请联系我社印制部
联系电话：（010）61207896　电子邮箱：zhijian@fltrp.com
凡侵权、盗版书籍线索，请联系我社法律事务部
举报电话：（010）88817519　电子邮箱：banquan@fltrp.com
法律顾问：立方律师事务所　刘旭东律师
　　　　　中咨律师事务所　殷　斌律师
物料号：278510001

About the Contributors

Aizhen Zhang is PhD and Associate Professor of English and Linguistics, Fujian Normal University, Fuzhou, China. She has been committed to the study of theoretical linguistics. Her latest articles include "Paradox and Logic of Natural Language" in *Journal of Xi'an International Studies University,* 2015, and "Semantic Fuzziness in the Perspective of Later Wittgenstein's Philosophy of Meaning" in *Journal of PLA University of Foreign Languages,* 2011.

Ambreen Shahnaz is a Lecturer at COMSATS Wah Campus as well as PhD Scholar at Fatima Jinnah Women University Rawalpindi. Her areas of interests are gender and language, language change and ELT. She has four research publications in international journals.

Bin Tang is Lecturer at the School of Foreign Languages of Southeast University, in Nanjing, China. He received his PhD in linguistics from Fudan University in Shanghai, China. His major areas of research interests include functional linguistics, discourse analysis and corpus-based language research.

Chengyu Liu is PhD and Professor of Linguistics at College of International Studies, Southwest University, Chongqing, China. His recent research interests include functional linguistics, discourse analysis, and translation studies. His recent publications include *A Functional-Cognitive Approach to Grammatical Metaphor* (monograph, Xiamen University Press, 2008), *Perspectives on Language* (co-edited with Wen Xu, Foreign Language Teaching and Research Press, 2012), *Academic Writing: Focus on Discovery* (co-authored with Martha Davis Patton, China Renmin University Press, 2015), *Language and Education* (trans.) (Vol. 9 of *Collected Works of M. A. K. Halliday*), Beijing Normal University Press, 2015).

Chunlei Yang is Associate Professor of Linguistics at Shanghai International Studies University, Shanghai, China. His research interests include theoretical linguistics (mainly syntax and semantics), computational linguistics and translation studies. He is one of the developers of Mandarin Grammar Online (ManGO). Recently, he has been working on contrastive linguistics and the deep linguistic processing of Mandarin Chinese based on Head-driven Phrase Structure Grammar (HPSG).

Dan Flickinger is Senior Researcher at the Center for the Study of Language and Information (CSLI) and project leader of the Linguistic Grammars Online (LinGO) Laboratory at CSLI, Stanford University, USA. His research interests include syntax and semantics in the framework of Head-driven Phrase Structure Grammar, Minimal Recursion Semantics (MRS) and deep linguistic processing. He is one of the main developers of several computational grammars including English Resource Grammar (ERG) and Mandarin Grammar Online.

Farah Riaz is Lecturer at COMSATS Wah Campus as well as PhD Scholar at COMSATS Islamabad Campus. Her areas of interest are business, management, finance and accounting. She has currently five conference papers and five journal publications; out of which three are in ISI indexed journals.

J R Martin is Professor of Linguistics at the University of Sydney. His research interests include systemic theory, functional grammar, discourse semantics, register, genre, multimodality and critical discourse analysis, focusing on English and Tagálog—with special reference to the transdisciplinary fields of educational linguistics, forensic linguistics and social semiotics. Professor Martin was elected a fellow of the Australian Academy of the Humanities in 1998, and was Head of its Linguistics Section from 2010-2012; he was awarded a Centenary Medal for his services to Linguistics and Philology in 2003. In April 2014 Shanghai Jiao Tong University opened its Martin Centre for Appliable Linguistics.

Jing Xu is Associate Professor in School of Foreign Languages and Literatures, Guizhou Minzu University. She got her PhD from Xiamen University, and has published nearly 20 papers in the areas of systemic functional linguistics, discourse analysis and English language teaching. She is now working on a provincial project *Research on Image-text Construction of Academic Institutional Identity and Cultivation on English Multi-literacy* (2014-2015), and is going to pursue her study at California State University, Sacramento as a postdoctoral fellow (1 Sept. 2015 - 1 Sept. 2016).

Jinjun Wang is PhD and Professor in School of Foreign Languages at Yunnan University, China. She has much interest in systemic functional linguistics, discourse analysis and sociolinguistics. For years, she has published books, dictionaries, and more than 40 journal articles, among which some made their appearance in international journals, such as *Discourse & Society*, *Discourse Studies*, *Language in Society* etc. Recently she has focused on environmental discourse analysis and the comparison of foreign language policies between China and ASEAN countries.

Juliane House is Emeritus Professor of Applied Linguistics, University of Hamburg and Director of Programs in Arts and Sciences at Hellenic American University, Athens, Greece. She was a founding member of the German Science Foundation's prestigious Research Centre on Multilingualism. She has published widely in the areas of contrastive pragmatics, discourse analysis, politeness, translation theory and English as a lingua franca. Her two latest books are *Translation: A Multidisciplinary Approach* (Palgrave Macmillan, 2014) and *Translation Quality*

Assessment: Past and Present, (Routledge, 2014).

Liangtao Lai is PhD in linguistics and Lecturer at the School of Foreign Languages, Shanghai Jiao Tong University, China. His research interests include systemic functional linguistics, educational linguistics, discourse analysis, and translation studies. He has published 14 papers and one book entitled *A Telos-oriented Model of Genre Analysis* (Xiamen University Press 2012), and has another book *Educational Linguistics: A Social Semiotic Approach* (Foreign Language Teaching and Research Press, 2015).

Lina Al-Mawajdeh is an MA holder graduated from Mutah University/Jordan in 2014. She is interested in comparative studies and sociolinguistics. Recently, she is a teacher at Ministry of Education, Jordan.

Michael Youles is a tutor at the Centre for English Language Education (CELE) at The University of Nottingham Ningbo, China (UNNC), teaching English for Academic Purposes since February 2009. His teaching career spans more than thirty years. In addition to teaching English, He also taught French and German, both to advanced level, while in the UK. Since coming to China, he has focused solely on teaching English and has developed a keen interest in certain aspects of the teaching of pronunciation.

Mohammad Al-Khawalda is Professor of Linguistics, Dept. of language and Linguistics, Mutah University/Jordan. He got his PhD in Linguistics-Syntax from Essex University/UK. In addition to his interest in syntax, he is interested in comparative studies, language & culture and translation.

Muhammad Kamal Khan is PhD and Assistant Professor of English at Shaheed BB University, Sheringal, Dir Upper, KP-Pakistan. Dr. Khan completed his PhD research at the School of English Language, Literature and Linguistics (SELLL), University of Newcastle, United Kingdom as visiting scholar. His research interests include Phonetics and Phonology, ELT and Teacher Training.

Qingye Tang is Professor in the English Department of School of Shanghai International Studies University. She got her MA degree from Central South University in 2000, PhD from Xiamen University in Foreign Linguistics and Applied Linguistics in 2005, and worked as a post-doctoral research fellow in Fudan University from 2006 to 2008; a visiting scholar in Florida University in 2008, and in Oxford University in 2010. The courses she taught include English Reading, English Writing, English Linguistics, English Rhetoric and Discourse Analysis. Her research interest involves systemic functional linguistics and discourse analysis.

Ryan T. Miller is Assistant Professor in the English Department at Kent State University. His research interests are second-language writing and reading. His research investigates development of academic and discipline-specific writing skills, and dual-language involvement and support of reading and its sub-skills.

Samina Amin Qadir, Vice Chancellor at Fatima Jinnah Women University, has extensive research publications. The researcher has attended many conferences worldwide and worked on administrative posts along with teaching.

Silvia Pessoa is Associate Teaching Professor of English and Sociolinguistics at Carnegie Mellon University in Qatar. Her research areas include literacy, academic writing development, and immigration studies. She has investigated the socio-cultural factors influencing literacy development in various settings and with various populations including immigrant adolescents in the U.S., college students in the U.S. and in Qatar, and migrant workers in Qatar.

Thomas D. Mitchell is Assistant Teaching Professor of English at Carnegie Mellon University in Qatar. His research interests include academic writing development, and the relationship between discourse, identity, and place.

Wei Zhang is PhD and Assistant Professor of Linguistics in the Department of English at The University of Akron, Ohio, USA. Her primary research interests are second language phonological acquisition, acoustic phonetics, TESOL teacher training, and TESOL program design.

Weizhen Chen is Professor of English & Linguistics, and Director of PhD Programs in English Language and Literature at Fujian Normal University, Fuzhou, China. He has over twenty publications in linguistics including two widely cited books *The Mirror of Human Mind: on Chomsky's Linguistic Ideas* (Academy Press, 1993) and *Categorization and Vagueness* (Fujian People's Publishing House, 2003).

Tangjin Xiao, PhD in linguistics and Professor of English language and literature, is Dean of College of Foreign Languages, Guizhou Minzu University, China. He has published over 40 academic papers in the areas of systemic functional grammar, translation, literature, and English teaching. His monograph is *English Modal Satellite Adverbs and Modality Supplementing in Discourse* (University of Electronic Science and Technology of China Press, 2009).

Xu Zhang is a postgraduate majoring in linguistics at College of International Studies, Southwest University. Her research interests include systemic functional linguistics and translation studies.

Bingjun Yang, formerly Professor at Southwest University, is now Professor of English linguistics at Shanghai Jiao Tong University. His research interests include systemic functional linguistics and translation studies. He has coauthored *Absolute Clauses in English from the Systemic Functional Perspective* recently published by Springer. He has published academic articles on such journals as *Translation Quarterly* (1999, 13-4; 2015, 4), *Language Sciences* (Elsevier Ltd., 2004, 3), *Journal of Personality Disorders* (The Guilford Press, 2007, 3),

Australian Journal of Linguistics (Taylor & Francis, 2014, 3), and *Journal of Quantitative Linguistics* (Taylor & Francis, 2015, 4)

Yongsheng Zhu is Professor of Fudan University and guest professor of Hangzhou Normal University. He has been Vice-chairman of China Association of Functional Linguistics ever since 1995. He served as Chairman of the Department of Foreign Languages at Suzhou University, Chairman of the Foreign Languages Department and Literature and Dean of the International Cultural Exchange School of Fudan University, Chairman of the board of the Confucius Institute at Stockholm University, member of the National English Teaching Advisory Committee, member of the Academic Accreditation Committee of the Chinese State Council, and member of the Executive Committee of the International Systemic Functional Linguistics Association. His research interests include systemic functional linguistics and discourse analysis.

Zhong Yang is professor of linguistics, School of Foreign Languages and Literature, Northeast Normal University. His research interests are functional linguistics and translation studies. He has published over 90 articles in academic journals and undertaken 5 research projects funded by the national or ministerial foundations. He has received the Tenth Annual Book Reward of China, first-class provincial reward for innovative teaching, and five provincial rewards for research in humanities and social sciences. He was the co-organizer of the 5th National Conference of Pragmatics, 7th National Conference of Functional Linguistics, and the organizer of the 6th National Conference of Cognitive Linguistics.

About the Editors

Liangtao Lai is PhD in linguistics and Lecturer at the School of Foreign Languages, Shanghai Jiao Tong University, China. He is also a member of the Academic Committee at the Martin Centre for Applicable Linguistics attached to the School. His research interests include systemic functional linguistics, educational linguistics, discourse analysis, and translation studies. He has published 15 papers and one book entitled *A Telos-oriented Model of Genre Analysis (Xiamen University Press 2012)*, and has another book *Educational Linguistics: a Social Semiotic Approach* in press.

Ahmar Mahboob teaches linguistics at the University of Sydney, Australia. Ahmar has a keen interest in critical language variation. His research focuses on different facets of how language variation relates to a range of educational, social, professional, and political issues. Ahmar has published seven authored/edited books, four special editions of journals, and over 60 papers and articles. He is the Co-Editor of TESOL Quarterly (with Brian Paltridge).

Pin Wang is PhD in linguistics and Lecturer in the School of Foreign Languages at Shanghai Jiao Tong University, China. He is also the Secretary of the Academic Committee at the Martin Centre for Applicable Linguistics attached to the School. His chief research interests are: Systemic Theory, Functional Grammar, and Functional Language Typology, with particular focus on classical languages (e.g. Sanskrit) and minority languages of China (e.g. Tibetan).

Contents

Part Three Social Linguistic Studies　173

Part Four Translation and Computational Linguistic Studies　249

Introduction

Since its establishment as an independent discipline in the early twentieth century, linguistics has undergone rapid development, as is witnessed by the great diversity of theories, methodologies, and practices in the area. This prosperity is, on the one hand, a blessing for all linguists considering the wealth of linguistic knowledge that we have gained, but on the other, leads to the segmentation of the discipline that should be an organic entirety. According to the Legitimation Coding Theory of Karl Maton (2014: 106), segmentalism in intellectual fields arises with the accumulation of new ideas or approaches that fail to integrate existing knowledge, which is caused by the strong classification and framing values both inside and outside the field. As an intellectual field, linguistics at its current state of development is also characterized by segmentalism, as is shown by the strong boundaries between different schools and subfields, and by the strong framing of research methods and procedures adopted in each school and subfield. Each school has its own premises, aim, methodology, theory, and practices that clearly demarcate its field and prevents trespassers with different backgrounds. As a result, different subfields have their own realms that are often mutually incompatible, which renders it difficult, if not impossible, to integrate them into a coherent unity. Scholars from different backgrounds no longer sit together to communicate; and even if we want, we find it difficult to understand each other as we speak different "languages". To facilitate further development of linguistics, we need to eliminate this segmentalism, cross the boundaries, and sit together to communicate with each other.

It is out of this belief that the Free Linguistics Conference (FLC) was initiated, which aims at providing a widely accessible forum for linguists in all areas of research to come together and share their diverse perspectives and findings. The 8th Annual International Free Linguistics Conference (the 8th FLC), held at the School of Foreign Languages, Shanghai Jiao Tong University, 26-27 September, 2014, is another significant step toward this aim. In this all-inclusive forum are congregated more than 180 scholars from more than 20 countries/regions. Presentations delivered cover a wide range of mainstream linguistics, including both theoretical linguistics (phonetics and phonology, lexicology, syntax, and semantics), and applied linguistics (such as sociolinguistics, educational linguistics, language teaching and acquisition, computational linguistics, translation studies, and discourse analysis), and involve more than ten languages such as English, German, Chinese, Arabic, Tagalog and Pashto. In one word, as trespassers of both geographical and intellectual borders, scholars with different intellectual backgrounds sit together, share their insights and discoveries, and make concerted efforts to further our studies of languages.

This book, *Multiperspective Studies of Language: Theory and Application*, is the fruition of the concerted efforts of the scholars presenting at the 8th FLC. It consists of 20 selected papers that are organized into four parts according to the subfields they belong to: theoretical linguistics, educational linguistics, social linguistics, translation studies and computational linguistics. All papers included in this volume were selected after going through a double-blind peer-review process.

Part One focuses on theoretical linguistic studies and includes six papers that deal with topics relating to phonology, lexis, grammar, and semantics. Zhong Yang's paper explores categorization in ancient Chinese philosophy and reveals the striking similarity between the experiential view of Chinese categorization and the view of modern cognitive linguistics and the importance of categorization as the basis of inference. Bingjun Yang shows the underlying similarity between the uses and structures of Chinese and English measure nominals and argues for the inappropriateness of the distinction between classifier and non-classifier languages as far as these two languages are concerned. Liangtao Lai reconsiders evidentiality within the SFL framework and maintains that evidentiality as a source of information is independent of epistemic modality, can be realized by various rank units and has different functions in specific contexts. Mohammad Al-Khawalda and Lina Al-Mawajdeh examine the conceptual and connotative meanings of body part words in Jordanian Arabic, and show the frequent use of their connotative meanings and the neglect of their conceptual meanings. Muhammad Kamal Khan examines the SOV word order and the complex syllable structure of Pashto as a proof of negation against the simplistic correlation between word order and syllable structure. The paper by Aizhen Zhang and Weizhen Chen reviews Russell's theory of types and Wittgenstein's logical symbolism as responses to Russel's set-theoretical paradox, and argues that Wittgenstein's theory of logical symbolism approaches Russell's paradox in a simpler yet more significant way than Russell's theory of types, though neither has achieved the goal of revealing the logic of natural language.

Part Two, comprising six papers, focuses on topics in educational linguistics, that is, it explores the applications of language studies in education. J. R. Martin introduces a practical model for managing specialized knowledge in schools based on the analysis of the power words, power grammar and power composition that characterize educational texts, and interpret the enacting of semantic waves that bridge between students' personal experience and esoteric knowledge. Yongsheng Zhu's paper reviews previous studies on the formative mechanisms of semantic waves and argues for spaciality as another mechanism in addition to theme, new information, temporality, semantic density and semantic gravity. Bin Tang draws on Martin's theorization of individuation (Martin 2010) to model the redistribution of literacy resources in society and explore its implications for school education. Wei Zhang's paper describes a Systemic Functional approach to content literacy incorporated in a TESOL teacher training program for in-service content teachers, with a view to raise their awareness of text complexity and their capacity of academic language teaching. Thomas Mitchell, Ryan Miller and Silvia Pessoa present a longitudinal case study of a student's development in his use of engagement resources (in SFL use of the term) to incorporate and interpret source texts and manage alternative voices in university history writing. Michael Youles proposes "pinyinising", an adaptation of "Hanyu Pinyin" on the basis of International Phonetic Alphabet, as an effective means to help Chinese students improve their pronunciation of the weak forms and linking in English speaking.

Part Three includes five papers that explore topics in social linguistics studies. Juliane House examines the role of English as a global lingua franca (ELF) and people's worry about its "threat" to multilingualism and translation, and suggests a compromise position of neither bedeviling ELF nor welcoming it naively and uncritically. Qingye Tang's paper examines the self-representation of old-generation Chinese migrant workers on the basis of a small interview corpus, and reveals their rejection of the name "migrant workers" as a stigma, their strong sense of in-group solidarity and sense of negative otherness against hostile outer groups. Jinjun Wang analyzes the matization and nominalization as two strategies for national identity construction as shown in news reports by Chinese and Canadian press about the takeover of Nexen Oil Company. Ambreen Shahnaz, Samina Amin Qadir and Farah Riaz explore gender construction in Pakistani children's literature on the basis of a corpus and reveal a strong presence of gender bias against females. Jing Xu explores strategies for inter-modal construction of institutional identity in multimodal discourses of print ads and academic journals, and argues for the role of semiotic modes other than language in identity construction.

Finally, Part Four includes three papers that focus on language translation and computation. Tangjin Xiao's paper suggests Pinyin expressions as a reflection of nominalization in Chinese-to-English translation of national culture, which can condense meanings, convey unique Chinese culture and help materialize discourse ideology. Chengyu Liu and Xu Zhang discuss Howard Goldblatt's manipulation in his translation of *Red Sorghum* (a masterpiece of the Nobel Prize winner Mo Yan) to cater to target readers' cultural preferences through a comparative transitivity analysis of the source and target texts. Chunlei Yang and Dan Flickinger introduce the methodology of grammar engineering for deep linguistic processing and their development of a computational Chinese grammar—Mandarin Grammar Online in the syntactic framework of head-driven phrase structure grammar using the semantic representation of Minimal Recursion Semantics.

Topics in this book not only cover different subfields, but are also discussed from multiple perspectives and grounded in different theoretical frameworks. Theories drawn upon in the book include systemic functional linguistics, cognitive linguistics, critical discourse analysis, social semiotics, sociology of education, set theory in mathematics, formal logic, computer science, and language engineering, etc. These are combined with a variety of research methods such as theoretical disputation, questionnaire, interview, corpus, statistics, longitudinal case study, mathematical demonstration, and modelling. These features are the result of the concerted efforts of the authors to break the borders between different subfields and share their findings with colleagues who work in other areas of language sciences. Thus, the book, like a piece of polyphonic music, is a sign of heteroglossia in which each author voices their respective positions and dialogizes with each other at the same time and reflects the foundation principles of the Free Linguistics Conference.

References

Maton, K. 2014. *Knowledge and Knowers: Towards a Realist Sociology of Education*. London and New York: Routledge.

Martin, J. R. 2010. Semantic variation: Modelling realisation, instantiation and individuation in social semiosis. In M. Bednarek and J. R. Martin (eds.), *New Discourse on Language: Functional Perspectives on Multimodality, Identity and Affiliation*. 1-34. London: Continuum.

Part One
Theoretic Linguistic Studies

An Exploration into Conceptions of Category in Ancient Chinese Philosophy

Zhong Yang

Northeast Normal University, China

1. Introduction

Categories refer to "the basic and general concepts of thought, language and reality" (Bunnin and Yu 2001: 142). Understood as such, categories are essential to cognition. The process of construing experience in terms of categories is fundamental in human cognition. The position of categorization in cognition is clearly expressed by Taylor (2003: vi): "All living creatures, even the lowest, possess the ability to categorize. In order to survive, a creature has to be able, at the very least, to distinguish what is edible from what is inedible, what is benign from what is harmful". He points out that categorization serves to reduce the complexity of the environment.

Categories as concepts construe experience, while subcategories reflect re-construal of experience. Sub-categorization as a cognitive process extends human knowledge. Both categories and subcategories are realized lexically. The study of categories has been an academic arena in many disciplines, including linguistics, psychology and philosophy. Aristotle started the philosophical exploration into categories. Almost in the same historical period, the School of Logicians in China's Warring States period explored the ideas of categories and sub-categories.

This paper first explores, based on data from some Chinese classics, the initiation of the ideas of categories and subcategories from a linguistic perspective and then discusses the function of categorization in reasoning and the position of speculating category in Chinese philosophy of language.

2. The conception of category in Moist thinking

In Chinese epistemology, the relation between language and reality was an important topic during the Warring States period. Due to drastic changes of the society, there appeared to be noncorrespondence between names and actualities. Philosophers at the time strived to rectify names (Jiang 2008). One of them was Mo Zi (?468-376 B.C.). He stressed that judgment or inference about things was based on classification. There are different ways to categorize things, but the features or the properties of a category must be specified. This idea is explicitly addressed in Jing Shuo Xia in *Mo* (1999: 28):

> What is the unique feature that distinguishes an ox from a horse? Does it make sense to say that the two are different because an ox has teeth and a horse has a tail? No. Both of them have teeth and a tail. They are not in the same class, because an ox has horns and a horse does not. It is horns that distinguish the two kinds. It would be confusing to take teeth and tail for distinguishers of the two classes. (牛与马唯异，以牛有齿，马有尾，说牛之非马也，不可。是俱有。不偏有偏无有。曰牛与马不类，用牛有角，马无角，是类不同也。若举牛有齿，马有尾，以是为类不同也，是狂举也。)

He emphasized the importance of categorization in judgment and argument in these remarks in Xiao Qu in *Mo* (1999: 29):

> To argue means to tell right and wrong, to examine similarities and differences, to judge the correspondence of names and actualities, to tell benign from harmful and to clarify confusion… Names must be in keeping with actualities, intentions must be expressed through proper wording, and causes must be explained. Communication is not possible without categories. (夫辩者，将以名是非之分，审治乱之纪，名同异之处，察名实之礼，处利害，决嫌疑。……以名举实，以辞抒意，以说出故。以类取，以类予。)

The above citations show clearly that Mo Zi speculated on the concept of category and its importance in linguistic communication.

3. The conception of subcategory in Gongsun Long's paradox "a white horse, not a horse"[1]

Gongsun Long (325 B.C.-250 B.C.) is one of the representatives of the School of Logicians during the Warring States period. One of his essays that have been passed on till today is "Discourse on a White Horse", of which he was most proud. Kong Chuan said to him, "I hear that you are truly learned, and I have long hoped that I can be your student. But I do not agree with you at the thesis 'A white horse, not a horse'. If you please discard that thesis I will plead for acceptance of me as a student of yours." Gongsun Long replied, "What you said is illogical.

I made my name because of my thesis is on a white horse. If I discard it then I have nothing to teach." (Gongsun 1999: 47)

"Discourse on a White Horse" was written in a dialogue form, composed of 493 characters. Here is the translated text:

A: Is it logical to say "A white horse, not a horse"?

B: Yes.

A: Why?

B: The word horse has sense of shape; the word white denotes a color. Denoting a color is different from denoting a shape. Therefore the saying is valid.

A: If there is a white horse, it cannot be said that there is no horse. If "there is a white horse" means "there is a horse", how can you say "A white horse, not a horse"?

B: If you want a horse, then either a yellow horse or a black one will do. If you ask for a white horse, then neither a yellow one nor a black one will do. When you say a white horse is a horse, you overlook color. When color is overlooked, a white horse is a horse. If you overlook color, a yellow horse or a black one will do, but if you consider color, neither will. That is why it is valid to say "a white horse, not a horse".

A: If you think a horse with color is not a horse, and there are no horses without color, then can you say there are no horses on earth?

B: Certainly all horses have color, thus there are white horses. If horses do not have color, how is it possible to have a white horse? So whiteness is separate in sense from horse. "A white horse" is composed of both white and horse. The integration of the sense white and the sense horse denotes the reference of the word horse. Therefore it is valid to say "a white horse, not a horse".

A: A horse without a white color is a horse, a white color exists independently from a horse. White horse is a compound name of horse and white. So it is not valid to say "a white horse, not a horse".

B: If you think "if there is a white horse, there is a horse" is valid, what about "if there is a white horse, there is a yellow horse"?

A: That is not valid.

B: So "there is a yellow horse" is different from "there is a horse". That is to say a yellow horse is different from a horse. If a yellow horse is different from a horse, then it is absolutely absurd on earth to say a white horse is a horse.

"If there is a white horse, there is a horse" is valid when color is overlooked. As whiteness is separate from horse, "a white horse" is not the same as "a horse".

Whiteness is not specific. It exists although it can be overlooked. "A white horse" denotes specific color of a horse. The white color of a horse is not whiteness as a separate category. "A horse" doe not denote color, so a yellow horse or a black one will do if a horse is needed. "A white horse" denotes color, so when a white horse is needed, neither a yellow one nor a black one will do. Since a name with color is distinctive from one without color, "a white horse, not a horse" is a valid thesis (translated by the author from "Discourse on a White Horse" in *Gongsun* (1999: 47-48).

The intention of the essay has been interpreted differently by Chinese philosophers. Chen (2007) holds that the purpose is for sophistry. Feng (1996) interprets that the intention of the essay is to argue for metaphysical concepts by objectifying abstract entities.

From a cognitive linguistic point of view, *horse* represents a category, *white horse*, a subcategory. The latter contains a distinguishing semantic feature [whiteness]. The more semantic features a linguistic sign contains, the narrower its scope of reference, and vice versa. Understood in this way, it is beyond doubt that the paradox is meant to argue that "a white horse" is not equivalent to "a horse". It can therefore be inferred that the intention of putting forward the paradox is to argue for the distinction between the concept of category and that of subcategory.

This interpretation can be supported by intertexual analysis of "Discourse on Hardness and Whiteness" by Gongsun Long. Below are the relevant remarks (cited and translated from "Separation of Hardness and Whiteness" in *Gongsun* (1999: 46):

A: Is it right to say hardness, whiteness, and stone represent three kinds of concept?

B: No.

A: Two kinds?

B: Yes.

A: Why?

B: "A hard stone" or "a white stone" contains two elements. ...Through seeing whiteness is perceived in a white stone leaving out hardness; through touching hardness is felt in a hard stone unnoticing whiteness... Hardness exists independently and in the meantime is possessed as a feature of things. It may be a feature of stones but it is not possessed by stones alone. So is whiteness. If it does not exist separately how can it whiten stones and other things？(曰：坚、白、石，三，可乎？曰：不可。曰：二，可乎？曰：可。曰：何哉？曰：无坚得白，其举也二；无白得坚，其举也二。视不得其所坚而得所白者，无坚也；拊不得其所白而得其所坚者，无白也。……坚未与石为坚，而物兼。未与物为坚，而坚必坚。其不坚石、物而坚。……白故不能自白，恶能白石、物乎。)

From these remarks it can be seen that Gongsun Long regards qualities as entities and analyzes the distinction and the relation between qualities and objects. In the two texts, whiteness is seen as separate entity distinctive from object and from other qualities. Once an object contains a particular quality, it represents a subcategory of the category to which it belongs. So "a white horse" is not equivalent to "a horse", "a white stone" not "a stone". What we find in Gongsun Long's discourses is that the object of analysis is a noun phrase rather than a noun analyzed by Mo Zi, such as horse and ox. Mo Zi addressed on the concept of category and the features that distinguish categories, while Master Gongsun Long's discourses touched upon the relation between category and subcategory, and qualities as entities within a subcategory. Epistemologically, cognition is finding relations between objects or entities within an object. The objects we are cognizant of include what we think of, refer to, or what is represented by a sign, including things, processes, relations, qualities, etc. (Schlick 2005).

4. Experiential basis of categorization

What is implied in Gongsun Long's discourses is an experientialist view of categorization. He speculated that the perception of hardness and whiteness is through different senses, namely, seeing and touching. Hardness and whiteness as separate entities do not exist independently from the human mind. Qualities as abstract entities result from interaction between man and nature.

This experientialist view of categorization is explicitly expounded later by Xun Zi (?313-238) (cited and translated from "Rectification of Names" in *Xun* (1999: 26):

On what basis can we differentiate things? On the basis of senses. Things of the same kind that have the same qualities are perceived through the senses as the same category. Analogy is valid when things of different kinds are compared. That is due to the fact that the conventional names can be understood. Eyes differentiate shape, volume, color, and texture. Ears distinguish various voices and sounds. The tongue tells all kinds of taste, such as sweet, bitter, salty, pungent, sour, etc. The nose gets fragrance, stink, stench, and other smells. The body feels pain, itching, heat, smoothness, sharpness, lightness and heaviness. The mind tells pleasantness, happiness, anger, sorrow, joy, like and dislike. The mind takes cognizance of all the information after the senses perceive information into categories.

（何缘而以同异？曰：缘天官。凡同类同情者，其天官之意物也同；故比方之疑似而通，是所以共有约名以相期也。形体、色理以目异；声音清浊，调竽、奇声以耳异；甘、苦、咸、淡、辛、酸、奇味以口异；香、臭、芬、郁、腥、臊、漏庮、奇臭以鼻异；疾、痒、凔、热、滑、铍、轻、重以形体异；说、故、喜、怒、哀、乐、爱、恶、欲以心异。心有征知。征知，则缘耳而知声可也，缘目而知形可也。然而征知必将待天官之当薄其类，然后可也。）

Wang (2007) points out that Xun Zi held an experientialist view of cognition, which is similar to the view of cognitive linguists today, "reality→cognition→language". He explicates Xun Zi's understanding of the cognitive process as "perception of categories through senses→cognizance of information by the brain→linguistic representations".

Lakoff (1989: 198) argues, in rejecting an objectivist view of meaning, that color categories do not exist independently from human cognition. "Colors arise from our interaction with the world[......] Colors are categories of mind that do not exist objectively in the world exclusive of seeing beings." He further points out that color results from human cognition in two respects: color categorization is partly a matter of cultural convention since different cultures have different boundaries for basic color categories; color categorization involves human physiology.

Halliday and Matthiessen (1999: 68) presents a similar view of categorization:

> Categorization is often thought of as a process of classifying together phenomena that are inherently alike, the classes being as it were given to us by the nature of the experience itself. But this is not what really happens. Categorization is a creative act: it transforms our experience into meaning, and this means imposing a categorical order rather than putting labels on an order that is already there.

In summary, we find close similarities between interpretations of the process and the basis of categorization by Gongsun Long and Xun Zi and the views of categorization held by contemporary Western linguists.

5. Categorization as basis of inference

Chinese philosophers conjecture that the idea of categorization can be traced back to the end of the Shang Dynasty and the beginning of the Zhou. *The Book of Changes* originated in that period. Methodologically, the book was based on classification. All phenomena were put into 64 categories, named *gua*, each of them into 6 kinds, named *yao*. Each category is represented by a combination of solid lines and dotted lines. Solid lines symbolize *yang*, dotted lines symbolize *yin*. *Yang* represents masculinity, positivity, and strength; *yin* represents femininity, negativity, and weakness. The diagram of the supreme (*taiji tu*) resembles the transformation of *yin* and *yang*. The book's main idea is to account for changes, to predict what would happen (Shi 2010).

While categorization as the basis of reasoning in *The Book of Changes* was still implicit, categories as basis of deductive reasoning was explicit in form in Aristotle's syllogism. A syllogism is a formally valid inference to a conclusion from two premises. For example:

> Major premise: All men are mortal.
> Minor premise: Socrate is a man.
> Conclusion: Socrate is mortal.

This syllogism contains two premises, in both of which there is a middle term *man (men)*. The major premise points out the quality of the category, while the minor premise identifies the subject as a member of the category. Then the conclusion states that the subject possesses the quality of the category. It is obvious that the whole process of deductive reasoning is formally based on a category. Logical studies in the past focus on the regularities of syllogism, while discussion of its categorical basis is rare.

In ancient Chinese philosophy, analogy as a form of reasoning, in contrast to syllogism, was frequently used. This can be exemplified by "Yan Zi as an Envoy to Chu". During the Warring States period, Yan Zi (?-500 B.C.) was sent by Qi as an envoy to Chu. He was a short man. Chu plotted to insult him from the start of the reception. A small door had been specially prepared for him upon his arrival at the palace. He refused wittily, saying that only one from the Kingdom of Dog goes through it. Then the king of Chu intrigued at the banquet to ridicule him. Someone was grabbed to the hall. The king asked who he was. The guards reported that he was a thief from Qi. The king turned to Yan Zi, "Are people from Qi good at stealing?" Yan Zi stood up and said, "I hear that tangerines that are grown in South Huai are called *ju* and in North Huai called *zhi* (trifoliate orange), the trees look alike but the fruits taste different. Why? Because the environments are different. Now this man was not a thief in Qi, but in Chu he is caught as a thief. Isn't it true that the environment of Chu produces thieves?" The king smiled and said, "It's no good kidding you." (Yan 1999: 60)

An analogy is a form of inference based on similarities between two categories. Halliday and Matthiessen (1999: 68) gives a most succinct account for the use of analogy:

> There would be indefinitely many ways of construing analogies among different elements in the total flux of experience; what our semantic resources enable us to do is to construe those analogies which yield categories resonating with what as a species, and as members of a particular culture, we have found to carry material and symbolic value.

In the above example, Yan Zi built a strong argument on analogical reasoning. The relation between plants and environment is mapped on to the domain of people and society. The basis of the analogy is the categorical distinction of *ju* and *zhi*.

In summary, analogy is a free form of reasoning. It is, different from syllogism, based on categories rather than one category. The similarities between categories in the analogy are construed by the speaker/writer and highlighted in the discourse. In other words, the similarities do not exist independent from human cognition. Analogies are instances of creative language use. That explains to a great extent why analogies are so abundantly used in Chinese classics and poetry.

6. Speculating categories as an embryonic stage of Chinese philosophy of language

In Section 2 it was pointed out that Gongsun Long revealed the relation between category and subcategory in arguing for the validity of his famous paradoxical proposition "a white horse, not a horse". That shows that early Chinese thinkers were already on the way to metaphysical exploration into form and meaning of language, a question that was discussed by Greek philosophers. It is worth mentioning, in passing, that there was not a link verb at the time that is equivalent to "be" in English. The character *shi* (是) was a pronoun, which became a link verb in Chinese approximately after 100 A.D. (Wang 1989). In ancient Chinese, propositions could be expressed without "*shi*", canonically in the pattern "… *zhe* (者), … *ye* (也)." There was, however, a character *fei* (非) to negate a sentence. Nevertheless, *fei* is not always equal in meaning to "be not". In addition, definition is canonically expressed by positive statements, not by negative statements. Based on these considerations it can be rejected that Gongsun Long's purpose for putting forward the paradox was simply for sophistry. He actually speculated on the relation between form and meaning, category and subcategory, things and properties as entities.

It was the School of Logicians that turned the relation between linguistic forms and actualities into content of speculation. In other words, the school of logicians initiated theoretical linguistics in China (Shao and Fang 1991). What is regrettable is that the teachings of the school had been discontinued due to complicated historical reasons while Confucianism and Daoism exerted strong influence for centuries. Neither Confucians nor Taoists clearly defined key concepts of their doctrines. "The Tao that can be expressed in words is not the true and eternal Tao; the name that can be uttered in words is not the true and eternal name" (Lao Zi 2008:59). The character *ren* (仁), which represents a key concept of Confucianism, appears 109 times in *The Analects* (Liu 2014) without definition. Philosophers of both schools emphasize true understanding and behavior in accordance rather than analysis. This leads to divergence of ancient Chinese philosophy and Greek philosophy. As explained by Liu (2014), what leads to divergence of "Logos" and "Tao", two similar fundamental concepts, is verbalization. What is verbalized can be analyzed. That is probably why in Chinese philosophy analysis is not attached as much importance as in Western philosophy. There are descriptions of omnipresence of Tao by followers of Lao Zi, but not definitions. As a result, Chinese people today talk about existence of Tao in all walks of life, Tao of governance, Tao of business, Tao of being, Tao of teaching, Tao of healthy life, Tao of friendship, etc., but few can generalize what that kind of Tao is.

In summary, speculation of category and subcategory is the starting point of Chinese philosophy of language. But due to irrelevance to governance, the ideas of the School of Logicians were not given due attention. Due to emphasis on the relation between understanding and behavior, the main streams of ancient Chinese philosophy neglect definition of key concepts. Consequently, Chinese metaphysical studies of language and reality stagnated after its embryonic stage.

7. Conclusion

The conception of category and subcategory is explored in classic Chinese philosophical texts. It is shown that the idea of category was discussed by Mo Zi, and the conception of subcategory addressed by Gongsun Long. The basis of categorization was discussed by Xun Zi, who held an experientialist view of cognition that is remarkably similar to the view of cognitive linguistics today. In addition, the contribution of categorization to inferences is analyzed, such as syllogism and analogy, both of which are based on categories. But analogies are based on categories, while syllogism on one category. The study of category was initiated by Aristotle in a logical-philosophical context. It is found that ancient Chinese philosophers, particularly the School of Logicians, also explored the concept of category and made use of categories in inference. In ancient Chinese philosophy, the study of category originated from the study of language and reality but it stagnated after its embryonic stage. Exploring categorical thinking in ancient Chinese philosophy may help to gain insights into convergence and divergence of Chinese and Western epistemology.

Acknowledgement

This paper is supported by China Fund for Humanities and Social Sciences under the project "A Study of Grammatical Metaphor in English and Chinese from the Perspective of Semogenesis" (Approval No.: 12BYY008).

Notes

1. The Chinese character 非 negates the predicate. In ancient Chinese at the time, there was not a link verb equivalent to "be", the character 是 was a pronoun then. This author translates " 白马非马 " into " A white horse, not a horse" rather than " A white horse is not a horse", because the latter as a contradictory statement does not convey the paradoxical meaning in the original proposition.

References

Bunnin, N. and Jiyuan Yu. 2001. *Dictionary of Western Philosophy*, Beijing: Renmin Press.

Chen, Bo. 2007. *What Is Logic?* (2nd ed.). Beijing: Beijing University Press.

Feng, Youlan. 1996. *A Concise History of Chinese Philosophy* (中国哲学简史). Beijing: Beijing University Press.

Gongsun, Long. 1999. *The Book of Master Gongsun Long* (公孙龙子). Bejing: Chinese Literature Press.

Halliday, M. A. K. and C. M. I. M. Matthiessen. 1999. *Construing Experience Through Meaning: A Language-based Approach to Cognition*. Beijing: World Book Publishing.

Jiang, Guozhu. 2008. *A History of Chinese Epistemology* (中国认识论史). Wuhan: Wuhan University Press.

Lakoff, G. 1989. *Women, Fire, and Dangerous Things: What Categories Reveal About the Mind*. Chicago and Lodon: The University of Chicago Press.

Lao, Zi. 2008. *The Book of Tao and Teh* (Revised ed.). Beijing: Beijing University Press.

Liu, Limin. 2014. The verbalization of "Tao" and "Logos": differences of Chinese and Western thinking from a linguistic perspective ("道" 与 "Logos" 之 "说" ——中西思想文化差异的语言视角). *Contemporary Foreign Language Studies* 6: 59-67.

Mo, Di. 1999. *The Book of Master Mo* (墨子). Beijing: Chinese Literature Press.

Schlick, M. 2005. *General Theory of Knowledge* (普通认识论). Beijing: The Commercial Press.

Shao, Jingmin and Jingmin Fang. 1991. *A History of Chinese Theoretical Linguistics* (中国理论语言学史). Shanghai: Eastern China Normal University Press.

Shi, Ningzhong. 2010. Proposition, definition and inference in ancient Chinese philosophy. *Frontiers of Philosophy in China*, 5(3): 414-431.

Taylor, J. 2003. *Linguistic Categorization* (3rd edition). Oxford: Oxford University Press.

Wang, Li. 1989. *A History of Chinese Grammar* (汉语语法史). Beijing: The Commercial Press.

Wang, Yin. 2007. *A Contrastive Exploration into Chinese and Western Semantic Theories* (中西语义理论对比研究初探). Beijing: Higher Education Press.

Xun, Kuang. 1999. *The Book of Master Xun*（ 荀子 ）. Beijing: Chinese Literature Press.

Yan, Ying. 1999. *Spring and Autumn Annals of Master Yan* (晏子春秋). Beijing: Chinese Literature Press.

Measure Nominals in English and Chinese from the Perspective of Systemic Functional Linguistics

Bingjun Yang

Shanghai Jiao Tong University, China

1. Introduction

"Describing a sentence as a construction of words is rather like describing a house as a construction of bricks, without recognizing the walls and the rooms as intermediate structural units" (Halliday and Matthiessen 2014: 362). Similarly, describing a group as a construction of words makes the description too simple, without revealing the internal structure and function of the group. This is particularly true to nominal group which functions as measuring in both English and Chinese, i.e. measure nominals under the category of Numeratives.

There are two types of Numeratives: quantifying Numerative which specifies either an exact number (e.g. *three books*) or an inexact number (e.g. *many books*), ordering Numerative which specifies either an exact place in order (e.g. *the second game*) or an inexact place (e.g. *a forthcoming game*). In theories other than Systemic Functional Linguistics (SFL henceforth), quantifying Numeratives are discussed under the category of count/mass nouns. It is generally believed that the count/mass distinction applies to most languages but differences are obvious, so those languages in which classifiers are not obligatory for nouns are called non-classifier languages and those in which classifiers are obligatory are called classifier languages (See Allan 1977; Wu and Bodomo 2009). Note that classifier here is different from the functional term "Classifier" in SFL, which refers to the subclass of a thing other than quantity (e.g. *electronic* in "electronic device"). Following such distinction, Chinese is treated by many scholars as a typical classifier language and English a typical non-classifier language.

In this article, we will argue against this distinction by revealing the similarities in structure and function of measure nominals in English and Chinese. First, we will provide a sketch of measure nominals in English and Chinese. Then we will discuss the structure and function of them from the perspective of SFL. Through the perspective of SFL, we will see why such a distinction as classifier and non-classifier language is not well-grounded for Chinese and English.

2. A sketch of measure nominals

2.1 Measure nominals in English

In English grammar books, nouns are divided into count nouns and mass nouns. Count nouns refer to entities which present themselves naturally in discrete and countable units, while mass nouns refer to substances which do not present themselves in such units. In the case of count nouns, a numeral can be put in front of the noun (e.g. *two books*). Mass nouns usually cannot be preceded by a numeral. In order to be counted, mass nouns have to be preceded by measure words, e.g. *three bottles of milk*. Such groups of English for mass nouns are called measure nominals. Measure nominals may include those groups formed for count nouns, but in this article we focus mainly on the construction "numeral + measure word + noun".

Measure nominals include both measure partitives and general partitives. The former relates to precise quantities denoting length, area, volume, and weight (e.g. *a mile of cable*), and the latter relates to other quantities (e.g. *a crowd of people*) (Quirk et al. 1985: 251). Measure words, if to include both measure partitives and general partitives, equal classifiers by other linguists (Allan 1977; Lehrer 1986). According to Lehrer (1986), classifiers in English can be put into the following categories by combining Keith Allan's taxonomies with Eloise Jelinek's proposal:

(1) Unit counters: *two head of cattle*
(2) Fractional classifiers: *three quarters of the cake*
(3) Number set classifiers: *dozens of birds*
(4) Collective classifiers: *two clumps of grass*
(5) Varietal classifiers: *two species of wheat*
(6) Measure classifiers: *one liter of wine*
(7) Arrangement classifiers: *two rows of beans*
(8) Metaphorical comparison classifiers: *a bear of a man*

This taxonomy is illuminating in understanding measure nominals, which usually denote a part of a whole. The structure of these nominals is basically the same, except that metaphorical comparison classifier is special and needs to be treated separately. However, a very important issue is what is the status of "of noun" in these nominals. "In most cases *of* cannot be replaced by another preposition, nor can it be paraphrased as a compound which reverses the order of the two nouns" (Lehrer 1986: 110). But is "of noun" a Postmodifier of the measure word? If so, is it a downranked prepositional phrase?

2.2 Measure nominals in Chinese

Wang Li, as a leading scholar in modern Chinese linguistics, was very interested in measure nominals. In his monograph published in 1985, Wang (1985: 260-275) proposed that measure nominals in Chinese can be put into six types: natural units (e.g. *liang zhi lao hu,* "two tigers"), collective units (e.g. *si yang guo pin,* "four kinds of fruit"), units of length, volume, weight and monetary units (e.g. *er qian ren shen,* "two qian of ginseng"), container (e.g. *yi bei jiu,* "a cup of liquor"), units about writing (e.g. *yi feng shu xin,* "a letter"), event units out of actions (e.g. *yi zhen ling sheng,* "a whirlwind"). A different categorization was then put forward by Lu Jianming (Lu 1987), who classified measure words in modern Chinese into four categories: action (e.g. *ci, tang, zhen*); time (e.g. *tian, nian, miao*); unit (e.g. *jin, chi*); nominal (e.g. *ge, zhang, zhi, tiao, wan, bei*). Lu's categorization avoids the overlapping and simplicity in Wang"s categories (e.g. units about writing as a subcategory), but the action type and the nominal type are still too general. Some measure words serve as typical cases in both the action type and the nominal type, e.g. "zhang" in *yi zhang gong* ("a bow", action) and *yi zhang zhuozi* ("a table", nominal).

About five years later, a more comprehensive categorization was put forward by Shi Xiyao. Shi (1992) put measure nominals in Chinese into two general categories: individual and collective. Measure nominals for individual things are related to the shape of a thing, the activity of an event, the prominent component of a thing, the container of a thing, the measuring unit of something, and the combining of something (Shi 1992: 38-46).

(9) Shape measure nominal: *yi pian xue hua* (a flake of snow)

(10) Activity measure nominal: *liang tiao shui* (two shoulders of water)

(11) Component measure nominal: *san tou niu* (three heads of cow)

(12) Container measure nominal: *si ping jiu* (four bottles of liquor)

(13) Unit measure nominal: *wu dun mi* (five tons of rice)

(14) Other measure nominal: *liu wei yao* (six tastes of medicine)

For shape measure nominals, the size of the shape or the shape itself may be perceived differently, so such expressions as *yi pian yun* (a piece of cloud) and *yi pian shu ye* (a piece of leaf) are all acceptable. However, some shape measure nominals are peculiar in that the measure words in them seem to be contradictory in meaning to the shape of the noun. For example, *yi tiao beizi* (a strip of quilt, the actual meaning is "a quilt") is acceptable but *yi pian beizi* (a piece of quilt) is not. Some nouns are quite different in shape but they may collocate with the same measure words. For example, *yi kuai shi tou* (a lump of stone) is acceptable and *yi kuai biao* (a watch) is too.

For activity measure nominals, some measure words which originally describe activity may collocate with nouns which are not directly related to activity. For example, in *liang tiao shui* the measure word *tiao* originates from the activity of shouldering water and in *wu zhang zui* the measure word *zhang* originates from the activity of opening mouth. But note that some usages may be different. For example, in *yi zhang zhuozi* the measure word *zhang* does not do anything with activity.

For container measure nominals, the choice of the measure word sometimes depends on the actual container in context. So *yi bei jiu* (one glass of liquor), *yi ping jiu* (one bottle of liquor), *yi wan jiu* (one bowl of liquor), *yi tong jiu* (one barrel of liquor) are all good collocations. The measure words may extend to any container that can hold the thing, so we have the following:

(15) yi bao jiu (one bag of liquor)

　　yi he jiu (one box of liquor)

　　yi xiang jiu (one case of liquor)

　　yi gang jiu (one jar of liquor)

　　yi chepi jiu (one wagon of liquor)

Note that some expressions seem to be container measure nominals but they are in fact metaphorical. For example, *yi lian yang guang, yi du zi mo shui, yi tao han shui*. The word *yi* (one) in such expressions basically means "whole" and it is not a numeral.

Measure nominals for collective things are further classified into two categories: those for pairs and those for groups.

(16) Pair measure nominals: *liang shuang xiezi* (two pairs of shoes)

(17) Group measure nominals: *liang pai liu shu* (two rows of willow)

Pair measure nominals are restricted to nouns in which two components of things always appear together, and the measure words for them include *dui, shuang, fu*, etc. For group measure nominals, the measure words vary with the nouns and there are a large number of such measure words in Chinese: *san fu pai* (three packs of poker), *san tao jia ju* (three sets of furniture), *san qun ren* (three crowds of people), *san luo tou fa* (three strands of hair), *san wo ma que* (three nests of sparrow), *san dui sha zi* (three piles of sand) etc.

So far we have briefly reviewed measure nominals in Chinese. The question is: whether a measure word is mandatory or not to measure nominals in Chinese? Before we can provide our answer to the question, it is helpful to turn to the distinction between classifier language and non-classifier language.

2.3 Classifier or non-classifier?

The languages of the world can be divided into two groups with regard to numeral classifiers: those that have classifiers, such as the majority of languages in East and Southeast Asia, and those that do not, such as most European languages, including English (Allan 1977; Greenberg 1990). To put it simple, a language in which a measuring expression is usually composed of a numeral and a noun is called a non-classifier language, and a classifier language is one in which a measure nominal is usually composed of a numeral, a classifier (i.e. measure word) and a noun. It is widely believed that in Chinese all nouns are like mass nouns in the sense that, in order for a noun to be counted, a measure word is mandatory.

Upon discussing measuring words in Chinese, some scholars identify two categories: classifier and massifier (e.g. Cheng and Sybesma 1998). The former forms a closed class and it is only used to distinguish nouns that are cognitively singularizable (i.e. count nouns). The latter does not form a closed class and it is used to create counting units for nouns that are cognitively non-singularizable. This view is illuminating in understanding measure words in Chinese. Soon after, Cheng and Sybesma (1999, 2005) argue that classifiers in Chinese are equivalent to a definite article, but Wu and Bodomo (2009) argue against this position on empirical grounds and propose that Chinese classifiers are not on the same footing as definite determiners. Some scholars even distinguish between classifiers and "true measure words", though they structurally both follow immediately after a numeral and appear before a noun (Lyons 1977; Li 2000). They hold this view for two reasons: true measure words usually occur with uncountable mass nouns but classifiers usually occur with count nouns; "true measure words" exclusively measure entities by unit but classifiers essentially sort entities by kind. Whatever argument it is, the general viewpoint is that Chinese is a classifier language.

To label Chinese as "classifier language" and English as "non-classifier language" is not well-grounded for the following reasons: both languages contain numerous classifiers but some are covert and some others are overt, and the choice of a classifier (the measure word) is entirely context-dependent; the structure and function of measure nominals where classifiers locate are basically similar between English and Chinese.

3. Context-dependency in using measure words

The choice of a classifier (the measure word) entirely depends on contexts. First, if to take various contexts into consideration, both English and Chinese contain countless things that are mass and numerous things that are countable. The cognitive foundation for countability is basically similar although cultural diversity may result in differences. Both English and Chinese regard things that cannot be individuated as uncountable, and things that can be individuated as countable. Consequently, we have many uncountable nouns such as "water, sand, grass, warmth" in English and their counterparts in Chinese.

Second, in contexts where the units can be inferred, the measure word is not necessary for Chinese, not for uncountable nouns in English either. Such contexts include idiomatic expressions and expressions to which measure words are redundant. See (18).

(18a) wu feng si yu (five wind and four rain, "proper and timely wind and rain")

wu hu si hai (five lakes and four seas, "all corners of the country")

(18b) six waters a cart (COCA)

40,000 soaps each day (COCA)

Third, the omission of measure words in Chinese and English results in various usages for different contexts rather than improper collocations. Count nouns in Chinese can be directly put after numerals without measure words while mass nouns in English can be used directly after numerals without measure words. This brings forth usages of different kinds, particularly true to spoken forms of the two languages. See (19).

(19a) san fang

(19b) three coffees

Instances in (19) may have a lot of meanings which varies with contexts. First of all, the nominal (19a) may mean: *san ge fang jian* (three rooms); *san dong fang zi* (three houses); or *san jian fang qian* (three antrums). Similar colloquial nominals can be found in Chinese where measure words are redundant. It is even abnormal to use measure words together with some nominals. For example: *wu xing* (five elements, i.e. metal, wood, water, fire and earth), *san sheng* (the three births, or reincarnations, past, present, future). Likewise, the meaning of (19b) in English also depends on context. It may mean: *three cups of coffee; three packs of coffee; three boxes of coffee; three cans of coffee...* In certain contexts, these nominals may sound quite strange to ordinary people. For example, to stevedores, (19b) may mean *three ships of coffee*; and to real estate staff, (19a) may mean *san dong zhu fang* (three buildings of houses). In other words, the presence of the measure word is optional rather than obligatory.

To sum up, the presence of the measure word is necessary for mass nouns in both English and Chinese, but mandatory only to cases where things need to be referred to as units. Mass things, if put into certain containers or divided into certain units, will be used in the same way as count nouns do. The presence of the measure word is redundant for count nouns in English, but count nouns can be used as measure words in other expressions (e.g. *a book of words*). Measure word is necessary for mass nouns in English, but mass nouns can be used as measure words in other expressions (e.g. *a cloud of words/smoke*). Now we can see that, it is not fixed but context-dependent in using measure words for nouns both in English and in Chinese. It is, therefore, not appropriate to say that measure words are mandatory for nouns in Chinese and mass nouns in English.

This view gains support from early studies like Allan (1980), who proposed eight levels of countability to be considered when dealing with English nouns. In that research, Keith Allan argued for the degree of uncountableness and he found that nouns in English "can be used both countably and uncountably in different NP environments" (Allan 1980: 541). Countability of nouns was not taken into account in Halliday (1994), but Halliday and Matthiessen (2004: 326; 2014: 385) suggested "cline of countability" for considering nouns, which ranges "from those nouns (and pronouns) which construe things as fully itemized, at one end, to those which treat them as totally unbounded at the other". Being countable or uncountable just reflects certain usages in certain typical contexts. When the elements of the context change, the degree of countability will alter, and will the necessity of using measure words.

After getting aware of context-dependency in the occurrence of measure words in English and Chinese measure nominals, we shall move back to the question mentioned above: whether *of noun* constitutes a downranked prepositional phrase to modify the measure word in English measure nominals? What is the function of "numeral + measure word" in English and Chinese? We will seek for answers to these questions by analyzing the structure and function of measure nominals from the perspective of SFL.

4. Analyzing metafunctional meanings of measure nominals
4.1 Experiential meaning of measure nominals

Structure and function, in general operation, go hand in hand and cannot be separated in SFL analysis. According to Halliday and Matthiessen (2014: 392), the internal structure of the measure expression (or other embedded numerative) in English can be drawn as the following:

a	cup	of	tea
Numerative			Thing
Premodifier	Head	Postmodifier	
β	α		

Figure 1   Internal structure of the measure expression (Halliday and Matthiessen 2014: 392)

We know that linguistic analysis by means of SFL should be carried out for the purpose of locating or revealing "meaning". However, when we take "cup" in "a cup of tea" as Head, it will be odd to locate a meaning of this nominal which focuses not on "tea". If "of tea" is Postmodifier, it is secondary in status to "cup". But in fact, it is not difficult to locate "tea" as the most important information in this nominal expression. In other words, the experiential and logical analysis of measure nominals provided in Halliday and Matthiessen (See Figure 1) needs to be reconsidered.

The problem becomes more apparent if we follow the analysis in Figure 1 to analyze the internal structure of the measure expression in Chinese, which is typical both for count nouns and mass nouns. See Figure 2 below.

一 yi a/one	杯 bei cup	茶 cha tea
Numerative		Thing
Premodifier	Head?	Postmodifier ?
β	α?	

Figure 2   Potential internal structure of the typical measure expression in Chinese

Closer examination of *yi bei cha* reveals that it is unreasonable to take *bei* (cup) as Head and *cha* (tea) as Postmodifier, for *cha* should be the word which carries the most important information. The group may be well-understood if *bei* is omitted but difficult to get across if *cha* is absent. One may argue that the two languages are different in measure nominals and we should analyze them in different ways. This is rational. Yet, all would agree that both "a cup of" and "yi bei" function as Numeratives, but why it seems all right to take "cup" as Head while it is quite unreasonable to take "bei" as Head. When "of tea" is taken as Postmodifier, it is downranked in status, lower than "cup". Likewise, when "cha" is treated as Postmodifier, it is downranked in status, lower than "bei". This is contradictory to the fundamental meaning of the nominal group, in which those function as Thing should be higher in status. So, an improved analysis is suitable for such expressions in Chinese (See Figure 3).

一 yi a/one	杯 bei cup		茶 cha tea
Numerative			Thing
Premodifier			Head
β			α

Figure 3　Improved internal structure of the typical measure expression in Chinese

Here in this analysis, Head is conflated with Thing, and the measure word comes together with the Numeral, functioning as Numerative and Premodifier. In other words, the measure word "bei" is part of the Premodifier and it should not be treated as Head. The Head and the Premodifier can be further modified by other modifiers respectively. In the same manner, "cup" in "a cup of tea" shall not be taken as Head.

The Numerative denotes the number of a Thing, while the Thing is always the most important information. In cases where the Thing is the default information known to language users, the Numerative may become more prominent. This applies to measure nominals both in Chinese and in English. Therefore, we may provide an improved analysis of "a cup of tea" in Figure 4.

a	cup	of	tea
Numerative			Thing
Premodifier			Head
β			α

Figure 4　Improved internal structure of the measure expression in English

Here we treat "a cup of" as an adjectival group, functioning as Numerative and Premodifier in the experiential meaning. In the default use of a measure nominal, the Thing ("tea" here in this example) is what to be modified. All those that denote the measuring of a Thing should be treated as modifiers. For example, "cup" and "tea" can be further modified: *two full cups of green tea.*

Such treatment finds supports from the history of English in the use of preposition "of". According to *Oxford English Dictionary* (OED), "of" displays about 63 distinct usages in the history of English. One of these usages is to indicate "quantity, age, extent, price, etc." See the following instance which was used in 1523:

(20) syxe foote of lengthe (six foot of length)

Can we say that "of lengthe" is a Postmodifier of "foote"? This is redundant both in meaning and structure, for "six foot" is already the exact length. Another explanation is to follow the usage illustrated by OED and say that "of" here functions as the indicator of "quantity", so "foote of" should be treated as a whole, functioning as Epithet. The modern measuring construction (e.g. a cup of tea) most probably inherits this usage, and we may consider "of" in "a cup of tea" as an indicator of quantity.

Such measuring constructions are quite different from other types of "of nominals" in English. For example, *the legs of three compasses, the legs of the table*. In these instances, "of nominals" function as Postmodifiers of "legs". The most important information conveyed in these instances is "legs", which functions as Head, conflating with Thing. Chinese counterparts of these nominals may further help explain the status of "of nominals" here (e.g. *zhi nan zhen de zhi zhen, zhuozi de tui*). In the counterparts, the most important information loads on "zhi zhen" or "tui" (legs).

4.2 Logical meaning of measure nominals

In the section above, we have already noted the logical structure of measure nominals in the four figures. Logical meaning, however, is more complicated than that. According to Halliday and Matthiessen (2014 390), "What the logical analysis does is to bring out the hypotactic basis of premodification in the nominal group, which then also explains its penchant for generating long strings of nouns." In the logical analysis, two kinds of structure are identified: univariate structure and multivariate structure. When the elements of a structure display as an iteration of the same functional relationship (α is modified by β, which is modified by γ, which is ...), it is univariate. For example: *investment trust cash management account* (Halliday and Matthiessen 2014: 390)

By contrast, when each element in a structure has a distinct function with respect to the whole, the structure is multivariate. For example:

(21) those two splendid old electric trains (Halliday and Matthiessen 2014: 364)

The functions of the elements in (21) are as follows: Deictic + Numerative + Epithet1 + Epithet2 + Classifier + Thing. The logical structure, therefore, is multivariate, with "trains" as the anchoring element.

The nominal group is unusual for we have to interpret its structure in both these ways simultaneously "to understand how it functions as a resource for construing complex things" (Halliday and Matthiessen 2014: 390). As to the measure nominal, the logical analysis in Figure 1 shows that the measure word is regarded as the central element in the logical structure (α). This measure nominal is a multivariate structure. The problem is, then, how to determine the status of "of noun" in the logical analysis of measure nominals. We can see no answer to this in Figure 1 and discussions related.

If to view measure nominals from a different perspective and take "a cup of" in "a cup of tea" as an adjectival group, the logical analysis will be without contradictions. See Figure 5 for an improved analysis of the logical meaning.

a	cup	of	tea
Premodifier			Head
β			α
ββ	βα		

Figure 5　Improved logical analysis of the measure expression in English

In this analysis, the only element that has not been explained is "of". Since we treat "a cup of" as a whole and "of" is only meaningful in structure, we may label it as "Relator". By contrast, in Chinese measure nominals, no relator is needed (See Figure 6).

一 yi	杯 bei	茶 cha
Premodifier		Head
β		α
β β	β α	

Figure 6　Logical analysis of the measure expression in Chinese

4.3 Interpersonal meaning of measure nominals

Expressions which contain typical measure words may not be used to measure. Such expressions carry strong interpersonal meaning and they are frequently used in English and Chinese. See (22) for some English expressions and their Chinese counterparts:

(22a) hundreds of, a bit of, rows and rows of, first/last of

(22b) cheng qian shang wan, yi ding dian er, yi pai pai, shou ge/zui hou yi ge

The interpersonal meaning of these expressions includes probability (*hundreds of, a bit of; cheng qian shang wan, yi ding dian er*), intensity (*rows and rows of, yi pai pai*) and temporality (*first/last of, shou ge/zui hou yi ge*). They are not measure nominals, for they do not measure anything but just describe degrees of probability, intensity or temporality.

Typical measure nominals such as "a cup of tea" do not carry much interpersonal meaning, except when "cup" is used out of expectation. For example, if the speaker/writer finds "tea" in a huge mug but uses "a cup of tea" to express that, he/she already conveys some comments.

When some modifiers which usually appear together with measure nominals are taken into consideration, the interpersonal meaning is quite obvious. We input "cup of" in the advanced search box of *Oxford English Dictionary* on CD-ROM (v. 4.0) published in 2009, and the following expressions pop up as part of the hundreds of instances. Chinese counterparts are also provided in brackets for comparison.

(23) a cup of hot tea (yi bei re cha)

　　　a cup of very peculiar-tasting tea (yi bei wei dao te bie de cha)

　　　a cup of pure water (yi bei chun jing shui)

　　　a cup of her ale (yi bei ta de mai ya jiu)

　　　a cup of such coffee (yi bei zhe zhong ka fei)

These instances show that modifiers can be naturally used before the Thing, conveying modality in them. The Epithet *hot* (re) in *a cup of hot tea* (yi bei re cha) indicates some degree of intensity in typical context. In some particular context (e.g. in outdoor places), it may function interpersonally in the same way as *good* (hao) do. The Epithet *pure* (chun jing) in (23) carries some degree of judgement concerning morality, and *very peculiar-tasting* (wei dao te bie) convey some degree of appreciation concerning desirability. As to the last two instances, *her* (ta de) and *such* (zhe zhong) show some degree of deicticity. Modifiers can be put before the measure word as well. See (24) from OED for example. Their Chinese counterparts are also provided for comparison.

(24) a comforting cup of bovril (yi bei shu shi de niu rou zhi)

　　　an excellent cup of coffee (yi bei shang cheng de ka fei)

　　　a refreshing cup of tea (yi bei ti shen cha)

　　　a bottomless cup of coffee (yi bei shen bu jian di de ka fei)

　　　a silent and thoughtful cup of tea (yi bei mo mo er you ti tie de ka fei)

In (24), the Epithets *comforting, excellent, refreshing* (shu shi, shang cheng, ti shen) convey some degree of judgement concerning morality. What is special here is that the last two measure nominals in (24) are not simple. The Epithets *bottomless* (shen bu jian di) and *silent and thoughtful* (mo mo er you ti tie) imply that the expressions are metaphorical. It is not easy to decide what element does the Epithet in each of (24) modify. Traditional grammar treats these Epithets as modifiers of "cup" but the Chinese counterparts already give us hints for a different interpretation. These Epithets modify the whole nominal group rather than "cup", for the focus is on the Thing in each of them. The interpersonal meaning of judgement therefore falls on the entire nominal. Besides modification shown in (23) and (24), measure word and Thing can be simultaneously modified by Epithets. See (25) and their Chinese counterparts in brackets.

(25) a giant cup of Irish breakfast tea (yi da bei ai er lan zao cha)

   a whole cup of hot coffee (yi zheng bei re ka fei)

   a second cup of hot tea (di er bei re cha)

   a little cup of real coffee (yi xiao bei zhen ka fei)

   the small cup of iced coffee (zhe xiao bei bing ka fei)

From the instances in (25), we may find that Epithets, Identifiers, Ordinatives, Deictics can all be used in the measure nominals, either before the measure word or before the Thing. Such uses carry interpersonal meanings of different degrees. The Chinese counterparts indicate that the Epithets in (25) modify measure word and Thing respectively. So the interpersonal meanings fall on the measure word and Thing. The interpersonal meanings will become more apparent if we follow Martin and White (2005/2007) and consider Judgement and Appreciation. To save space, we are not going to discuss that here.

5. Conclusion

Whether to use or not to use a classifier may not be grammatically determined (Li 2000), but it could be discourse and/or pragmatically sensitive (Hopper 1986). Since countability is a matter of degree (Allan 1980) which varies with contextual elements, it is not constructive to look into measure nominals from the perspective of mass/count distinction. From what we have observed, transference of countability needs to be carefully considered. A typical uncountable noun can be transferred to be countable, and vice versa (e.g. *two coffees, a cloud of smoke*).

Functional analysis of measure nominals in English and Chinese further reveals that such a distinction as classifier language and non-classifier language should be withdrawn in discussing measure nominals. The distinction may be useful in certain context, but the choice of measure words is a matter of context. Both English and Chinese contain numerous count nouns and mass nouns, and both languages may or may not use measure words in expressing measuration. The group "of noun" that follows the measure word in a measure nominal does not modify the measure word at all, and it is not a downranked phrase. The word "of" after the measure word can be taken as Relator in measure nominals and "measure word + of" functions as an adjectival group. Frequent occurrence of some usages in certain context may induce us to overgeneralize in studying measure nominals. What we should keep in mind is that typical usages in certain contexts are only typical in those contexts, and it is context dependence that should be highly respected upon discussing linguistic issues from the social-cultural perspective. A more constructive and meaningful way of studying measure nominals is to categorize the potential contexts and principles of identification via such theories as SFL.

References

Allan, K. 1977. Classifiers. *Language*, 53, 281-311.

Allan, K. 1980. Nouns and countability. *Language*, 56, 541-567.

Cheng, L. L.-S. and R. Sybesma. 1998. *Yi-wan Tang, Yi-ge Tang*: classifiers and massifiers. *Tsing Hua Journal of Chinese Studies*, 3, 385-412.

Cheng, L. L.-S. and R. Sybesma. 1999. Bare and not-so-bare nouns and the structure of NP. *Linguistic Inquiry*, 30: 509-542.

Cheng, L. L.-S. and R. Sybesma. 2005. Classifiers in four varieties of Chinese. In G. Cinque and R. Kayne (eds), *The Oxford Handbook of Comparative Syntax*. 259-292. Oxford: Oxford University Press.

Erbaugh, M. S. 1986. Taking stock: The development of Chinese noun classifiers historically and in young children. In C. Craig (ed.), *Noun Classes and Categorization*. 399-436. Amsterdam: John Benjamins Publishing Company.

Greenberg, J. H. 1990. Dynamic aspects of word order in the numeral classifier. In K. M. Denning and S. Kemmer, *On Language: Selected Writings of Joseph H. Greenberg*. 227-240. Stanford: Stanford University Press.

Halliday, M. A. K. 1994. *An Introduction to Functional Grammar* (2nd edition). London: Edward Arnold.

Halliday, M. A. K. and C. Matthiessen. 2004. *An Introduction to Functional Grammar* (3rd edition). London: Edward Arnold.

Halliday, M. A. K. and C. Matthiessen. 2014. *Halliday's Introduction to Functional Grammar* (4th edition). London and New York: Routledge.

Hopper, P. 1986. Some discourse functions of classifiers in Malay. In C. Craig (ed.), *Noun Classes and Categorization*. 309-325. Amsterdam: Benjamins.

Lehrer, A. 1986. English classifier constructions. *Lingua*, 68, 109-148.

Li, W. 2000. The pragmatic function of numeral-classifiers in Mandarin Chinese. *Journal of Pragmatics*, 32, 1113-1133.

Lu, J. 1987. On numeral-classifier with adjectives inserted between. *Language Teaching and Research*, 4, 53-73.

Lyons, J. 1977. *Semantics*. Cambridge: Cambridge University Press.

Martin, J. R. & P. R. White. 2005/2007. *The Language of Evaluation: Appraisal in English*. London and New York: Palgrave Macmillan.

Quirk, R., S. Greenbaum, G. Leech, and J. Svartvik. 1985. *A Comprehensive Grammar of the English Language*. London: Longman.

Shi, X. 1992. Origin and use of measure words for thing. *Language Teaching and Research*, 2, 38-46.

Wu, Y. and A. Bodomo. 2009. Classifiers determiners. *Linguistic Inquiry*, 40: 487-503.

Wang, L. 1985. *Modern Chinese Grammar*. Beijing: The Commercial Press.

Reconsidering Evidentiality from a Systemic Functional Perspective

Liangtao Lai

Shanghai Jiao Tong University, China

1. Introduction

Evidentiality was first observed by Franz Boas (1911: 423) during his study of Kwakiutl, an American Indian language. He noted that in the grammar of this language, there are special suffixes used to indicate the source of information. The term "evidential" first appeared in his posthumous publication *The Grammar of Kwaktiutl* (Boas 1947), which indicates a small set of suffixes used to express the source of knowledge and the degree of certainty. Jacobson (1957) discussed evidentials in his book *Shifters, Verbal Categories and Russian Verb*. Since then, the two terms evidential and evidentiality have been adopted and have generated considerable discussion. Based on the examination of corpora from hundreds of languages, linguists from all over the world have explored the category from different perspectives and published various papers and monographs.

However, there remains much controversy regarding the essential meaning of the term. There are two major camps in this regard. Scholars such as Jakobson (1957), Bybee (1985), Friedman (1986), Aikhenvald and Dixon (2003), Fitneva (2001), de Hann (2000, 2005a, 2005b), and Cornillie (2009) hold that evidentiality only refers to the source of information and is a semantic category independent of modality. Other linguists, such as Palmer (2001), Chafe (1986), Nichols (1986), Anderson (1986) and Willet (1988), maintain that evidentiality refers to the speaker's attitude to knowledge as well as the source of information. In other words, attitude is the nuclear meaning of evidentiality, whereas source of information is the peripheral meaning. Still other scholars (e.g. Hu 1994), trying to reach a compromise, argue that the term evidentiality has two senses: a narrow one indicating the source of information, and a broad one indicating both the source of information and the speaker's attitude to knowledge.

In view of this confusion, it seems advisable to study evidentiality from a new perspective. This study is intended to examine evidentiality within SFL's framework and explore its significance for discourse analysis. It is hoped that such an SFL-based study can provide insights complementary to current achievements and help further our understanding of this category.

2. Theory

As a functional theory of language, SFL (cf. Halliday 1978; Halliday and Hasan1985; Halliday 1994; Halliday and Matthiessen 2004; Martin 1992; Matthiessen 1995) considers language as a meaning potential and studies language in specific situational and cultural contexts from an inter-organism perspective. According to SFL, language is stratified into semantics, lexicogrammar and phonology, while context into register and genre, with a lower stratum realizing an upper one. As a meaning-oriented theory of language, SFL prefers a top-down perspective, proceeding from genre/register, to semantics and lexicogrammar, and finally to phonology.

SFL holds that language has three metafunctions: ideational, interpersonal and textual. The ideational metafunction consists of two parts: an experiential part and a logical part. The former indicates the use of language to construe experience in the real world and to reflect events, persons and things as well as circumstantial factors such as time and space, while the latter indicates the use of language to express the logical relations between two or more units of meaning. At the lexicogrammatic stratum, ideational metafunction is mainly realized by the transitivity system. The interpersonal metafunction is the use of language to enact social relationships, i.e. to express the speaker's social role, identity, status, attitude, motivation as well as his judgement and evaluation of things, and to influence the attitude and behavior of other people. It is realized by mood and modality resources, adjuncts as well as evaluation resources. The textual metafunction is the function of language to organize words and sentences into a relevant discourse. It relates language to the context, so that a speaker can only generate a text in compliance with its context. The three metafunctions are of equal importance and form a trinity.

3. Methodology

In this study, on the basis of SFL theory, the theoretical status and denotation of evidentiality are first examined. The theoretical findings are then applied to the analysis of two texts that involves plenty of evidentiality resources.

One of the texts is an extract of a paper from the *Journal of Pragmatics 33* titled "Epistemic Marking and Reliability Judgements". The evidentials (linguistic resources for realizing evidentiality) in the text are identified and the sources of information discussed. Then the overall function of the evidentials is analyzed. The contributions of evidentiality to the ideational, interpersonal and textual metafunctions of the text are explored respectively. The other text is a news report randomly extracted from the website of the *New York Times* (NYT) published in June 24, 2008, titled "South Korea Warns against Further Beef Protests". The method of analysis is basically the same.

4. Evidentiality defined from an SFL perspective

4.1 Ontological status of evidentiality

As a social-functional theory of language, SFL views language as a meaning potential. The study of evidentiality from an SFL perspective implies a social-functional approach with the focus on meaning. In addition, following SFL's preference of top-down perspective, an SFL-based study of evidentiality is one which first explores the semantic nature of the category, followed by the examination of its realization resources at the lexicogrammatic stratum. This means that in SFL, the ontological status of evidentiality will be most appropriately considered as a semantic rather grammatical, category. In this paper, the term "evidentiality" refers to such a semantic category, whereas the term "evidential" refers to the lexicogrammatic resources that realize the semantic category.

4.2 Denotation of evidentiality

In the discussion of the denotation of evidentiality, most scholars refer to one or more of the notions "information source", "evidence", and "justification" (e.g. Bybee 1985; Anderson 1986; Crystal 1991; Aikhenvald 2003, 2004). Other scholars also refer to epistemic notions such as "probability", "degree of certainty", "reliability of the knowledge", "speaker's commitment to the truth of knowledge", or "attitude towards knowledge", in addition to "information source" or "evidence" (e.g. Mithun 1986; Mayer 1990; Chafe 1986; Chafe and Nichols 1986; Palmer 2001). It seems that a consensus has reached concerning at least one part of the denotation of evidentiality, that is, its indication of the source of information (Boye and Harder 2009). The controversy lies in the explanation of the relation between evidentiality and epistemic modality and the interpretation of the phrase "information source".

Epistemic modality generally refers to the "evaluation of the chances that a certain hypothetical state of affairs under consideration (or some aspect of it) will occur, is occurring, or has occurred in a possible world" (Nuyts 2001b: 21). According to Palmer (2001: 24):

Epistemic modality and evidentiality are concerned with the speaker's attitude to the truth-value or factual status of the proposition and may thus be described as "propositional modality". The basic difference between epistemic modality and evidential modality is that with epistemic modality speakers make judgements about the factual status of the propositions, whereas with evidential modality they indicate what is the evidence that they have for it.

Palmer's view is representative of the truth-functional approach to both evidentiality and epistemic modality. Such an approach generally holds that meaning is nothing substantially more or less than the truth conditions they involve. Emphasis is placed upon reference to actual things in the world to account for meaning, with the caveat that reference more or less explains the greater part (or all) of meaning itself. It's from such an approach that Palmer talks about "truth value" and "factual status", that Chafe and others talk about "degree of certainty", "reliability", "probability", and "attitude" in their definitions of evidentiality. In addition, "evidence" or "information source" is treated as a sort of justification for the truth conditions of the propositions concerned. It is evidentiality in this sense that is considered as closely related to epistemic modality and considered as either a subtype of epistemic modality or as a subtype of propositional modality together with epistemic modality.

The truth-functional approach to semantics dates back to the logical-philosophical-psychological tradition of linguistics, as opposed to the sociological-anthropological tradition, from which SFL is derived (Hu et al. 2005). SFL views language as a social semiotic system and considers the meaning of linguistic resources as the function they play in a specific context rather than their truth conditions as against the reference in the real world. Considered from such a social-semiotic point of view, it would be better to interpret "information source" from the perspective of Bakhtin's dialogism (Bakhtin 1981). Different information sources can be considered as the indication of different voices (in Bakhtin's sense of the term). Different information sources in a text are different voices negotiating the meaning of the text. "Information source" in this sense is independent of the notions "truth conditions", "reliability", "degree of certainty", "attitude towards knowledge", or "speaker's commitment to the truth of the knowledge". As a result, it is untenable to combine "information source" in this sense with these other notions. Evidentiality can consequently be defined as indicating information source that shows the voices involved in the negotiation of meaning of a text. In this sense, evidentiality is a semantic category independent of epistemic modality.

5. Realization of evidentiality

5.1 Top-down perspective vs. bottom-up perspective

An SFL approach is a top-down one proceeding from context, to semantics and lexicogrammar, and then to phonology, with an upper stratum realized by a lower one. From such a perspective, the semantic category evidentiality is realized by different lexicogrammatic resources, which are called evidentials.

As there is a relation of multiple-correspondence between language form and meaning (that is, one form can realize several meanings and one meaning can be realized by different forms), the same semantic category of evidentiality can be realized by different lexicogrammatic forms. On the other hand, a lexicogrammatic form that realizes evidentiatity may also realize other meanings (other semantic categories). From a top-down perspective, then evidentiality as a semantic category has different forms of realization, which may vary from one language to another. In the examples below, the same category of evidentiality "opinion" is realized by a clause *he holds*, a phrase *in his view* and a word-group *his view* respectively.

(1) He holds that the hypothesis is well grounded.
(2) In his view, the hypothesis is well grounded.
(3) His view that the hypothesis is well grounded needs justification.

On the contrary, a bottom-up perspective proceeds from the lexicogrammatic stratum (the form level) to the semantic stratum. From such a perspective, a lexicogrammatic form that realizes the source of information can also realize other meanings, for example, attitude towards knowledge, or degree of certainty. This is the approach adopted by scholars such as Palmer (2001 [1986]), Chafe (1986) and Ifantidou (2001), who recognize a "broad sense" of the term. For example, Ifantidou (2001: 5-8), when discussing the functions of evidentials, defined evdientials as some lexicogrammatic forms and then argued that these forms had several functions such as expressing the source of information and the degree of certainty. As "evidential" is a formal category, what she was studying is a formal category that can express several meanings rather than the semantic category of evidentiality. Thus, Ifantidou (and her predecessors such as Chafe and Palmer) confused the formal category of evidential with the semantic category of evidentiality. The point is that a form can only be called an evidential when it is used to realize evidentiality or source of information. When it is used to realize the degree of certainty, or speaker's attitude towards knowledge, it is no longer an evidential but a modal form. Therefore, it is not viable to argue that evidentials have several semantic functions which indicate both the source of information and the speaker's attitude or degree of certainty.

As these scholars take form as their starting point and they find that the form can realize both source of information and speaker's attitude, they need to handle the relationship between the two semantic categories. There are two possible solutions: either they may claim that a lexicogrammatic form, which mainly realizes the source of information, can also realize the speaker's attitude, and therefore treat modality as a subclass of evidentiality (cf. Matlock 1989; Dendale and Tasmowski 2001); or they may argue that a lexicogrammatic category that mainly realizes modality can also realize the source of information, and thus treat evidentiality as a subclass of modality (cf. Palmer 2001 [1986]; Mushin 2001: 24-25; Willet 1988: 52).

5.2 Grammaticalization of evidentials

In SFL, lexis and grammar are treated as of the same stratum. Specifically, lexis and grammar are considered as constituting a cline; lexis is the most delicate grammar, while grammar is lexis with low delicacy (Halliday and Matthiessen 2004: 42-46). This implies that as the realization forms of evidentiality, evidentials may be either grammatical or lexical. In addition, units of all ranks at the lexicogrammatic stratum may serve as evidentials, including clauses (and clause complexes), phrases/groups, words and morphemes. Different languages may adopt different forms of realization. If that be the case, it is unviable to define evidentiality and classify evidentials based on any one type of rank unit (e.g. morphological realization). English has no morphemic evidentials, though many other languages have. In the following examples, the information sources are realized by a clause, a prepositional phrase and a word respectively.

(4) I heard she got married.
(5) According to Chafe's formulation then, the semantics of evidentiality is about the matching of our type of knowledge, established on the basis of some source, against some measure of reliability.
(6) Adults presumably are capable of purely logical thought.

Some scholars, however, restrict evidentials to inflectional morphemes that are similar to tense markers. They discuss the grammaticalization of evidentiality and its criteria, treat these criteria as universal and as the basis for language typology, and contend that some languages have evidentials while others do not. For example, Mushin (2001: 40-49) discussed the grammaticalization of evidentiality in Quechua, Makah and Chinese Lhasa Tibetan and established some criteria accordingly; Lazard (2001) explored the definition of evidential grammaticalization, and concluded that English and French have no evidentials; the evidential markers discussed by Aikhenvald (2003) are also inflectional morphemes. As the realization forms are too restricted to reflect the reality of language use, such an approach reduces the significance of evidentiality as a linguistic category. This point is also supported by de Hann's work (2005a, 2005b), which shows that evidentiality is marked across languages in a wide variety of forms in addition to morphological ones.

6. Evidentiality in relation to the three metafunctions

6.1 Evidentiality and ideational metafunction

Evidentiality indicates the source of information. All information derives from the real world, including the external objective world and the internal subjective world of the speaker, and would involve certain processes (events), participants (persons or things) and circumstantial elements. In SFL, the experiential part of the ideational metafunction is described as representing physical and mental experiences in the real world, or more specifically, reflecting events, persons and things as well as circumstantial factors such as time and space (Halliday 1994). It can be seen that evidentiality in the sense of information source is a part of the experiential metafunction.

The experiential metafunction is realized by the transitivity system, which construes the world of experience into a manageable set of process types, including material, behavioral, mental, verbal, relational, and existential ones (Halliday and Matthiessen 2004: 170). However, it seems that only mental and verbal processes can realize evidentiality. Mental processes fall into four subtypes: perception, cognition, desideration, and emotion, of which only the first two can be used to indicate information source. Perceptive processes include visual (e.g. see, notice), auditory (e.g. hear, overhear), olfactory (smell) and other sensory ones, all of which can function as evidentials. Cognitive processes that can realize evidentiality include the "opinion/belief/expectation" type (e.g. think, believe, and expect), imagination type (e.g. imagine, dream), memory type (e.g. remember, recall), and inference/reasoning/assumption type (e.g. guess, assume, seem) (cf. Halliday and Matthiessen 2004: 210). Verbal processes are processes of saying. Relevant here are the quoting and reporting subtypes (e.g. say, report, write, announce). Thus, on the basis of the processes available for their realization, evidentiality meanings can be classified in the following way (see Table 1).

Table1　Processes realizing evidentiality

	Perception	Visual, auditory, olfactory, other
Mental	Cognition	Opinion/belief/expectation; imagination; memory; inference/reasoning/assumption
Verbal	Quoting, reporting	

It should be noted that the classification refers to the types of evidentiality meanings rather than types of realization forms. Each type can be realized by lexicogrammatic forms other than verbs. For example, they may be realized by circumstantial elements of the means, reason, or angle type (Halliday and Matthiessen 2004: 259-277). In this case, the original verbs can either be nominalized or combined with a preposition, or be transformed into adverbials to indicate the information source independently. In this way, *in my view* and *I think* will be considered as belonging to the same type, i.e., the cognition-opinion type. Each type may also be realized by nominal groups, clausal adverbials or clause connectives. See the examples below.

(7) I see her coming down the hill. (perception: visual)

(8) I hear someone knocking at the door. (perception: auditory)

(9) The breeze smelled exactly like Vouvray—flowery, with a hint of mothballs underneath. (perception: olfactory)

(10) So you believe that the story is better at dealing with real-life human emotions. (cognition: opinion)

(11) Imagine you are a billionaire and have a large house. (cognition: imagination)

(12) I guess I was thinking about it in different way. (cognition: inference)

(13) I remember I met him two years ago in a party. (cognition: memory)

(14) Somebody told me that I mustn't repudiate my own non-fiction. (verbal: reporting)

(15) According to Chafe's formulation then, the semantics of evidentiality is about the matching of our type of knowledge, established on the basis of some source, against some measure of reliability. (verbal: reporting as circumstance of angle)

(16) Adults presumably are capable of purely logical thought. (cognition: assumption as circumstance)

(17) Rumors go that he is a betrayed husband. (verbal: reporting)

(18) Similarly, the use of daylight in shopping complexes appears to increase sales. (cognition: reasoning based on previous discussion)

6.2 Evidentiality and interpersonal metafunction

When evidentiality (information source) is viewed from the perspective of Bakhtin's dialogism (Bakhtin 1981) rather than from a truth-functional perspective, it can be understood as enacting different voices that work together to negotiate the meaning of the text (cf. Section 4.2). Verbal communication is dialogic in the sense that it always takes up in some way what has been said or written before and anticipates response from some actual or potential readers/ listeners. This dialogistic perspective leads us to examine, on one hand, the degree to which speakers/writers acknowledge the voices of these prior speakers and in the ways in which they engage with them. Thus, we are "interested in whether they present themselves as standing with, as standing against, as undecided, or as neutral with respect to these other speakers and their value positions" (Martin and White 2005: 92). On the other hand, such a perspective leads us to the anticipatory aspect of the text—to the signals speakers/writers provide as to how they expect those they address to respond to the current proposition and the value position it advances. "Thus we are interested in whether the value position is presented as one which can be taken for granted for this particular audience, as one which is in some way novel, problematic or contentious, or as one which is likely to be questioned, resisted or rejected" (Martin and White 2005: 92). From a dialogistic perspective, then evidentiality as information source can be understood as resources of intersubjective positioning that enable speakers/writers to negotiate relationships of alignment/disalignment with previous value positions or voices referenced by the text and also with the text's putative addressee.

In SFL, the part that deals with dialogistic resources is the engagement system (Martin and White 2005; White 2005). Specifically, the engagement system deals with "those meanings which in various ways construe for the text a heteroglossic backdrop of prior utterances, alternative viewpoints and anticipated responses" (Martin and White 2005: 97). The engagement meanings are taxonomized into four classes ("disclaim", "proclaim", "entertain", and "attribute") according to the particular dialogistic positioning associated with given meanings and the effect of the difference choices of meaning. Disclaim means that the textual voice positions itself as at odds with, or rejecting, some contrary position, which includes "deny (negation)" and "counter (concession)". Proclaim means that by representing the proposition as highly warrantable, the textual voice sets itself against, suppresses or rules out alternative positions; it is subclassified into "concur", "pronounce", and "endorse". Entertain implies that "by explicitly presenting the proposition as grounded in its own contingent, individual subjectivity, the authorial voice represents the proposition as but one of a range of possible positions—it thereby entertains or invokes these dialogic alternatives" (e.g. it seems, the evidence suggests, apparently, in my view) (Martin and White 2005: 98). While entertain values present the internal voice of the speaker/writer as the source, attribute values present some external voice. Attribute means that "by representing proposition as grounded in the subjectivity of an external voice, the textual voice represents the proposition as but one of a range of possible positions—it thereby entertains or invokes these dialogic alternatives" (Martin and White 2005: 98). It is subclassified into "acknowledge" (e.g. X said/believes, in X's view) and "distance" (e.g. X claims that, it rumors that). "Disclaim" and "proclaim" contracts the dialogic space, whereas "entertain" and "attribute" expands the dialogic space.

However, in many utterances, evidentiality meaning is simply absent. These are bare assertions which do not overtly reference the information sources, and therefore do not overtly reference other voices or recognize alternative positions. As a result, the communicative context is represented as monoglossic and dialogistically inert, at least for the brief textual moment taken up by the utterance. See the examples below for the evidentiality meanings interpreted from a dialogistic perspective.

(19) Mr President, once again I think we are being denied as a parliament the opportunity to make our opinions known concerning the recommencement of whale hunting. (entertain)

(20) He now poses little threat to the world, according to Robert. (attribute, acknowledge)

(21) The defense claimed that the evidence was inadmissible. (attribute, distance)

(22) As Professor Fawcett has shown, the hypothesis is wrong. (proclaim, endorse)

(23) I contend that the theory does not hold water. (proclaim, pronounce)

(24) I see her coming down the hill. (entertain based on "my" visual evidence)

(25) The evidence shows a burglary had taken place. (proclaim, endorse)

(26) In this paper, I challenge this view for two reasons. (disclaim, deny)

(27) That mismatch seems worse than it was ten years ago. (entertain)

(28) He always works very hard. (bare assertions without evidentiality meaning)

6.3 Evidentiality and textual metafunction

The close relation between evidentiality and textual metafunction is most clearly shown by conjunctives indicating cause-condition and those indicating manner, for example, *consequently*, *therefore*, *as a result*, *otherwise*, *thus*, *similarly*. They can show that the succeeding prepositional information is a kind of reasoning based on the co-text, and thus helps maintain the cohesion and coherence of the text. See the examples below.

(29) I mustn't say anything about it. Otherwise, I'll get shot by the lady who just shut the door. (inference based on a reason contrary to the previous one)

(30) Similarly, the use of daylight in shopping complexes appears to increase sales. (likewise inference based on previous reasons)

More importantly, in a text, information sources of different types can form evidence chains that interact with each another. These interacting chains integrate the different propositions in the text into a whole and make the text coherent. For example, in an academic paper, references to the same source in the body part form a verbal-quoting/reporting chain with the corresponding entry in the bibliography part. These chains interact with each other and contribute to the unity of the whole paper. The textual metafunction of these chains will be illustrated in more detail in the succeeding case analysis section.

7. Case analysis

In this section, two texts are analyzed to demonstrate the construal of the different types of evidentiality meanings, to illustrate the ways of intersubjective positioning for reader alignment in texts, and to show the contribution of evidentiality resources to textual unity. The first text is an extract from a paper in the *Journal of Pragmatics 33* titled "Epistemic Marking and Reliability Judgements"; the second is a piece of news report titled "South Korea Warns Against Further Beef Protests" extracted from the website of *New York Times* on June 24, 2008.

Text 1

The prevailing view of the semantic contribution of epistemic devices is that they all serve to express the attitude (i.e., certainty or degree of commitment) of the speaker to what is said, and are thus properly treated within the domain of epistemic modality (Lyons, 1977; Kratzer, 1981, 1991; Palmer, 1986). Epistemic modality is defined as the expression of "the speaker's opinion or attitude toward a proposition that the sentence expresses or the situation that the proposition describes" (Lyons, 1977: 452), or equivalently, "the degree of commitment by the speaker to what he says" (Palmer, 1986: 51). Palmer (1986) furthermore argues that "the whole purpose [of source-of-information markers] is to provide indication of the degree of commitment of the speaker: he [sic] offers a piece of information, but qualifies its validity for him in terms of the type of evidence he has" (1986: 54). In other words, speakers convey their degree of confidence in the information not only by using markers that directly express confirmation, certainty, or doubt, but also by using markers that reveal source of information, that is, the mode of creation and acquisition of the information (hearsay, perception, deduction, etc.). Source-of-information markers have even been formally analyzed as epistemic modals (Izvorski, 1997).

In this paper, I challenge this view for two reasons. First, as hearers, we cannot always be passive receptacles of speakers' opinions. Sometimes we need an indicator such as source-of-information that allows us to make judgments ourselves about the reliability of what is said. Second, source of information does not have consistent implications for the reliability of information. These arguments are formulated having in mind grammatical epistemic marking (whose basic meaning is debated) but I suspect that they can be applied to lexical devices as well and I use examples from English. The discussion, furthermore, emphasizes the hearer's interpretation of what is said and thus crucially assumes that this interpretation is the same as the speaker's.

(Source: *Journal of Pragmatics* 33 [2001])

Ideationally, most of the evidentiality resources in Text 1 are of the verbal-quoting/reporting type, including *(Lyons, 1977; Kratzer, 1981, 1991; Palmer, 1986), (Lyons, 1977: 452), (Palmer, 1986: 51), Palmer (1986) furthermore argues, he [sic], (1986: 54), (Izvorski, 1997). In other words* can be considered as indicating verbal explanation in another way, thus also of the verbal type; *I challenge… for two reasons* indicates mental reasoning, belonging to the cognition-reasoning type; *I suspect* belongs to the cognition-opinion type. The verbal-quoting/reporting resources in the first paragraph form an evidentiality chain, which is further related to the references part at the end of the paper. This chain interacts with *I challenge… for two reasons* in the second paragraph, as the views related to the two types of evidentiality resources are in opposition. As a whole, the evidential resources help make the text a coherent unity.

Interpersonally all evidentiality resources in the first paragraph are of the "attribute-acknowledge" type, which show the author's objective presentation of the view of a specific group. However, as this view is only held by that specific group, the information source opens the dialogic space and implies that there may be other people who hold different views. In the second paragraph, the author explicitly retorts this view through the clause *I challenge*, which is of the disclaim-denial type. The author positions himself as being at odds with the proceeding view and contracts the dialogic space in order to emphasize his own view. After the first reason is formulated, the author denies a contrary position, which is followed by a bare assertion. The second reason is presented in basically the same way, except that an "entertaining" process *I suspect* is used to alleviate the absoluteness of the author's argument so as to provide space for alignment with putative readers who think otherwise. As a whole, the evidentiality resources, together with other engagement resources, help the author present two groups of opposing views, and help position himself with one side by retorting the other.

Text 2

South Korea Warns Against Further Beef Protests

By CHOE SANG-HUN

Published: June 25, 2008

SEOUL—President Lee Myung-bak, attempting to reassert his authority after weeks of demonstrations against his decision to resume imports of American beef, said Tuesday that his government would not tolerate further violent protests.

Mr. Lee's announcement came as Seoul was discussing when President Bush should visit South Korea in a follow-up to Mr. Lee's visit to the United States in mid-April.

Officials here had indicated that Mr. Bush would visit Seoul next month after the Group of 8 summit meeting in Japan. But the beef deal set off widespread anti-government protests, prompting some officials to worry that a Bush visit might lead to further demonstrations.

"The government must deal sternly with illegal and violent protests, as well as rallies that challenge the state's system," Mr. Lee told a cabinet meeting on Tuesday—a comment that contrasted with the low-key, apologetic stance he had taken in recent weeks

Yu In-chon, the government spokesman, said after the cabinet meeting: "It's time for people to put out the candles and return to work."

The demonstrations forced Mr. Lee to ask Washington to revise the original beef deal. In a new accord unveiled Saturday, the United States agreed to export only beef from cattle younger than 30 months, to soothe South Koreans' fears of mad cow disease.

Protest organizers vowed to keep rallying until Mr. Lee agreed to a complete renegotiation of the pact, although the size of the protests, some of the largest since the end of military rule in the 1980s, has been decreasing.

Asked about Mr. Bush's possible trip to Seoul, Dana Perino, the White House spokeswoman, said on Monday that Washington will announce details "soon."

The ban on American beef was first imposed in 2003, when a case of mad cow disease was detected in the United States.

South Korea has yet to publish a legal notice of the revised beef deal, the final step needed to resume U.S. imports.

Justice Minister Kim Kyung Han, meanwhile, said Tuesday that prosecutors will investigate people who have been flooding businesses with anonymous phone calls threatening to begin boycotts unless the companies withdrew advertisements from the nation's three major conservative dailies, which have criticized the protests.

Ideationally, all evidentiaility meanings in this news report are of the verbal-quoting type. However, they function at two different levels of the text. Specifically, *By CHOE SANG-HUN* and *Seoul* indicate the information source of the whole text, whereas the remaining evidentials indicate information sources of the corresponding utterances. It can be said that the latter group is subordinate to the former. The latter can be further classified into two subgroups: words by Korean officials (including *President Lee Myung-bak...said*, *Officials here had indicated*, *Mr. Lee told*, and *Yu In-chon, the government spokesman, said)*, and words by the official of the United States (*Dana Perino, the White House spokeswoman, said*). This 4:1 ratio indicates that the news report is mainly based on what had happened in South Korea, which is consistent with the evidential *"Seoul"* of the whole text. The quotations from the South Korean officials form an evidentiality chain, which is closely related to and interacts with the information source of the United States as they are quotations from the two sides concerning the same issue. Both of the interacting chains are anchored to the information sources of the whole text. Thus, it can be seen that the evidentiality resources help make the whole text coherent.

Interpersonally, the evidentiality resources of the text fall into two types. *By CHOE*

SANGHUN and *Seoul* are of the entertaining type as they represent the text-internal voice of the author. They indicate that the whole text only represents the value positioning of the author and the news agency even though it pretends to be neutral. The authorial voice of the whole text is only one of a range of possible positions. On the other hand, the processes of quoting from both South Korean and American officials are of the "attribute-acknowledge" type. This implies that the propositions concerned are represented as external voices other than the authorial internal voice. The author simply acknowledges these external voices neutrally without choosing to stand on one side, thus attempting to keep solidarity with as many putative readers as possible. However, when the fact is taken in to consideration that no voices of the demonstrators are represented, it can be seen that this way of value positioning is not as neutral as it seems. In addition, in the news report, there are many bare assertions which are dialogically inert and represented as a truth of fact. However, they are assertions of the author and the news agency (CHOE SANG-HUN, Seoul, etc.), who have employed various evaluation resources explicitly or implicitly to help evaluate the events in the news report. A dialogic reading of the evidentiality meanings helps reveal the strategies employed in news reports for value positioning in a seemingly neutral representation.

8. Conclusion

In this paper, evidentiality is studied from the perspective of systemic functional linguistics. The denotation of evidentiality is examined, its realization forms at different rank units are explored, and the relationship between evidentiality and the three metafunctions are discussed. The construal of evidentiality is illustrated through the analysis of two texts. As an outcome, the following conclusions can be drawn.

From a systemic-functional perspective, evidentiality is a semantic category that refers to the source of information of a proposition. When interpreted from a social/dialogistic perspective rather than a truth-functional one, the information sources in a text show the different voices that work together to negotiate the meaning of the whole text, rather than the truth-conditions or factual status of the propositions concerned.

Evidentiality as a semantic category has different realization forms (evidentials) at the lexicogrammatic stratum. They can be distributed at different lexicogrammatic ranks, such as morpheme, word, word group (phrase), and clause/clause complex. Evidentialtiy in different languages have different forms of realization. The restriction of evidentials to inflectional morphemes reduces the significance of the category as it does not adequately reflect the reality of language use.

As information source is derived from our experience of life, evidentiality is the experiential part of the ideational metafunction of a language. Based on the process types available for realizing information source, evidentiality meanings can be divided into two large types: mental and verbal. Mental sources include perception (which can be subclassified into visual, auditory, olfactory, and other sensory types) and cognition (which can be subclassified into opinion/ belief/ expectation, imagination, memory, inference/reasoning/assumption types). Verbal sources include quoting and reporting types. As these are types of evidentiality meanings, information sources realized by forms other than process verbs can be grouped accordingly based on their specific meanings.

From the perspective of Bakhtin's dialogism, interpersonally evidentiality can be understood as indicating different voices that work together to negotiate the meaning of a text. Evidentiality resources are resources of intersubjective positioning that enable speakers/writers to negotiate relationships of alignment/disalignment with previous value positions referenced by the text and with the text's putative addressee. Based on the particular dialogistic positioning associated with given meanings and the effect of the different choices of meaning, evidentiality as intersubjective positioning resources can be classified into disclaiming (including denial and countering), proclaiming (including concurring, pronouncing, endorsing), entertaining, and attributing types (including acknowledging and distancing).

In terms of textual metafunction, some evidentials may function as conjunctives in a text. In addition, different sources of information in a text can form evidence chains that interact with each other, and help make the whole text into a coherent unity.

Acknowledgement

This paper is supported by The Startup Fund for Young New Teachers of Shanghai Jiao Tong University (Approval No. 14X100040038) and the Fund for Academic Innovation of School of Foreign Languages, Shanghai Jiao Tong University (Approval No. WF117114001).

References

Aikhenvald, A. Y. 2003. Evidentiality in typological perspectives. In A. Y. Aikhenvald, M. Robert and W. Dixon (eds.), *Studies in Evidentiality*. 1-31. Amsterdam/Philadelphia: John Benjamings Publishing Company.

Aikhenvald, A. Y. 2004. *Evidentiality*. Oxford: Oxford University Press.

Anderson, L. B. 1986. Evidentials, paths of change, and mental maps: typologically regular asymmetries. In W. Chafe and J. Nichols (eds.), *Evidentiality: The Linguistic Coding of Epistemology*. 273-312. Norwood: Ablex.

Bakhtin, M. M. 1981. *The Dialogical Imagination* (translated by C. Emerson and M. Holquist). Austin: University of Texas Press.

Boas, F. 1911. Kwakiutl. In F. Boas (ed.) *Handbook of American Indian Languages*. 423-557. Washington:

Government Printing Office.

Boas, F. 1947. *The Grammar of Kwaktiutl*. Philadelphia: American Philosophical Society.

Boye, K. and P. Harder. 2009. Evidentiality: linguistic categories and grammaticalization. *Functions of Language,* 16 (1), 9-43.

Bybee, J. L. 1985. *Morphology: A study of the Relation Between Meaning and Form*. Amsterdam/ Philadelphia: John Benjamins Publishing Company.

Chafe, W. 1986. Evidentiality in English conversation and academic writing. In W.Chafe and J. Nichols (eds.), *Evidentiality: The Linguistic Coding of Epistemology*. 261-272. Norwood: Ablex.

Chafe, W. and J. Nichols. 1986. *Evidentiality: The Linguistic Coding of Epistemology*. Norwood: Ablex.

Cornillie, B. 2009. Evidentiality and epistemic modality: on the close relationship between two different categories. *Functions of Language,* 16 (1), 44-62.

Crystal, D. 1991. *A Dictionary of Linguistics and Phonetics*. Oxford: Blackwell.

De Haan, F. 2000. Evidentiality and epistemic modality setting boundaries. *Southwest Journal of Linguistics,* 18, 83-101.

De Haan, F. 2005a. Semantic distinctions of evidentiality. In M. Haspelmath, M. S. Dryer, D. Gil and B. Comrie (eds.), *The World Atlas of Language Structures*. 314-317. Oxford: Oxford University Press.

De Haan, F. 2005b. Coding of evidentiality. In M. Haspelmath, M. S. Dryer, D. Gil and B. Comrie (eds.), *The World Atlas of Language Structures*. 318-321. Oxford: Oxford University Press.

DeLancey, S. 2001. The mirative and evidentiality. *Journal of Pragmatics,* 33, 369-382.

Dendale, P. and L. Tasmowski. 2001. Introduction: evidentiality and related notions. *Journal of Pragmatics,* 33, 339-348.

Fitneva, S. A. 2001. Epistemic marking and reliability judgements: Evidence from Bulgarian. *Journal of Pragmatics,* 33, 401-420.

Friedman, V. A. 1986. Evidentiality in the Balkans: Bulgarian, Macedonian, and Albanian. In Chafe, W. and J. Nichols (eds.), *Evidentiality: The Linguistic Coding of Epistemology*. 168-187. Norwood: Ablex.

Halliday, M. A. K and C. M. I. M. Matthiessen. 2004. *An Introduction to Functional Grammar*. London: Edward Arnold.

Halliday, M. A. K. 1978. *Language as Social Semiotic: The Social Interpretation of Meaning*. London: Edward Arnold.

Halliday, M. A. K. 1994. *An Introduction to Functional Grammar*. London: Edward Arnold.

Halliday, M. A. K. and R. Hasan. 1985/1989. *Language, Text and Context: Aspects of Language in a Social Semiotic Perspective*. Geelong: Deakin University Press.

Hu, Z., Y. Zhu, D. Zhang, and Z. Li. 2005. *An Introduction to Systemic Functional Linguistics*. Beijing: Beijing University Press.

Hu, Z. 1994. Evidentiality in language (yuyan de kezhengxing). *Foreign Language Teaching and Research,* 1994 (1), 9-15.

Ifantidou, E. 2001. *Evidentials and Relevance*. Amsterdam/Philadelphia: John Benjamings Publishing Company.

Jacobson, R. 1957. *Shifters, Verbal Categories and Russian Verb*. Cambridge: Harvard University, Dept. of Slavic Languages and Literatures, Russian Language Project.

Lazard, G. 2001. On the grammaticalization of evidentiality. *Journal of Pragmatics,* 33, 359-367.

Martin, J. R. 1992. *English Text: System and Structure.* Amsterdam/Philadelphia: John Benjamins Publishing Company.

Martin, J. R. and P. R. R. White. 2005. *The Language of Evaluation: Appraisal in English.* New York: Palgrave Macmillan.

Matlock, T. 1989. Metaphor and the grammaticalization of evidentials. *Berkeley Linguistics Society,* 15, 215-225.

Matthiessen, C. M. I. M. 1995. *Lexicalgrammatical Cartography: English Systems.* Tokyo: International Language Sciences Publishers.

Mayer, R. 1990. Abstraction, context, and perspectivization—evidentials in discourse semantics. *Theoretical Linguistics,* 16, 101-163.

McCready, E. and N. Ogata. 2007. Evidentiality, modality and probability. *Linguistics and Philosophy,* 30 (2), 147-206.

Mithun, M. 1986. Evidential diachrony in Northern Iroquoian. In W. Chafe and J. Nichols (eds.), *Evidentiality: The Linguistic Coding of Epistemology.* 89-112. Norwood: Ablex.

Mushin, I. 2001. *Evidentiality and Epistemological Stance: Narrative Retelling.* Amsterdam/Philadelphia: John Benjamings Publishing Company.

Nuyts, J. 2001a. Subjectivity as an evidential dimension in epistemic modal expressions. *Journal of Pragmatics,* 33, 383-400.

Nuyts, J. 2001b. *Epistemic Modality, Language, and Conceptualization: A Cognitive-pragmatic Perspective.* Amsterdam/Philadelphia: John Benjamings Publishing Company.

Palmer, F. R. 2001 [1986]. *Mood and Modality* (2nd edition). Cambridge: Cambridge University Press.

Plungian, V. A. 2001. The place of evidentiality within the university grammatical space. *Journal of Pragmatics,* 33, 349-357.

White, P. R. R. 2005. An introductory tour through appraisal theory. Available at http://www.grammatics.com/appraisal/ (retrieved on November 10, 2011)

Willet, T. 1988. A crosslinguistic survey of the grammaticalization of evidentiality. *Studies in Language,* 12, 51-97.

Conceptual and Connotative Meaning of Body Parts: Examples from Jordanian Arabic

Mohammad Al-Khawalda[a] and Lina Al-Mawajdeh[b]

[a]Mutah University, Jordan; [b]Mutah University, Jordan

1. Introduction

The meaning of words and expressions is an attractive field of study. The traditional assumption is that words have sense-units, or "meanings", which are typically known as static "lexical entries" (Allwood, 2003). These lexical entries combine in accordance with grammatical rules to form meaningful sentence.

It is common knowledge in literature that words contain additional meanings beyond their lexical or dictionary meaning. Generally, when dealing with words, a distinction is often made between "lexical, i.e. conceptual or denotative" meaning and "connotative or associative" meaning. The former refers to the meaning described in dictionaries, which is the basic literal meaning, while the later is the other meaning associated with the word in certain cultures or contexts. For instance, the lexical or denotative meaning of the word "snake" in *Merriam Webster Dictionary* is "any of numerous limbless scaled reptiles (suborder Serpentes syn. Ophidia) with a long tapering body and with salivary glands often modified to produce venom which is injected through grooved or tubular fangs". In addition to this conceptual meaning, the word "snake" could have many other associative or connotative meanings attached by different people in different cultures such as "evil, danger, killing", etc.

Connotation has a strong correlation with culture. The feelings, images, and memories that exist about a word in a certain culture make up its *connotation*. This is why the connotation of a certain word could differ from one society to another. For instance, in Arab culture, one of the connotations of "the moon" is *"beauty or a beautiful girl"*. So, if a person saw a beautiful girl, he/she can say "I saw a moon". However, this connotation of the moon is not available in Russian and most western societies. According to Wikipedia (2014) "a connotation is a commonly

48

understood subjunctive cultural or emotional association that some word or phrase carries, in addition to the word's or phrase's explicit or literal meaning, which is its denotation". This is why it has been agreed that learning a new language is not independent of learning about the culture in which the language is used, as the *language of the people reveals a lot about their culture*. The relationship between language and culture is therefore a unique one and the effect of culture on language is undeniable. Evans (2006: 509) points to this relation and uses the expression "cultural-specific lexical concepts" to refer to words and expression which cannot be understood by language learners of other cultures. Culture is shared and maintained through the use of language. As a result, culture reflects in language and vice versa. For instance the linguistic terms used in different occasion such as greeting, congratulating, consolation, etc. are culturally oriented. On the other hand, culture is a set of linguistic terms used in different occasions. Language, habits, behaviors, etc. are acquired from culture. It is therefore a well known fact that language and culture are two interrelated concepts, as language is a component part of culture. Wierzbicka (1994) claims that when dealing with language we will find out that socio-cultural layer, or the component of culture is the background of its real existence. Generally, a cultural group is described as a speech community. In other words, language is used to identify cultural grouping. Even in small communities and countries one can identify the cultural subgroups by their language. That explains why Gibbs (1999: 153) argues that "theories of human conceptual systems should be inherently cultural in that the cognition which occurs when the body meets the world is inextricably culturally-based". The difference between languages does not consist only in differences in pronunciation, vocabulary or grammar, but also in the usage of certain expressions which signals that community (Patricia, 1986). According to The World Intercultural Property Organization (WIPA) (2011), traditional cultural expressions are handed down from one generation to another, either orally or by imitation, (ii) reflect a community's cultural and social identity, (iii) consist of characteristic elements of a community's heritage, (iv) are made by "authors unknown" and/or by communities and/or by individuals communally recognized as having the right, responsibility or permission to do so, (v) are often not created for commercial purposes, but as vehicles for religious and cultural expression, and (vi) are constantly evolving, developing and being recreated within the community (WIPA Report 2011: 1).

Accordingly, within the same language, one may find words and expressions used by a certain group within the language community but not by another group. Obama (2010) states that "Language is the mirror of culture, as it reflects not only real world around us, not only real life conditions, events, and experiences, but also a public conscience and self-conscience of the nation, mentality, national character, way of life, customs and traditions, habits, moral, system of values, vision, world outlook, and world perception."

Swiderski (1993) points out that mastering a language requires a great knowledge of the culture in which this language is used. Without that knowledge of culture, the ability of the learners is incomplete.

Arabic language is full of expressions which often prove difficult for learners to master. They are even difficult for native speakers of Arabic if they are not part of such sub-culture in which these expressions are used. Allwood (2003: 43) provides an account of what he refers to as "meaning potential", according to him, a word's meaning potential is all the information that the word has to convey either by a single individual, or on the social level, by the language community.

The context has its importance to decide the semantic value of words. Evans (2006) points out that the semantic values associated with words are flexible, open-ended and highly dependent on the utterance context in which they are embedded. In other words, the meaning associated with a word in any given utterance appears to be, in part, a function of the particular linguistic context in which it is embedded (Croft 2000 in Evans 2006: 492). Evans (2006: 503-504) uses the expression "lexical profile" to describe the associative meaning of a given word. He states that any lexical concept has a lexical profile.

While any given usage of a lexical concept will have its own unique selectional requirements, general patterns ("tendencies") can be established, and form part of the conventional knowledge associated with a particular lexical concept. General selectional patterns in Lexical concepts, cognitive models and meaning-construction terms of semantic, collocational and grammatical tendencies are what I refer to as a lexical profile.

To clarify his point, he gives the following example and discusses his lexical concept and lexical profile.

His time (death) is fast approaching.

It seems that the connotative meaning of a word is generally connected to or can be inspired from its lexicalized meaning. Lee and Dapretto (2006) points out that lexicalized meaning plays an important role in figurative and connotative readings of a word.

Vainik (2011) argues that in every language there are lexical expressions using body parts to describe human emotion, feeling, reaction, etc. There is a general agreement that there is an interaction with both the physical and social environment in which body parts play a vital role. Nissen (2011) investigates metaphor and metonymy of "mouth" in English, Danish and Spanish.

In his cross-linguistic and cross-cultural perspective, he emphasizes that non-lexical uses of mouth in these three languages are pervasive. His results support the view that metaphor and metonymy are powerful in generating figurative expressions which are connected with body parts.

2. Background and scope of this study

Arabic is one of the Semitic languages (namely Arabic, Amharic, Hebrew, Tigrinya, and Aramaic) spoken by approximately 200 million people in the Arab world which extends from the northern part of Africa to the southwestern part of Asia. Jordan is one of the Arab countries in the Asian part. All Arabs speak one language which is Arabic. However, a sort of variations can be found among these countries, and that is why in linguistic studies scholars refer to regional varieties, such as Jordanian Arabic, Saudi Arabic, Egyptian Arabic, etc. Jordanian Arabic exists only as a spoken variety. Jordan, like other Arab countries, exhibits a diglossic situation with Jordanian Arabic as the variety used at informal settings and Standard Arabic as the variety used at formal settings. Within each country, it is possible to find some regional or cultural variations according to certain cultural communities.

Data for the study was taken from the north eastern Jordan. The use of body parts in this area (and many other parts) in speech is distinguishable. In the Jordanian Arabic Culture, Body parts are used to describe human emotion, behavior and all aspects of personal characteristics. However, a systematic study of the lexical and connotative/associative meaning of human body parts emphasizing their relationship with the lexicalized meanings within the culture is yet to be exploited. There have been some attempts here and there which deal with the usage of body parts figuratively, metaphorically and in proverbs in different societies to express similar or different meanings. Lakoff and Johnson (2001) point to the metaphoric usage of body parts which they call "personification". According to them, this type of metaphor is considered marginal for the European culture, namely, metaphors which regard objects as having a human body: "There are well-known expressions like the *foot* of the mountain, a *head* of cabbage, the *leg* of a table, etc." (ibid. 54-55). This paper has nothing to do with "personification", but emphasizes the relationship between lexical and connotative meaning as stated by Asher (2010), that connotative meaning has its root or has derived from lexical meaning. "Linguists working on word meaning have discovered many fascinating facts about the meanings of words. In particular, they have described various sorts of what appear to be modifications of lexical meaning due to the demands of a certain predicational environment" (Asher 2010: 1). That is, to my knowledge, this work is unique in its aim and scope.

3. Subjects and methodology

The subjects of the study are Jordanian Arabic native speakers from Almafraq district of north east Jordan. 100 subjects aged between 30-50 years participated in this work. Sex and educational levels were ignored since the study is on cultural-bound expressions. Each of them was given a list of 25 expressions for which they were to provide relevant cultural-based interpretations or meanings. The questionnaire was served informally to ensure natural and spontaneous responses.

4. Data and discussion

In this section, the data are some of the cultural expressions connected with body parts used in the speech of north eastern of Jordanians (some of them are used all over Jordan and in other Arab countries). These expressions denote color, size, shape, etc. of the body parts. I will provide a roughly literal translation to clarify the lexical meaning of these expressions. It is worth noting here that in Arabic the third person singular pronoun is used as a default. For instance, *eed* (hand), *eeduh* (his hand). Our examples can be used with all pronouns, for instance, instead of *eeduh* (his hand), we can say *eedha* (her hand), etc. The data are divided according to body parts.

4.1 eed (hand)

The hand is the part of the body used to do, carry, catch things, etc. It is the instrument for performing manual work and labour whether good or bad.

4.1.1 eeduh Taweelah (his hand is long/he has a long hand).

All the subjects (100%) did not refer to the lexical meaning of this expression, that is, "he has a long hand", the opposite of "short". They interpreted it as "thief" or "burglar". This connotative meaning can be related to the lexical meaning. The "burglar" uses his hand to steal and he can reach things wherever they are. The Arabic word *taweel* is more or less equivalent in meaning to the English "long or tall" which could be a good characteristic of persons to reach things. In some languages, the hand is involved in the activity of burglar. In Thia, for instance, *mue gaaw*, lexically means "a hand with glue on it" but the connotative meaning is "burglar".

4.1.2 eeduh fatHah (his hand is open)

Similar to the example in Section 4.1.1, all the subjects referred to the associative meaning of this expression. They interpreted it as "he spends money" while its lexical meaning (his hand is open) was ignored. To spend or waste things cannot be from a closed thing, it would definitely be from something that is loosely opened. In other words, if you have money or anything in your hand and you keep it closed, you won't lose your money. However, if you continue to open your hand unnecessarily, you will waste what is in your hand. Accordingly, the associative meaning of this expression is semantically related to the lexical meaning.

4.1.3 eeduh naDefah (his hand is clean)

Unlike the previous expressions, the lexical meaning of this expression is present in the responses received. 30% of the subjects used the lexical meaning side by side with the connotative meaning. The connotation of *eduh naDefah* is that he does not steal or try to benefit from his position in an illegal way. Generally, this expression is used to describe honest people who occupy certain jobs or position in government or business establishments without taking undue advantage of their position to gain money or properties illegally. Stealing and cheating are considered dirty behavior. Being clean (the opposite of "dirty") is an indication of purity. It is from this idea that the expression gains its interpretation.

4.1.4 eeduh bayDa (his hand is white)

None of the subjects referred to the literal color meaning of the hand in this context. All of them gave the connotative meaning which is "a helpful person". That is, this expression is used to describe someone who helps others to overcome their problems, e.g. to find a job. The strange thing is that the opposite "his hand is black" does not exist in Jordanian Arabic. It seems that the connection between white and purity and innocence could be behind this usage.

4.1.5 eeduh xafefah (his hand is light (opposite of heavy))

Again, none of the subjects referred to weight which signals the literal interpretation of the expression. This expression has more than one associative meaning: the first, which is positive, is "skillful person", while the second, which is negative, is "burglar". 40% of the subjects stated that it means "skillful person". 10% mentioned that it means "skillful burglar" while the rest (50%) stated that it means both "a burglar and a skillful person". All these are related to the same idea (skillful person) whether in making or stealing things. Since "light" means easy to move, "light hand" indicates that such hand can move easily and quickly.

4.1.6 eeduh eθqelah (his hand is heavy)

The lexical meaning of this expression was absent in our subjects' interpretations. There was agreement among the subjects that this expression means "unskillful person" or someone who is so slow in doing things. As can be noted, this expression is in contrast with that in Section 4.1.5. Again the associative meaning has its root in the lexical meaning. It is not easy to move heavy things just as heavy hand cannot be moved smoothly and quickly.

4.2 qalb (heart)

The heart is the most notable part which is used intensively to describe someone's state of mind, his feelings, thoughts, ideas, etc. It is interpreted as an index for all types of emotional states and behaviors.

4.2.1 qalbuh asswad (his heart is black)

All the subjects interpreted this expression according to its associative meaning. It means "a vengeful person". They agreed that this expression is used to describe "bad person", someone who hates others and wishes them bad and misery. Black, the opposite of white, is a color which represents evil and bad things in Jordanian culture. Moreover, the heart is considered the organ of feelings and emotions. That is, when the heart is described as black, it means that it is full of evil things. So, this expression has a direct semantic connection with the lexical meaning of the color "black".

4.2.2 qalbuh abyaD (his heart is white).

This expression has the opposite meaning of the expression in Section 4.2.1. Naturally, white is the opposite of black. It is used to describe someone who loves other people and does not harbor any evil thoughts about them. White is the color which represents honesty and purity. Accordingly, this expression acquires its meaning. That is, when the heart is described as "white" it means no evilness and honesty.

4.2.3 qalbuh ekbeer (his heart is big)

None of the subjects refer to the size, i.e. the "bigness" of the heart. The connotative meaning of this expression is that the person loves others and is a loveable person, characterized by forgiveness. Traditionally (in Jordanian culture), love is attributed to heart, and for it to be wide or big means it can accommodate more and more. The combination of these two words means "he loves others (many people)". It implies that he hates no body. This expression indicates the opposite meaning of the expression *qalbuh aswad* in Section 4.2.1.

4.2.4 qalbuh mayet (his heart is dead)

Lexically it could mean death. But all our subjects used the associative meaning which is "having no feeling, no love, no sympathy, etc." It should be noted here that this expression is not used in the case of negative feelings such as "hate". Generally it is used when someone shows no interest in the opposite sex. Therefore, the fact that the associative meaning is derived from the lexical meaning is clear. Death ends all sorts of feelings, and since, as stated above, feeling is connected with the heart, the death of the heart means the end of all feelings.

4.2.5 galbuh axDar (his heart is green)

This expression is almost the opposite of the one in Section 4.2.4. It means that his heart is full of feelings, looking for love, attracted to pretty girls. Generally, this expression is used when an old man shows a sort of interest in pretty girls or has a desire to get married. Green is a symbol of life in Jordanian culture, and is generally connected with grass or trees. So when we compare green grass with dried one, the meaning of "green heart" becomes clear.

4.3 elsan (tongue)

The tongue is one of the most important organs in the human body. It is responsible for speech production. When described with the use of adjectives, it can reflect the type or quality of speech in Jordanian Arabic.

4.3.1 elsanuh Heloo (his tongue is sweet)

For something to be sweet is generally pleasant. Therefore, when the tongue which is the organ of speech is described as being sweet, it means it utters pleasant words. It is used when using words to attract others, mainly females. All the subjects were unanimous on this interpretation.

4.3.2 elsanuh Taweel (his tongue is long)

In this expression, the denotative meaning was ignored by respondents. None of them talked about the size (length) of the tongue. This expression means that the person referred to has the habit of attacking others using bad words. He doesn't show respect to anyone and doesn't feel shy to use taboo words on others. Lexically, any long thing can reach more in comparison with the short. That is, his tongue can attack or reach anybody.

4.3.3 elsanuh maqtuu (his tongue is cut off)

This expression is used to describe someone who is not able to defend himself or respond directly when being attacked verbally by others. He does not like talking. The lexical meaning is not present in the interpretations supplied by our subjects. As stated above, the tongue is the organ of speech. When it is cut, the person cannot speak. From this lexical meaning, the associative meaning logically follows.

4.4 ain (eye)

The "eye" is the organ of sight. From the look of someone we can have a clue about his feelings, whether he hates, admires, loves, envies, etc. the thing or the person he looks at. The heart reflects whether he is happy, sad, or angry.

4.4.1 anuh Hamra (his eye is red)

The lexical meaning of this expression appears here side by side with its connotative meaning. 70% of the subjects used both readings, the lexical (his eye is red) and the connotative (he is a brave or courageous person). The other 30% of the subjects used only the connotative meaning. It should be noted here that if we use the plural form "his eyes" we mean the color and there is no connotative meaning. It seems that when some animals such as a wolf or dog get angry or ready to attack, his eyes are getting red. So, being brave and courage are connected with redness.

4.4.2 anuh Harah (his eye is hot [chili])

The lexical meaning of the above expression was ignored by all subjects. All subjects used the connotative which means that "he envies others" (envious or begrudging). Culturally, the person who envies others could harm them. As soon as he looks at a certain attractive part, that part will be damaged or deteriorated. Hot is connected with chili, which could be harmful or cause troubles when taken. It seems that the connotative meaning comes from this idea.

4.4.3 anuh bardah (his eye is cold [not chili])

All the subjects used the connotative meaning. This expression is the opposite of the previous one in Section 4.4.2. It means that this person does not envy others or cause harm to them when looking at them. It seems the connotative meaning comes from the fact that cold is the opposite of hot, while hot indicates harmfulness. By analogy, cold means harmless.

4.5 θum (mouth)

The mouth is the organ or the cavity which is important for speech production and for eating. Both reflect the personality and the characteristic of the person.

4.5.1 θumuh fateH (his mouth is open)

Both lexical and connotative meanings were used here. The connotative meaning is "he needs more and more (what he has is still insufficient). Generally, when this expression is used to describe a person, it implies that the person needs financial help. 55% of the subjects used the connotative meaning to explain this expression, 45% used both. However, this expression doesn't mean he is "greedy". Open implies that you can fill or add. If the door is open, you can enter. If a box is open, you can add or fill it with things, etc. From this lexical meaning, this expression acquires its connotative meaning.

4.5.2 θmuh waase (his mouth is wide)

80% of the subjects used the associative meaning (i.e he always needs more and more, or cannot be satisfied) to explain this expression. 20% of the subjects use both lexical and associative meanings. It seems that the connotative meaning comes from the fact that "wide and big" things cannot be filled easily. They need more and more filling. The difference between the two associative meanings lies on the fact that the second implies the first. That is, either what he has is insufficient, or he is greedy.

4.6 asnan (teeth)

The teeth are the parts of the body which help in cutting food. Moreover, they are considered as an indication of age. In most cases, when a person gets old, he starts losing his teeth.

4.6.1 asnanuh Haatah (toothless person) (his teeth fell down)

94.2% of our subjects used the associative or connotative meaning to explain this expression which means he has an experience. Only 8% used both lexical and associative meanings. Losing teeth is connected with aging, that is, old people lose their teeth. Moreover, old age is connected with having experience. So, as can be noted, the connotative meaning of the expression has its root in its lexical meaning. If somebody tries to deceive or cheat somebody else, the other person touches his teeth and says *isnaani Haatah* (my teeth fell down) to show that he has an experience with such tricks and cannot be cheated.

4.6.2 sinuh Tayb (his tooth is good)

The lexical meaning of this expression is that he has no problems in his teeth. The associative meaning which all the subjects pointed out is that "he eats a lot" (good in eating or he likes food). So, if you look at somebody who eats more than expected, you say *sinnuh taybah* (his tooth is good). Of course the ability to eat is connected with teeth. If you have any problem in your teeth, definitely you will have a problem in eating. The associative meaning has its semantic relation with the lexical meaning.

4.7 aDum (bone)

Generally the appearance of a person depends on his/her skeleton. If he/she suffers from any health problem in any part of his skeleton, definitely it will affect his physical shape and normal life. Strong bones mean a strong person while weak bones (i.e. osteoporosis) mean a weak person.

4.7.1 aDmuh gasi (his bone is hard)

All the subjects went for the connotative meaning of this expression. The connotative meaning is that the fellow cannot fail or be defeated. He can survive all types of problems and challenging situations. This interpretation does not generally mean physical strength. The expression is commonly used in relation to, for instance, having financial challenges, loss of beloved ones or fortune, etc. In other words, the fellow can cope with and overcome such situations. "Hard" simply means strong, while a hard thing is something which cannot be broken easily. The connotative meaning of this expression is derived or semantically related to its lexical meaning.

4.7.2 aDmuh Tary (his bone is soft)

This expression is almost the opposite of that in Section 4.7.1. Only the connotative meaning is present in the subjects' interpretations. The lexical meaning is that his bone is not strong, and can be easily broken. Soft bone is connected with infants or kids. The associative meaning of this expression is that "the fellow can be easily defeated, he has no experience, he is susceptible to failure, etc. It implies that it is difficult for him to face or come over any problem, or he has no experience to cope with difficult situations. The association between its lexical and connotative meanings is clear.

Table 1 below is a summary of the lexical and connotative meanings of body parts investigated in the study.

5. Conclusion

As can be noted, none of our above examples is interpreted according to its lexical meaning alone. The associative or connotative meaning is the dominant one. Moreover, the cultural impact is clear in such usages. That is, social believes, ideas etc. are reflected in the connotative interpretations of the expressions. The lexical and connotative meanings of the body parts are related to size, color, or certain types. Although the associative or connotative meaning is dominant, the lexical meaning is present, serving as the anchoring point to the connotative meaning. However, generally in their daily speech, Jordanian people use body parts instead of adjectives. So if you ask a certain person, instead of saying "he is a burglar", they would say "his hand is long". Then if you ask "what do you mean?", he would say "burglar". It seems that color and size have the same semantic impact. For instance, "Taweel" (tall or long) has a bad connotation whether we use it with "tongue" or "hand". With the former it means "a bad person who insults others and uses bad words", and with the later it means "burglar", i.e. a bad person. Another example the color "white". When used together with hand, it means "a helpful" person, and when used with heart, it means "a kind, lovable" person. Both mean a good person. This could be an indication that the connotative meaning has its root in lexical meaning.

Table 1   Summary of lexical and connotative meanings of body parts

Expression	Lexical meaning	Connotative meaning
eeduh Taweelah	His hand is long	Thief, burglar
eeduh fatHah	His hand is open	Spend or waste his money
eeduh naDefah	His hand is clean	Does not steal or get money illegally
eeduh bayDa	His hand is white	A helpful person
eeduh xafefah	His hand is light (not heavy)	Skillful person
eeduh eΘqelah	His hand is heavy	Unskillful person

Expression	Lexical meaning	Connotative meaning
qalbuh asswad	His heart is black	Full of hate, wishes others misery
qalbuh abyaD	His heart is white	Full of love and purity
qalbuh ekbeer	His heart is big	Love others
qalbuh mayet	His heart is dead	No feeling-no longer interested in the opposite sex
galbuh axDar	His heart is green	Full of feelings, looking for love, shows interest in the opposite sex.
elsanuh Heloo	His tongue is sweet	Use nice expressions, good in praising others
elsanuh Taweel	His tongue is long	Attack others, use negative words, shows no respect to others
elsanuh maqtoo	His tongue is cut off	Passive in speech, weak in defending himself
inuh Hamra	His eye is red	Brave, courageous person
anuh Harah	His eye is hot (chili)	Envy others, causing harm to others as a result of looking to what they gain.
anuh bardah	His eye is cold	Doesn't envy others
Өumuh fateH	His mouth is open	Needs more, not satisfied
Өmuh waase	His mouth is wide	Cannot be satisfied
Asnanuh Haatah	Toothless person	Has experience
sinuh Tayb	His tooth is good	Eats a lot, good in eating
aDmuh gasi	His bone is hard	Strong person, can face all types of problems
aDmuh Tary	His bone is soft	Affected by any situation

6. Limitations of the study

This work is limited in its scope and aim. It covers only seven parts of the body although all parts of the body can be involved in the study. Some of the mentioned body parts and others alike that do have sexual connotations are deliberately avoided in this paper. In addition, there is a limitation in the subjects of the study because it is assumed that these are cultural expressions and the number would not affect.

References

Allwood, J. 2003. Meaning potentials and context: some consequences for the analysis of variation in meaning. In H. Cuyckens, R. Dirven and J. Taylor (eds.), *Cognitive Approaches to Lexical Semantics*. 29-66. Berlin/New York: Mouton de Gruyter.

Asher, N. 2010. Lexical meaning in context: an introduction. PhD programme cognitive science research training group, *Adaptivity in Hybrid Cognitive Systems*. University of Osnabrück.

Evans, V. 2006. Lexical concepts, cognitive models and meaning construction. *Cognitive Linguistics* 17, 4, 491-534.

Croft, W. 2000. *Explaining Language Change: An Evolutionary Approach*. London: Longman.

Gibbs, R. 1999. Taking metaphor out of our heads and putting it into the cultural world. In R. Gibbs and G. Steen (eds.), *Metaphor in Cognitive Linguistics*. 145-166. Amsterdam: John Benjamins Publishing Company.

Lakoff, G. and M. Johnson. 2001. *Metaphors We Live by*. Chicago: University of Chicago Press.

Lee, S. S. and M. Dapretto. 2006. Metaphorical vs. literal word meanings: FMRI evidence against a selective role of the right hemisphere. *Neuro Image, 29*, 536-544.

Nissen, U. 2011. Contrasting body parts: metaphor and metonymy of mouth in Danish, English and Spanish. In Z. Maalej and N. Yu (eds.), *Embodiment via Body Parts: Studies from Various Cultures*. 71-92. Amsterdam: John Benjamins Publishing Company.

Obama. 2010. Available at http://voices.yahoo.com/language-culture-5185683.html.

Patricia, C. 1986. The acquisition of communicative style in Japanese. In B. Schieffelin and E. Ochs (eds), *Language Socialization Across Cultures*. 213-250. Cambridge: Cambridge University Press.

Swiderski, R. M. 1993. *Teaching Language, Learning Culture*. Westport, CT: Bergin & Garvey.

Vaink, E. 2011. Dynamic body parts in Estonian figurative description of emotion. In Z. Maalej & N. Yu (eds.), *Embodiment via Body Parts: Studies from Various Cultures*. 41-70. Amsterdam: John Benjamins Publishing Company.

Wierzbicka, A. 1992. *Semantics, Culture, and Cognition: Universal Human Concepts in Culture-Specific Configurations*. New York: Oxford University Press.

Wikipedia. http://en.wikipedia.org/wiki/Culture# Language_and_culture. Retrieved on April 14, 2012.

Wikipedia, http://www.authorstream.com/Presentation/UzielR-1272069-someone-like-you-connotation-exercise/. Retrieved on April 16, 2012.

William, C. 2000. *Explaining Language Change: An Evolutionary Approach*. London: Longman.

WIPO (The World Intellectual Property Organization). 2011. Intellectual Property and Traditional Cultural Expressions/Folklore. Available at http://wo.ala.org/tce/faq/. Retrieved on May 2, 2012.

SOV Word Order and Complex Syllable Structure in Pashto: A Proof of Negation

Muhammad Kamal Khan
Shaheed BB University, Pakistan

1. Introduction

This paper describes two characteristics of Pashto language as evidence to some of the implicational universals in the literature. It is concerned with the description of Pashto, firstly, as a representative SOV language and, secondly, its complex syllable structure which allows consonant clusters at both onset and coda levels.

A number of studies regarding dependencies among different levels of language have pointed out that languages with SOV word order tend to have simple syllable structure (e.g., CV[C]) and vice versa (Lehman 1973; Donegan and Stampe 1983; Gil 1986; Plank 1998; Fenk-Oczlon and Fenk 2004; Tokizaki 2011; Tokizaki and Kuwana 2012). This correlation between SOV word order and simple syllable structure has been typologically demonstrated by checking data from a number of languages and the phenomenon has been described as implicational universal: *an SOV word order implies a simple syllable structure*. The present study, by checking data from Pashto, however, shows that the very phenomenon does not exist in the case of the subject language. Pashto language is introduced briefly in the next paragraph. Section 2 provides the historical background to the basic word order as the foundation of such universals. Section 3 covers various aspects of Pashto word order establishing it as a strict head final (SOV) language. The next section summarizes important features of SOV-related tendencies. On the basis of the previous sections, Section 6 ascertains the position of Pashto as "proof of negation" to the discussed implicational universals. Finally, the last section concludes the discussion by raising some important questions related to the topic.

Pashto belongs to the Eastern Iranian sub-group of Iranian language family, an important group of Indo-Iranian branch of Indo-European origin (Payne 1987; Tegey and Robson 1996).

The language is spoken by approximately 50 million native speakers (Rehman 2009; Khan 2012) as it is spoken natively by considerable population in some major cities of Pakistan and Afghanistan.

Pashto has many interesting features and therefore has inspired some researchers to explore it. Although the language has not been much explored, its unique reverse sonority clusters (Bell and Saka 1982; Levi 2004) and its interesting second place clitics (Roberts 2000; Rehman 2014) have been discussed in detail. Similarly, the syntactic and phonological features of the language offer enough evidence for further discussion on the correlation between syllable structure and word order. Now, before exploring these features of Pashto in detail, an overview of the historical background of the correlation between SOV word order and simple syllable structure and the consequent implicational universals is pertinent.

2. Historical background

According to a number of linguists (e.g., Greenberg 1963, 1966; Lehmann 1971, 1973, 1978; Vennemann 1972; Hawkins 1983; Croft 1990), among linguistic components, syntactic component is the most significant component for the basis of linguistic typology. The basic order of the fundamental syntactic elements (i.e. subject, verb and object) is used as the central component in typological analysis.

As per linguists, there are many reasons why syntactic pattern is taken up as the basis for linguistic typology. Firstly, syntax regulates and makes use of different orders of words within a sentence. Such regulating of words is more significant than morphological and phonological characteristics of those words. Secondly, syntax contributes mainly to the fundamental meanings of the sentence. Thirdly, word order is the easiest way to observe the sequence of units within a sentence (Croft 1990). Moreover, *verb* is central in human languages and the addition of an object to a verb decides the word order of a particular language. Additionally, verb has the ability to form sentence solely and, therefore, it is the most important component of a sentence (Lehmann 1978). The simplest sentence is made of a verb or a verb and a subject or object. Languages of the world may be classified as either OV or VO according to the patterns of their verb in the basic syntactic structure. Keeping in mind this central role played by the basic syntactic components, typologists have based their typological implications on basic word order (BWO). Moreover, BWOs are correlated with particular structural features of languages for the classification of languages.

Greenberg (1966), whose WO universals have considerable impact on the typological study of languages, gives the following three types of BWO:

a) Verb + Subject + Object   (VSO)
b) Subject + Verb + Object   (SVO)
c) Subject + Object + Verb   (SOV)

Hawkins (1983) calls this classification as "Greenbergian Trichotomy". On the other hand, Lehmann (1971) mentions two possible BWOs, the VO (Verb+ Object) and OV (Object+ Verb). He considers the order of only two fundamental elements (i.e., verb and its object). He classifies languages on the basis of these two BWO types (VO languages such as English and OV languages like Japanese). Based on the idea of Lehmann, Vennemann (1972) reformulates the "Greenbergian Trichotomy" into the two possible BWOs by collapsing the VSO and SVO into one VO type. He gives this the notion of Natural Serialization Principle (NSP). NSP has contributed a lot in defining the basic languages into two types and providing logical explanation to BWO change.

The definition of BWO by Lehmann (1971, 1978) and Vennemann (1972, 1974, 1975) (i.e., the combination of *verb* and *object*) is considered fundamental by many typologists for the classification of languages. Although *subject* is also given importance for considering the BWO of languages, the division of languages into two categories (OV and VO) is considered more appropriate by linguists and, therefore, used for the classification of languages as well. Now, before surveying the proposed tendencies and features of relevant BWO, let me present the case of Pashto word order. The tendencies and implicational universals suggested for SOV languages are highlighted in Section 4.

3. Basic word order in Pashto

The syntactic features of Pashto have been explored by a number of studies (Penzl 1955; Shafeev 1964; Tegey and Robson 1996; Roberts 2000; Khan 2012). Ranging from simple reference grammar to detailed analysis of the syntactic structure, these studies explore the BWO of Pashto. Babrakzai (1999), Tegey and Robson (1996) and Roberts (2000) find that verbs always occur at the end of Pashto sentences. They mark Pashto to be "fairly rigidly" head-final language.

From the work of Shafeev (1964), the World Atlas of Language Structures (WALS)[1] provides details of Pashto as an SOV language. Similarly, the Syntactic Structures of the World's Languages (SSWL)[2] has the value of "yes" for the property of Subject+ Object+ Verb for Pashto and reports on Pashto as an SOV language. The above mentioned studies are mostly based on different varieties of Pashto (e.g., Kandahari and Kabuli dialects) but in all of these varieties, there is no variation of BWO. Here I give a brief analysis of BWO in Yousafzai dialect (the standard dialect of Pashto (Hallberg 1992; Rehman 2009; Khan 2012)).

As discussed above, Pashto maintains the head-finality as the most important constraint in its word order. Consider the following examples:

(1) ahsan   pəlet   ma:ʈkɽo

     S   O   V

Ahsan (MASC SG)   *plate*   *break-did(PAST PERF)M3SG*

     "Ahsan broke the plate."

(2) barja:l   ki:ʈa:b   wa:i

     S   O   V

Baryal   *book*   *read-do(TRANS)PRES F3SG*

     "Baryal reads a book."

(3) xor   maʃu:m   xkol kɽo

     S   O   V

The sister   *baby*   *kiss-did (PAST PERF) M3SG*

     "The sister kissed the baby."

(4) ba:tʃa   pətəŋ   əluzawi:

     S   O   V

Bacha   *kite fly- do (TRANS)PRES F3SG*

"Bacha is flying the kite."

Roberts (2000) discusses the possibility of the order OSV within some contexts subject to cliticization and topicalization. But such freedom is only possible in the past tense. In simple declarative sentences, the head-finality is the most important constraint and it is on the top of the hierarchy of syntactic constraints in Pashto. Note the following example:

(5) maʃu:m   mor ʈa   pəleʈ   war kɽo

     S   IO   DO   V

Child   *mother to*   *plate*   *give-do (Past Perf)*

     "The child gave the plate to the mother."

The word order is considered a bit flexible in ditransitive sentences by Roberts (2000) in sentences like the above. But such a relaxation is only possible with certain conditions:

- This is only possible with ditransitive verbs.
- The grammatical function of the arguments is clear from the context.
- The relevant case marking is given (as the particle [ʈa] along with the IO shows the

position of IO wherever it is placed).

Since there are certain conditions involved, we cannot declare this relaxation as a canonically possible one. In the future tense of Pashto, the crucial role is played by the clitic *ba*. Roberts calls it a second place clitic in Pashto as it is placed second to the noun in the sentence. He says that the future tense is created with the help of split agreement of the compound verb in Pashto. The relevant thing for our discussion is that such split agreement in future even maintains the same SOV order.

(6) gwəl   ba   maṇa   xwri:

    S   O   V

Gul(MASC) FUT   apple   eat(Present) MASC3S

   "Gul will eat apple."

The above sentence simply shows that the future tense reconfirms the canonical SOV pattern for the language. In the light of the above brief analysis and as suggested by other sources, we argue that SOV (Subject+ Object+ Verb) is the only order which is available in unmarked and syntactically simple sentences in all three tenses of the language. There are some languages which allow some word orders other than the canonical ones in some contexts. Pashto is not among such languages because it is fairly rigidly SOV. Only in sentences of diatransitive verbs, Pashto allows OSV but in such cases certain conditions (e.g., topicalization) are also to be fulfilled by the contexts. Finally we determine the following points:

1. Subject moves to Spec IP which is the leftmost position of the projection.
2. Objects follow their subjects.
3. The top ranking of HD-RT reflects the rigid behavior of the language of the head finality position in a clause.

Since it is an established fact that Pashto is an SOV language, the coming section highlights the tendencies and features proposed by the studies for such types of languages in the literature.

4. SOV word order and the implicational universals

In typological linguistics, languages are classified according to their structural types and there are studies which have proposed some tendencies and restrictions on certain possible language types. This section briefly discusses the major contributions based on the correlation between word order and syllable structure.

Lehmann (1973), among other morphological, syntactic and phonological correlations and implications, suggests that VO languages have complex syllable structure, while in contrast, the languages with OV word order have simple syllable structure. Table 1 gives his point here:

Table 1　Comparison between VO and OV languages

VO Languages	OV Languages
Have complex syllable structure Syllables are closed and end with consonants CCCVCCC Consonants clusters possible at both side of the nucleus	Simple syllable structure Syllables end in vowels, no consonant cluster possible at the end CV Mostly one consonant comes at the beginning

He provides examples from Japanese, Turkish, Quechua and Sanketi for OV languages and Classical Hebrew, Portuguese and Squamish for VO languages. Similarly, Donegan and Stampe (1983, 2004) and Donegan (1993) also contribute to the discussion of correlation between word order and syllable structure by comparing Munda and Mon-Khmer languages. They suggest that the syllable structure of SOV (Dependent-Head) languages is likely to be simple, i.e. (C)V. In contrast, languages with SVO (Head-Dependent) have complex syllable structure, i.e. (C)(C)V(G)(C) where G stands for glides. The crux of their comparison is shown in Table 2 below.

Table 2　Monda andMon-Khmer Languages

	MUNDA	MON-KHMER
Word order	SOV Dependent-Head	SVO Head-Dependent
Syllable canon:	(C)V(C)	(C)(C)V(G)(C)

It is illustrated by the table that languages with SOV order have simple syllable structures and languages with SVO maintain the complex syllable structure. Gil (1986) tests the same correlation between syllable structure and word order within data of 170 sample languages from Stanford Phonology Archives and the UCLA Phonological Segment Inventory Database.

Apart from the works given above, there are some databases which imply correlations from the data recorded by them. Universals Archives[3] lists 2029 *implicational universals* regarding various structures of languages. There are two universals which are important here. The same universals have been mentioned by some studies as evidence for their claims that there is a correlation between word order and syllable structure (e.g., Tokizaki and Kuwana 2012). These universals are given below in Table 3 and 4.

Table 3   Universal 196 of Universal Archives

Original:	OV languages tend to have simple syllable structure
Standardized:	IF basic order is OV, THEN syllable structure is simple (tending towards CV)
Formula:	OV $\Rightarrow$ simple syllable structure
Comments:	-

Table 4   Universal 207 of Universal Archives

Original:	VO languages tend to have complex syllable structure
Standardized:	IF basic order is VO, THEN syllable structure is complex (permitting initial and final consonant clusters)
Formula:	VO $\Rightarrow$ structure complex syllable
Comments:	_

From the above two universals, it is implied by the experts that there is a considerable difference between SOV and SVO languages based on their syllable complexity.

Fenk-Oczlon and Fenk (2004) analyze the same correlation between syllable structure and word order and argue that OV word order is rightly correlated with other linguistic features, like a very small number of phonemes per syllable and agglutinative morphological language structure. More recently, Tokizaki and Kuwana (2012) conclude from the data given by WALS- World Atlas of Language Structure that such correlations are certainly possible in which the simple syllable structure of SOV word order can be attested. They are of the view that there exists a possibility of such correlations and that the tendency of phonology and morphology is correlated with syntax. They listed a number of languages with constant OV order and counted the possible coda consonants. These languages show that OV languages have more limited variety of consonants in coda than VO languages.

The above studies suggest that there is a tendency of simple structure by SOV languages. Now, let us analyze the case of Pashto syllable structure which we witnessed to be a representative SOV language in Section 3.

5. The case of Pashto syllable structure

The highlighted studies in Section 4 suggest that an SOV language may have simple syllable structure (i.e. CV(C)). This section explores Pashto syllable in this regard.

A Pashto syllable ranges from a single vowel to the maximum of three consonants in the onset and two in the coda positions. There is the possibility of a total of twelve syllabic patterns in this language (Khan 2012). Pashto syllable contains at least one vowel as the peak in the nucleus which may be preceded or followed by consonant sounds. In Pashto the nucleus is always filled by a vowel because the language does not have any syllabic consonant. The nucleic vowel may be preceded by three and followed by two consonants to the maximum. The syllabic patterns of Pashto are given in Table 5 below.

Consonant clusters are possible at all three positions (word initial, medial and final positions) but maximum consonant combinations as clusters are possible at the word initial position. There is no restriction for onset consonants and a large number of consonants are possible at the coda level as well. Khan (2012) has calculated 108 combinations of consonant clusters possible in the base word forms in Pashto. Pashto phonology has also inspired researchers for a very interesting feature of reverse sonority clusters (Bell and Saka 1982; Levi 2004; Khan 2012). Its syllables are quite rich in terms of two-consonant clusters. Khan (2012) has given positions and combinations of consonant clusters in the language. These are given as an appendix at the end.

The above breakdown of Pashto clusters exhibits the richness of Pashto in terms of consonant clusters. Here the syllable structure of Pashto is summarized as follows.

- Pashto syllable structure is complex.
- It allows both closed and open syllables.
- The language is quite rich in terms of two-consonant clusters.
- The language not only allows consonant clusters but it also allows reverse sonority cluster.
- The maximum syllabic template of the language is (C)(C)(C)V(C)(C).

Table 5   Syllabic Templates in Pashto

Syllabic Patterns	Example	Glossary
V	[o]	sirrah
VC	[as]	mare
VCC	[aks]	jealousy
CV	[xa:]	okey
CVC	[xog]	sweet
CVCC	[ʃənd]	barren/impotent
CCV	[ɣlA:]	Theft
CCVC	[gra:n]	difficult/expensive
CCVCC	[dzwənd]	life
CCCV	[xwlə]	mouth
CCCVC	[ʃxwan] as in [sxwan. der]	bull
CCCVCC	[ʃxwand]	chewing

6. A proof of negation

As discussed in Section 4, the SOV word order has been correlated with simple syllable structure by a number of studies in literature. But by checking data from Pashto in Sections 3 and 5, it is evident that this is not always true. Pashto is an SOV language but it does have a rich variety of complex syllable structures and allows many consonant clusters. It is specifically rich in terms of two consonant clusters and allows a number of reverse sonority clusters also. The phenomena of Pashto give the "proof of negation" to such implicational universals based on the correlation between OV word order and simple syllable structure (and therefore, VO order and complex syllable structure too).

Pashto certainly does not agree on such a correlation and asserts that there is no such relationship between word order and syllable structure. It provides us with enough evidence to believe that the frequency, combinatory and distributional possibilities of consonant clusters are not always the property of only SVO languages. This leads us to raise many background questions such as: can word order be the foundation of such correlations? Is the word order of languages not changeable? If yes, how about the syllable structure? Can we theoretically justify such a correlation and finally the implicational universals? What does the modern theory (such as Optimality Theory) say about the nature of such implicational universals? And many more.

Although we are not in a position to argue on the basis of the data from just one language, we suggest the re-examination of such correlations and universals. For detailed investigation, the data must be added from enough sample languages. Samples must be carefully selected so that every language family has equal opportunity to represent the classifications and relevant features.

7. Conclusion

The case of Pashto presented in this paper casts serious doubts on the correlations between word order and syllable structure. Such a conclusion ultimately leads us to question the validity of implicational universals and correlation between syntactic and phonological structures. For further in-depth study of the phenomena, the inclusion of larger data of languages is recommended. Follow-up research may also be concentrated on the relationship between syllable structure and word order in different language families across time and space.

Notes

1. http://wals.info/ (accessed on August 20, 2011)
2. http://sswl.railsplayground.net/browse/languages/Pashto (accessed on Sep 26, 2011)
3. http://typo.uni-konstanz.de/archive/intro/index.php (accessed on July 20, 2010)

References

Babrakzai, F. 1999. *Topics in Pashto Syntax.* Doctoral Dissertation: University of Hawai'i at Manoa.

Bell, A. and M. M. Saka. 1982. Reversed sonority in Pashto initial clusters. *The Journal of the Acoustical Society of America, 72,* S100.

Croft, W. 1990. *Typology and Universals, Cambridge Textbooks in Linguistics* (2nd edition). Cambridge: Cambridge University Press.

Derbyshire, D. C. and G. K. Pullum. 1979. A select bibliography of Guiana Carib languages. *International journal of American Linguistics, 45* (3), 271-276.

Donegan, P. 1993. Rhythm and vocalic drift in Munda and Mon-Khmer. *Linguistics of the Tibeto-Burman Area, 16* (1), 1-43.

Donegan, P. and D. Stampe. 2004. Rhythm and the synthetic drift of Munda. *The Yearbook of South Asian Languages and Linguistics, 2004,* 3-36.

Donegan, P. J. and D. Stampe. 1983. Rhythm and the holistic organization of language structure. *CLS Parasession on the Interplay of Phonology, Morphology and Syntax, 19,* 337-353.

Fenk-Oczlon, G. and A. Fenk. 2004. Systemic typology and crosslinguistic regularities. In V. Solovyev and V. Polyakov (eds.), *Text Processing and Cognitive Technologies.* 229-234. Moscow: MISA.

Gil, D. 1986. A prosodic typology of language. *Folia Linguistica, 20,* 165-232.

Greenberg, J. H. (ed.). 1966. *Some Universals of Grammar with Particular Reference to the Order of Meaningful Elements* (2nd edition). Cambrigde Mass.: MIT Press.

Greenberg, J. H. 1963. Some universals of grammar with particular reference to the order of meaningful elements. *Universals of Language, 2,* 58-90.

Hallberg, G. 1992. *Sociolinguistic Survey of Northern Pakistan Volume 4 Pashto. Waneci, Ormuri.* National Institute of Pakistan Studies, Quaid-i-Azam University Islamabad.

Hawkins, J. A. 1983. *Word Order Universals.* New York: Academic Press.

Khan, M. K. 2009. *A Comparative Study of Pashto and English Linguistic Taboos.* Lahore: University of Management and Technology.

Khan, M. K. 2012. *Pashto Phonology: The Relationship Between Syllable Structure and Word Order.* Muzaffarabad: University of Azad jammu and Kashmir.

Lehmann, W. P. 1971. On the rise of SOV patterns in New High German. In *K.G.* Schweisthal (ed.), *Grammatik, Kybernetik, Kommunikation (Festschrift Alfred Hoppe), 19*-24.

Lehmann, W. P. 1973. A structural principle of language and its implications. *Language,* 47-66.

Lehmann, W. P. 1978. *Syntactic Typology: Studies in the Phenomenology of Language* (Vol. 10). Austin: University of Texas Press.

Levi, S. V. 2004. *The Representation of Underlying Glides: A Cross-linguistic Study.* Unpublished PhD dissertation, University of Washington.

Payne, J. 1987. Iranian languages. In B. Comrie (ed.), *The World's Major Languages.* 514-522. Oxford: Oxford University Press.

Penzl, H. 1955. *A Grammar of Pashto: A Descriptive Study of the Dialect of Khandahar, Afghnistan.* Washington D.C.: American Council of Learned Society.

Plank, F. 1998. The co-variation of phonology with morphology and syntax: a hopeful history. *Linguistic Typology, 2*, 195-230.

Rehman, G. 2009. A comparative study of Pashto and English phonology for English language learning. Unpublished M. PhD Thesis, University of Management and Technology, Lahore.

Rehman, G. 2014. *Verbal Clitics in Pashto.* Muzaffarabad: University of Azad Jammu and Kashmir.

Roberts, T. 2000. *Clitics and Agreement.* Unpublished Doctoral Dissertation, Massachusetts Institute of Technology.

Shafeev, D. A. 1964. *A Short Grammatical Outline of Pasht.* (edited and translated by Herbert H. Paper). The Hague: Mouton and Co.

Tegey, H. and B. Robson. 1996. *A Reference Grammar of Pashto.* Washington DC: Center for Applied Linguistics.

Tokizaki, H. 2011. Correlation between Word Order and Phonology: Variation in Dialects and Languages. In *Variation and Typology: New trends in Syntactic Research*, 68.

Tokizaki, H. and Y. Kuwana. 2012. Limited consonant clusters in OV languages. In P. Hoole, L. Bombien, M. Pouplier, C. Mooshammer and B. Kühnert (eds.), *Consonant Clusters and Structural Complexity.* Berlin: Mouton de Gruyter.

Vennemann, T. 1972. Analogy in generative grammar: the origin of word order. In *Proceedings of the 11th International Congress of Linguists.* Bologna.

Vennemann, T. 1974. Topics, subjects and word order: from SXV to SVX via TVX. *Historical linguistics, 1*, 339-376.

Vennemann, T. 1975. An explanation of drift. In C. N. Li (ed.), *Word Order and Word Order Change.* Austin: Texas University Press. 269-305.

Russell's Paradox and the Logic of Language

Aizhen Zhang[a] and Weizhen Chen[b]

[a]Fujian Normal University, China;

[b]Fujian Normal University, China

1. Introduction

Paradox in a broader sense refers to any statement or tenet contrary to received opinion or belief. In a narrow sense, it only refers to a statement or proposition which on the face of it seems self-contradictory, though, on investigation, it may prove to be well-founded. Russell's paradox is the most famous of the logical or set-theoretical paradoxes, which has dealt a blow both to Frege's theory of the foundations of mathematics, and the naïve set theory created by Georg Cantor. Ever since it was discovered by Russell, the attempt to avoid the paradox has prompted a great deal of work in logic, philosophy and linguistics. Even today, it is still topical, and will not go away in the future (e.g. Moorcroft 1993; Du 2012).

Interestingly enough, young Wittgenstein ends *Tractatus* 3.333 by announcing summarily that he has made Russell's paradox *vanish*. There is an intention in his proposition that his formula solves the paradox better than Russell's theory of logical types. However, at first, Bertrand Russell himself ignored this solution of his paradox (Sutrop 2009). Moreover, it is also disregarded both by the Russellians and most Wittgensteinians, discussed neither in the special studies on Russellian contradiction (Quine 1963; Garciadiego 1992; Link 2004) nor in the comparison of Whitehead and Russell's *Principia* and Wittgenstein's *Tractatus* (e.g. Rao 1998).

This paper, thus, tries to first explore Russell's paradox and then explain how Russell and Wittgenstein approach this problem in different ways. With an in-depth analysis of the paradox and the possible solutions, this paper also attempts to address the following issues: Does Wittgenstein's solution fundamentally unravel the logical problems of language? Or at least, does he successfully render the theory of types superfluous as he himself has claimed? If yes, what status do symbolic language and natural language have in his earlier and later philosophy?

By approaching these problems, it is hoped that this paper will shed some light on the study of Wittgenstein's philosophy as well as the logic of natural language.

2. Russell's paradox and Russell's theory of types

Central to any theory of sets is a statement of the conditions under which sets are formed. Apart from simply listing the members of a set, it was initially assumed that any well-defined condition (or precisely specified property) could be used to determine a set. In other words, for any formula $\varphi(x)$ containing *x as a free variable, there will exist the set* $\{x: \varphi(x)\}$ whose members are exactly those objects that satisfy $\varphi(x)$. This is, however, where Russell discovers the contradiction. In a letter to Frege, he raises the problem as follows:

> Let "w" be the predicate: to be a predicate that cannot be predicated of itself. Can "w" be predicated of itself? From each answer, the opposite follows. Likewise, there is no class (as a totality) of those classes which, each taken as a totality, do not belong to themselves. From this I conclude that under certain circumstances a definable collection does not form a totality. (Russell 1902)

An alternative formulation of the paradox that is closer to real-life situations and may be easier to understand for non-logicians might as well be dramatized as the "Catalogue Paradox". Suppose a library has to compile catalogues of all its books. Since the catalogue is itself one of the library's books, some librarians include it in the catalogue for completeness; while others leave it out as it being one of the library's books is self-evident. Now imagine that the library is going to compile a bibliographic catalogue of all (and only those) catalogues which don't list themselves in the catalogue. The question is, "Should it list itself?" On one hand, we cannot include it in its own listing, because then it would include itself, which then should belong to the other catalogue, that of catalogues that do include themselves. On the other hand, if we leave it out, the catalogue is incomplete, for it should include all the catalogues that don't list themselves. Either way, it can never be a true catalogue of catalogues that do not list themselves. Hence the paradox.

Russell's paradox has had profound ramifications for the historical development of class or set theory. It makes the notion of a universal class (a class containing all classes) extremely problematic. It also brings into considerable doubt the notion that for every specifiable condition or predicate, one can assume that there exist a class of all and only those things that satisfy that condition. The properties version of the contradiction—a natural extension of the classes or sets version—raises serious doubts about whether one can be committed to objective existence of a property or universal corresponding to every specifiable condition or predicate.

Russell's own response to the paradox comes with his aptly named *Theory of Types*. Believing that self-application lies at the heart of the paradox, Russell tries to solve the problem by stratifying terms in an ascending ordered hierarchy of types: objects terms have type 0, predicate terms that apply to objects (as in "This apple is red") have type 1 or are first-order, predicates of predicates (as in "Redness is an color") have type 2 or are second-order, and so on, indefinitely. To make it easier to understand, we could call this solution "simple theory of types" and list the logical types defined by Russell in the following way (c.f. Han 2007):

> objects of type0: individuals (stuff different from set, function or proposition etc.)
> objects of type1: classes of individuals (or the function of individuals)
> objects of type2: classes of classes of individuals (or the function of the function of
>   individuals)
>
> ...

As we can see in this system, a set is regarded as being of a higher type than its member. In this way, it becomes possible to refer to all objects for which a given condition (or predicate) holds only if they are all at the same level or of the same "type". Take propositional function $\varphi(fx)$ for example, which could be expressed as "*x is tall*", by which we can yield sentences like "*John is tall*", "*Jack is tall*" etc. But if the function takes itself, i.e., "*x is tall*", as the argument, producing a sentence like "'*x is tall' is tall*", it is a meaningless combination of words.

Therefore, Russell stipulates that no term of any type can be applied to any other term of the same or higher type, but that for any terms in any well-formed proposition of the logic, only a predicate term of type $n+1$ can be applied to a predicate or object term of type n. Thus, we can only legitimately ask whether the object of Type n is a member of the objects of Type $n+1$, instead of asking whether the object of Type n is a member of itself. By doing so, we can avoid Russell's paradox, which is formulated in symbolic logic by means of sentences containing predicates that purport to express formal logic, semantic, or set theoretical self-non-applications.

This solution is motivated in large part by the adoption of the so-called *vicious circle principle*. As Whitehead and Russell explain.

> An analysis of the paradoxes to be avoided shows that they all result from a kind of vicious circle. The vicious circles in question arise from supposing that a collection of objects may contain members which can only be defined by means of the collection as

a whole. Thus, for example, the collection of propositions will be supposed to contain a proposition stating that "all propositions are either true or false." It would seem, however, that such a statement could not be legitimate unless "all propositions" referred to some already definite collection, which it cannot do if new propositions are created by statements about "all propositions." We shall, therefore, have to say that statements about "all propositions" are meaningless. ... The principle which enables us to avoid illegitimate totalities may be stated as follows: "Whatever involves all of a collection must not be one of the collection"; or, conversely: "If, provided a certain collection had a total, it would have members only definable in terms of that total, then the said collection has no total." We shall call this the "vicious-circle principle," because it enables us to avoid the vicious circles involved in the assumption of illegitimate totalities. (Whitehead and Russell 1950: 37)

As is well known, we can't introduce an object or property with a definition that depends on that object or property itself. Otherwise we are committing an error of circular argumentation. In addition to ruling out definitions that are explicitly circular, like "An object has property P iff it has a property no different from P", it also rules out definitions that quantify over domains which include the entity being defined. Russell's paradox, in a way, stems from the definition of the set N, a set that contains all sets that are not members of themselves. This kind of definition by itself is problematic, for it defines a new set in terms of the totality of all sets, of which this new set itself would be a member.

If we consider proposition in terms of propositional function, this principle in effect states that before a function can be defined, one must first specify the function's domain, namely, those objects to which the function will apply. Otherwise, it will lead to contradiction. Consider again the previous example cited by Russell. In the sentence "*All propositions are either true or false*", if "all propositions" here includes the sentence "*All propositions are either true or false*", then we will have "'*All propositions are either true or false' is either true or false*", which is thus similar to liar paradox, a paradox arising from saying of itself by making judgment on oneself.

3. Wittgenstein's solution to Russell's paradox

Wittgenstein (1947) summarizes the whole of Russell's Theory of Types as "A function cannot be its own argument, because the functional sign already contains the prototype of its own argument and it cannot contain itself". And he attacks it as "superfluous", commenting that $F(F(fx))$ is not an example of a function taking itself as its own argument, because, to him, with an adequate symbolism, $F(F(fx))$ is simply not permissible instead of not possible. That is to say, in logical syntax, "$F(F(fx))$" simply does not exist. This is how he explains it.

...in this, the outer functions F and the inner function F must have different meanings; for the inner has the form ψ (fx), the outer the form ψ (φ (fx)). Common to both functions is only the letter "F", which by itself signifies nothing. (Tractatus 3.333)

As we know, a functional sign is simply the sign of the function; the function being what the sign signifies. In "F(F(fx))", the outer "F" signifies a function, while the inner "F" the argument of the function defined by the outer "F". So, Wittgenstein pinpoints the root problem of Russell's paradox as applying the same sign to different symbols, which are supposed to be differentiated by different signs like, φ or ψ.

Here, Wittgenstein's approach is relying heavily on the distinction between *sign* and *symbol*:

The sign is the part of the symbol perceptible by the sense. Two different symbols can therefore have the sign (the written sign or the sound sign) in common—they then signify in different ways... Thus, there easily arise the most fundamental confusions (of which the whole of philosophy is full). (Tractatus 3.32-3.327)

So, for Wittgenstein, the equivocations permitted by the same sign conventionally representing different symbols makes ordinary language a logician's nightmare. They are also the source of philosophical difficulties, where many sign-symbol confusions are less easy to uncover or disentangle. Consider again Russell's paradox. As is pointed out by Kelly Dean Jolley (2004), F(F(fx)) appears to be a case of function acting as its own argument, but if we consider the logical syntactic application of the sign, we see that the functions share the same sign "F", but not the same symbol. The outer "F", considered in its significant use, has two blank spots; the inner "F" has only one. Hence, the two signs are different symbols. However, this formula, on the one hand, requires "F" to refer to the same object signified by the same symbol or the same function; on the other hand, it also demands that "F" should refer to two different objects signified by two different symbols, i.e., function φ(fx), and function ψ(φ(fx)) with φ(fx) as its argument. Under such circumstance, contradiction is bound to arise.

Wittgenstein thus summarizes in 3.332 that for an adequate symbolism, "no proposition can say anything about itself, because the propositional sign cannot be contained in itself (that is the 'whole theory of types')". In other words, now that paradox in effect involves a proposition or a function saying about itself, we can simply avoid the problem by ruling out self-referential (reflexive) sentences. So, according to Wittgenstein's interpretation of Occam's razor, Russell's theory of types is unnecessary, and logically meaningless.

But what an "adequate symbolism" or a proper "sign language" in Wittgenstein's sense is all about is actually not systematically or sufficiently elaborated in his works. Perhaps Wittgenstein himself doesn't know exactly what are sufficient for an adequate symbolism or sign language, but from the account in *Tractatus*, we can infer that the essence of a proper symbolism, according to Wittgenstein, is the distinction between *sign* and *symbol*. As the confusion of the two is very often the cause of philosophical problems, Wittgenstein stipulates:

> In order to avoid these errors, we must employ a symbolism which excludes them, by not applying the same sign in different symbols and by not applying signs in the same way which signify in different ways. A symbolism, that is to say, which obeys the rule of logical grammar—of logical syntax". (Tractatus 3.325)

In short, Wittgenstein concludes that errors of contradiction arising from type-transgressing, vicious circle, self-application, etc. could all be avoided with this simple stipulation. Furthermore, he also points out that it is nonsensical to make attempts to solve "problems" that have traditionally been regarded as philosophical. He believes that by adopting a correct view of the logic of language that excludes all philosophical discourse as nonsense, we can avoid being troubled by philosophical puzzles. That is to say, we can hope to resolve philosophical "problems" by recognizing that there are no such problems and that philosophical "propositions" are nonsensical pseudopropositions involving logically meaningless abuses of language.

4. Paradox, symbolism and natural language

With the help of logical symbolism, we can indeed solve a lot of logical as well as semantic paradoxes. Consider the following two classical paradoxes in history:

(1) Russell's paradox. Russell's paradox actually arises from this tricky question: If N is defined as the set of all sets that are not members of themselves, is N a member of itself? To put it in a more visible way, If $N \in N$, we then have N= {n1, n2, n3,...N...} . Here, as can be easily seen, the propositional sign N is contained in itself.

(2) Liar's Paradox. Liar paradox formulates a proposition that says of itself that it is a lie or it is false. If the sentence is true, then it is false, since it says of itself that it is false; if the sentence is false, then it is true, since then it falsely says of itself that it is false. We can again convert this problem into a sequence of sentences that can show, in a more direct way, how the contradiction violates Wittgenstein's stipulation of sign and symbol. Consider **S1**:

S1: What I am saying is false.

As in accordance with the liar paradox, "what I am saying" refers to **S1**, we can replace "what I am saying" with **S1**, and have

[S1[S1 what I am saying is false] is false]

where **S1** contains itself and a paradox arises. This sentence again can be rewritten as, in much the same way,

[S1[S1 [S1what I am saying is false] is false]is false]

So, it is also arguable that we have a paradox here as this process can go on and on, with the value of the sentences oscillating between true and false.

More examples of semantic paradoxes can be listed to show the feasibility of Wittgenstein's solution to paradox. Think of the following two sentences:

(a) I doubt everything.

(b) I know I know nothing.

Obviously, if the sign "everything" in **(a)** contains the proposition **(a)**, we then have **(a)** = {*I doubt* [...**(a)**...]}, which leads to a similar paradox.

As for **(b)**, which is less perspicuous, it can be reformulated as:

(c) I know I don't know anything.

Likewise, if **(c)** is contained in "anything" in the proposition, we will have **(c)**={*I know I don't know*[...**(c)**...]}, which is also a paradox.

However, can we then come to the conclusion that the fact that the propositional sign is contained in itself will necessarily give rise to paradoxes? The answer is not that simple, though. Look at the following examples:

(d) I like everything.

As has been done above, **(d)** can be also analyzed as **(d)** ={*I like*[...**(d)**...]} if **(d)** is contained in "*everything*." But what is interesting now is that there is nothing wrong even if **(d)** is contained in itself.

It is therefore a big temptation to take reflexivity or self-reference plus negation as the sufficient and necessary condition of a paradox. But consider the following sentence:

(e) I don't like anything.

For the convenience of analysis, (e) can be transformed into (e) ={*I don't like* [...(e)...]}, when (e) is contained in itself. Nevertheless, it makes senses if one, say, a misanthropist, doesn't like anything, including this proposition. Negation plus self-reference once again appears to be insufficient to explain the whole phenomenon of paradox.

A more interesting example made up by Kripke (1975) is (f):

(f) Most (i.e., a majority) of Nixon's assertions about Watergate are false.

Seemingly, nothing is intrinsically wrong with (f), nor is it ill-formed. However, in certain context, it could also become contradictory. Consider (g):

(g) Everything Jones says about Watergate is true.

Suppose that (f) is Jones's sole assertion about Watergate, or alternatively, that all his Watergate-related assertions except perhaps (f) are true. Then it requires little expertise to show that (f) and (g) are both paradoxical: they are true if and only if they are false. (f) perfectly shows that it would be fruitless to look for an ***intrinsic*** criterion that will enable us to sieve out, as meaningless, or ill-formed, those sentences which lead to paradox. The fact is simply that no syntactic or semantic feature of (f) guarantees that it is unparadoxical.

It is true that Wittgenstein's logical symbolism, or the idea of an adequate symbolism, can indeed explain and solve Russell's paradox in a much simpler way than Russell's Theory of Types, but it is not the panacea to the logical problems in natural languages, or at least, all the logical problems of paradoxes. The above analysis can at most indicate that reflexivity might lead to self-referential paradoxes, which, unfortunately, reveals very little about the operation of logic in natural language, for it cannot identify the particular formula or context that decisively turns a sentence into a paradox.

So far, we have come to the position to understand something that is often misunderstood as the divide for earlier and later Wittgenstein: the status of symbolic language and natural language. Does earlier Wittgenstein hold that symbolic language is better than natural language, which lead to the effort to construct an ideal language more precise and logic than natural language? The answer from Russell is no doubt representative of the common interpretation. In *Introduction* to *Tractatus*, Russell remarks,

Mr. Wittgenstein is concerned with the conditions for a logically perfect language—not that any language is logically perfect, or that we believe ourselves capable, here and now, of constructing a logically perfect language, but that the whole function of language is to have meaning, and it only fulfils this function in proportion as it approaches to the ideal language which we postulate.

But this obviously goes against Wittgenstein's intention. In *Tractatus* 5.5563, Wittgenstein clearly states that "In fact, all the propositions of our everyday language, just as they stand, are in perfect logical order." This kind of point of view is once again recycled in *Philosophical Investigation* §98,

On the one hand it is clear that every sentence in our language 'is in order as it is'. That is to say, we are not **striving after** an ideal, as if our ordinary vague sentences had not yet got a quite unexceptionable sense, and a perfect language awaited construction by us.—On the other hand it seems clear that where there is sense there must be perfect order.—So there must be perfect order even in the vaguest sentence. (Wittgenstein 1968)

Convinced that the ideal order is there in every sentence of natural language, Wittgenstein by no means thinks of symbolic language as better than natural language. For him, type-transgressing, namely, mistakes in natural language that can never occur in symbolic language, cannot occur in any language, whether symbolic or natural. If a sentence in a natural language is meaningless, the explanation cannot be that the sentence type-transgresses. It is no more possible to type-transgress in a natural language than in a symbolic language. Any natural language sign in which a symbol can be seen is meaningful. A meaningless natural language sign is one in which no symbol can be seen. But this means that it is also one that will not type-transgress: it is not ill formed but rather unformed (c.f. Jolley 2004).

As we see it, for Wittgenstein, the difference between the symbolic language and the natural language is that the symbolic language can be used to show the symbols seen in the signs of a natural language. When there are no symbols to be seen in the signs, then the signs of natural language are meaningless—but not because something has happened in them that cannot happen in the symbolic language, but rather because nothing has happened in them at all. And that is why there is no representing them in the symbolic language. The problem is not that the symbols in its signs type-transgress, the problem is that there are no symbols in its signs. Meaningless sentences, because of type-transgressing, no more exist in natural language than in symbolic language (c.f.

Jolley 2004).

However, the way symbolic language is better than the natural one is that we can gather the logic of language from the symbolic language in an easier or more direct way than from the natural language. Wittgenstein in *Tractatus* 4.002 put it in this way, "everyday language is a part of the human organism and is just as complicated. It is humanly impossible to gather the logic of ordinary language from it directly." Anscombe (1959) has rightly pointed out that Wittgenstein tries to understand the logic of natural language by studying and constructing logical symbolism.

5. Postscript

The above discussion shows that Wittgenstein's theory of logical symbolism approaches Russell's paradox in a simpler yet more significant way than Russell's Theory of Types, but still hasn't achieved the goal of revealing the logic of natural language, or at least we can say that given natural language in use, reflexive paradox hasn't *vanished* as declared in *Tractatus*. However, it by no means indicates that natural language is logically imperfect, nor does it imply that we should totally give up the attempt to construct some symbolic language to explain the logic of natural language.

We also show that Wittgenstein consistently believes that natural language is in perfect logical order, as is supported by the fact that human beings can acquire, understand and use an indefinite number of sentences within a limited period of time without much deliberate effort despite the complexity of grammar and ambiguity of word meanings. The difference between earlier and later Wittgenstein lies in the fact that the earlier Wittgenstein strives to reveal the perfect logic in natural language by constructing a systematic theory of symbolic language, whereas later Wittgenstein seems to have given up this attempt and tries to explain the logical problem, or the "*grammar*" problem of language (a frequently used term in *Philosophical Investigation*) in terms of "forms of life".

What should be especially noted is that later Wittgenstein challenges the need to have a systematic approach to any paradoxes. He says one should try to overcome the superstitious fear and dread of mathematicians in the face of a contradiction. According to him, the proper way to respond to any paradox is by an ad hoc reaction instead of any systematic treatment designed to cure it and any future ills. We can either claim some paradoxes are meaningless, some are neither true nor false, and some are simply not sentences. Whichever choice is made, it needn't be backed up by any theory that shows how to systematically incorporate the choice. After all, the language can't really be incoherent because we've been successfully using it all along, so why all this fear and dread? In a word, to understand the logic, or "grammar", of natural language, we need resort to the forms of life people are living in. This is simply the call from Wittgenstein.

References

Anscombe, G. E. M. 1959. *An Introduction to Wittgenstein's Tractatus*. London: Hutchinson University Library.

Du, G. 2012. Development in the study of Russell's paradox. *Journal of Hubei University*, 5, 1-6.

Garciadiego, A. R. 1992. *Bertrand Russell and the Origin of the Set-theoretic "Paradoxes"*. Basel, Boston, and Berlin: Birkhäuser Verlag.

Han, L. 2007. *A Companion to Tractatus*. Beijing: The Commercial Press.

Jolley, K. D. 2004. Logic's caretaker—Wittgenstein, logic, and the vanishment of Russell's paradox. *The Philosophical Forum*, 3, 281-309.

Kripke, S. 1975. Outline of a theory of truth. *The Journal of Philosophy*, 72, 690-716.

Link, G (ed.). 2004. *One Hundred Years of Russell's Paradox: Mathematics, Logic, Philosophy*. Berlin: Walter de Gruyter.

Moorcroft, F. 1993. Why Russell's paradox won't go away. *Philosophy*, 68, 99-103.

Quine, W. V. O. 1963. *Set Theory and its Logic*. Cambridge: The Belknap Press of Harvard University Press.

Rao, A. P. 1998. *Understanding Principia and Tractatus: Russell and Wittgenstein Revisited*. San Francisco, London, and Bethesda: International Scholar Publications.

Russell, B. 1902. Letter to Frege. In J. van Heijenoort, (ed.), *From Frege to Godel: A Source Book in Mathematical Logic, 1879-1931*. 124-125. Cambridge: Harvard University Press.

Sutrop, U. 2009. Wittgenstein's Tractatus 3.333 and Russell's paradox. *Trames*, 2, 179-197.

Whitehead, A. N. and B. Russell. 1950. *Principia Mathematica* (2nd edition). Cambridge and London: Cambridge University Press.

Wittgenstein, L. 1947. *Tractatus Logico-philosophicus*. London: Kegan Paul, Trench, Trubner and Co., Ltd.

Wittgenstein, L. 1968. *Philosophical Investigations*. Oxford: Basil Blackwell.

Part Two
Educational Linguistic Studies

Exploring Content: Building Knowledge in School Discourse

J. R. Martin

University of Sydney, Australia;

Shanghai Jiao Tong University, China

1. Knowledge blindness

For more than a decade now, researchers drawing on systemic functional linguistics (hereafter SFL) and legitimation code theory (hereafter LCT) have been engaged in transdisciplinary research into knowledge building in education (Christie and Martin 2007, Christie and Maton 2011). Martin and Maton (2013) report on one significant phase of this research, which focused on secondary school history and biology. The papers in that volume specifically address what Maton (e.g. 2013, 2014) refers to as "knowledge blindess", which he characterizes as the tendency for progressivist and constructivist educators to focus on generic processes of learning, and sideline the issue of how the nature of knowledge itself both constrains and enables teaching/learning. From a linguistic perspective this blindspot is reflected in the largely "intransitive" discourse abounding in publications and conferencing, where ongoing reference is made to processes of reading, writing, speaking, listening, viewing and learning[1] without specification of the "object" of these processes. It is as if students are reading and listening and viewing to learn to understand to write to pass so they can continue reading and listening and viewing to understand to write to pass and so on, without reference what is being taught, learned and assessed – namely the discipline specific knowledge of subjects (their content if you will).

In this paper I approach this issue from the perspective of SFL and the genre-based literacy of the so-called "Sydney School" (Derewianka and Jones 2012, de Silva Joyce and Feez 2012, Rose and Martin 2012). I begin by introducing the context variable field, which SFL uses to map the knowledge at play in everyday life, in specialized trades, crafts, hobbies and recreational activities, and in management, government and academe—in short, in all walks of life. I next focus on secondary school science, by way of elaborating the specialization of knowledge in that field. Then, in closing, I consider the way in which the understandings arising from this perspective can be used in the design of principled pedagogic activities such as those evolving in the Reading to Learn (hereafter R2L) programs developed by David Rose (Rose and Martin, 2012).

2. Field

In SFL meanings can be explored from a number of different perspectives. These include the level of abstraction at which analysis is undertaken (i.e. phonology/graphology, lexicogrammar, discourse semantics, register and genre in Martin and Rose 2003, 2008) and the kind of meaning involved (i.e. ideational, interpersonal, textual). Note that context is modeled as register and genre, which are treated as abstract levels of meaning. A schematic outline of these perspectives is presented as Figure 1.

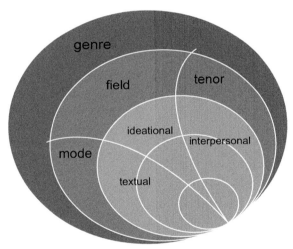

Figure 1   The intersection of stratification and metafunction in SFL
(viewing diagonally from top to bottom the co-tangential circles represent genre, register, discourse semantics, lexicogrammar and phonology/graphology)

Martin (e.g. 1992) treats field as involving a set of activity sequences which work together to enact one or other walks of life (in the home, at work, at prayer, at play etc.). Each field additionally involves specialized taxonomies of the people, places and things involved in these activities, organized by classification (type and sub-type relations) and composition (whole and part relations). These people, places and things, whether abstract or concrete, may in addition be graded in relation to one another in arrays (e.g. professional ranks such as Lecturer A, Lecturer B, Senior Lecturer, Associate Professor, Professor, or measurements such as cup, pint, quart and gallon).

In the penultimate chapter of Martin and Rose (2008) a multimodal text concerning mulga trees from a secondary school geography textbook is analysed (Scott and Robinson 1993); throughout the textbook words and pictures cooperate to build knowledge of Australian desert environments and their fauna and flora (touched upon in Martin 2013a). Two pages further the book moves on from mulga plains to spinifex plains. The main bush found there is commonly referred to as spinifex (although botanically it is Triodia species, not Spinifex species), and even more commonly as hummock grass (because of its mound-like shape when young) or porcupine grass (because of its sharp pointed blades). Compositionally speaking we can distinguish the plant's roots (very deep), stem (full of resin), blades (curled), flowers and seeds (as sketched out in Figure 2 below).

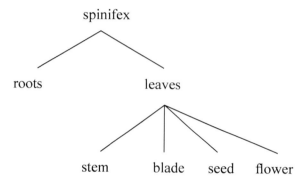

Figure 2   Composition of a spinifex bush

The desert environments this species inhabits, the spinifex plains, are construed in the textbook through classification (using their flora and fauna, fertility and rainfall as criteria)—as desert ranges & rocky outcrops, plains or rivers, and if plains, then as mulga plains, spinifex plains or saltbush & blue bush plains. By intersecting this classification of arid lands with a classification of the living things found there, we arrive at a geographic perspective on the kind of thing spinifex is, as outlined in Fig. 3 below (where square brackets mean "or" and curly brackets "and"). The crucial point I am making in Figures 2 and 3 here is that from the perspective of the field of physical geography, simply recognising a spinifex bush, as a visitor to central Australia or in a photograph, is not enough; in addition, its uncommon sense composition and uncommon sense classification are central to its meaning in this field.

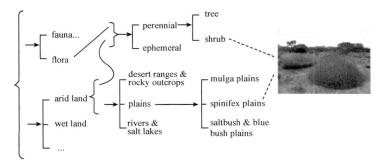

Figure 3   Physical geography classification of spinifex bush (flora x environment)

Beyond its composition and classification the spinifex bush is involved in a number of activity sequences which are fundamental to its survival in its desert environment (for the explanation genres mounting these sequences see Unsworth 1997; Veel 1997). There are processes of transpiration and photosynthesis to consider, including the spinifex bush's adaption for these in its desert environment (the fact that each blade of this grass has its own root which penetrates three or more meters into the soil for example, or the curled leaves which curtail water loss but are annoyingly painful for the humans which run into them). And turning from day time to life time, we can consider its life cycle—moving from its generation as a young hummock, to a mature clump (hollowing out with a dead centre as its grows outwards and thereby creating a favorite sleeping spot for kangaroos), to its loss of foliage when it burns intensely in fire, to its regeneration from its roots (or fire-induced germination from seeds). An outline of this cycle is presented as Figure 4.

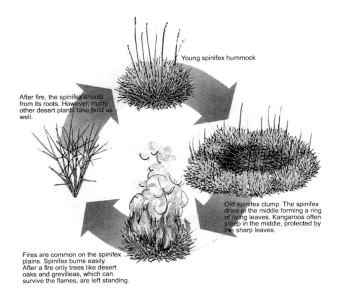

Figure 4   Life cycle of the spinifex (Scott and Robinson 1993: 25)

From the perspective of Legitimation Code Theory (LCT) the strength of the semantic density of the entity spinifex, as understood in physical geography, includes its "valeur" in the composition and classification taxonomies exemplified above, alongside the role it plays in any sequences in which it is involved (see Maton 2013). There is thus much more to the meaning of the term than a simple definition affords (Halliday and Martin 1993, Martin 1989, Wignell et al. 1990)—relatively strong semantic density (conceived in terms of the number of semantic relations in play) is involved as well.

3. Semantic waves

Maton (2013, 2014) introduces the notions of semantic gravity (the degree to which meaning relates to its context) and semantic density (the degree of condensation of meaning), LCT concepts that can be usefully considered from the perspectives of technicality and abstraction in SFL (e.g. Martin 1990, 1993, Wignell 1998, 2007a, b). In the phase of classroom discourse below for example the technical term cilia is unpacked as little hairs (a relatively concrete phenomenon from everyday life), thereby strengthening its semantic gravity and weakening its semantic density.

(1)

T: Okay B... what are the 'cilia'. What was it? No? A... do you know what cilia is? No? D...?
   Someone must know what they are...

S: Hairs.

S: The little hairs?

T: The little hairs.

After some further discussion the teacher aggregates the uncommon sense meaning of cilia as part of a table on the board.

cilia	Hair-like projections from cells lining the air passages	Move with a wavelike motion to move pathogens from the lungs until it can be swallowed into the acid of the stomach

Maton suggests mapping the dynamics of knowledge building of this kind by means of a graph plotting the strength of sematic gravity and semantic density (the y axis) over time (the x axis). A semantic wave characterizing the explanation of cilia noted above is outlined in Figure 5 below.

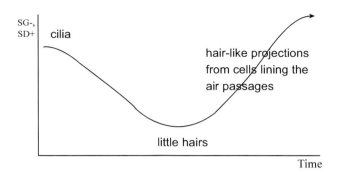

Figure 5   Profiling the explanation of cilia as a semantic wave (after Martin 2013b)

4. Power words, power grammar, power composition

4.1 Power words

From the perspective of SFL waves of semantic gravity and semantic density of this kind implicate all dimensions of field—classification (i.e. what kind of organism cilia are), composition (i.e. where in organisms they are found and how they are themselves composed) and sequencing (i.e. what processes they participate in), as specified in Martin (2013b). At stake in the lesson phase examined here is the classification of cilia as a part of a cell (classification and composition) and the role they play expelling pathogens (implication sequencing). The relevant classification taxonomy is outlined in Figure 6, which positions cilia as an kind of organelle protruding from eukaryotic cells, subclassified as motile or not, and if motile as flagella (involving a whip action for propulsion, e.g. sperm) or cilia (involving a wave motion, e.g. cilia in air passages).

organelle

    cilia (proturbence from eukaryotic cell)

        ⌐motile (undulipodia)
        │   ⌐flagella (whip action for propulsion)
        │   └cilia (wave motion)
        └non-motile (primary-sensory antennae)

Figure 6   Classification of cilia as a type of organelle

As we can see, building up the specialized knowledge of an uncommon sense field such as biology involves large numbers of technical terms (*cilia, cells, pathogens* etc.). Critically, each term implicates specialised uncommon sense relations of classification, composition and sequencing. Specialised knowledge is not in other words a word salad—a collection of unfamiliar words; rather, the relations among the technical terms are critical. In our work with secondary school teachers (Macnaught et al. 2013) we have highlighted the strong semantic density afforded by technical terms and the relations among them by referring to them as **power words** (i.e. words that confer the authority of the knowledge they encode as disciplinary power).

4.2 Power grammar

What about grammar? Is uncommon sense grammar at stake here too? Consider the following passage which focuses on the defining feature of the eukaryotic cells cilia protrude from, namely their enclosing membrane:

(2) Cells are wrapped in a cell membrane, which controls what goes into and comes out of the cell. Material made of small particles moves in and out of cells through pores in the cell membrane. Sometimes this movement requires energy. This movement is necessary to supply substances needed by the cell and to remove wastes. (Haire et al. 2004: 103)

The function of the cell membrane is to control what enters and leaves the cell. Three ranking clauses (*what goes into // and comes out of the cell // material made of small particles moves in and out of cells*) describe this process in terms of an entity participating in an action in a setting; and in each case the entity is realized by a nominal group, the action by a verbal group and the setting by a prepositional phrase. In Halliday's terms (e.g. 1998, 2004) in these clauses we have a matching relation between semantics and grammar, a realisation relation which he refers to as congruent. The grammar directly encodes the meaning.

Table 1   Congruent realization of cell membrane function in grammar

entity	action	setting
nominal group	*verbal group*	*prepositional phrase*
what	*goes*	*into (the cell)*
(what)	*comes*	*out of the cell*
material made of small particles	*moves*	*in and out of cells…*

The text then makes four further references to this process (*sometimes this movement requires energy // this movement is necessary // to supply substances needed by the cell // and to remove wastes*). In each, the semantic figures involving the entities, actions and settings tabulated in Table 1 (what goes, comes, moves) are now realized as a nominal group (*this movement*) rather than a clause. Halliday refers to incongruent realisations of this kind as metaphorical, with grammatical categories in tension with semantic ones (with grammar symbolizing meaning in other words rather than directly encoding it). The metaphorical realisation here condenses meaning as a nominal group and thereby opens up the meaning potential of nominal groups for this package of meaning. The semantic figures in Table 1 for example are condensed into clauses in which "this movement" becomes an entity that requires energy, supplies substances and removes wastes. This realignment of semantic and grammatical categories is outlined in Table 2.

Table 2   Metaphorical realization of cell membrane function

[entity action setting]	action	entity
nominal group	*verbal group*	*nominal group*
this movement	*requires*	*energy*
this movement	*supply*	*substances...*
(this movement)	remove	wastes

As just illustrated, grammatical metaphor is a fundamental resource as far as uncommon sense construals of the world are concerned. In particular we need to highlight its special role in the definitions which establish technical terms and in explanations. Returning to the focus on Australia's arid lands with which we started this paper, consider the following passage:

(3) The loss of vegetation due to overgrazing has caused soil erosion. Soil erosion is the loss of the soil and nutrients which make the grasses and trees grow. Wind and water remove the soil. Once the soil is eroded, the land cannot be used for production. These areas become "deserts" of unusable land. Desertification, as the spread of deserts is called, is a major world problem. (Scott and Robinson 1993: 61)

In this text two terms are defined, soil erosion and desertification. Both terms involve grammatical metaphor—with soil erosion condensing the congruently realized figure unpacked as *soil is eroded* and desertification packing up the congruently realized figure *these areas become deserts*. Equally important is the fact that the definitions of both these terms themselves involve grammatical metaphor—with **the loss** *of the soil and nutrients...* defining soil erosion and **the spread** *of deserts* defining desertification. This interaction between grammatical metaphor and technicality is further explored in Martin (1990, 1993).

Table 3   Grammatical metaphor in relation to definitions (nominalizations italicized)

term	definition
soil *erosion*	the *loss* of the soil and nutrients which make the grasses and trees grow
desertification	the spread of deserts

As far as explanation is concerned, grammatical metaphor plays an equally critical role. Consider for example the following implication sequence:

animals overgraze the land

(so) land loses vegetation

(so) wind and water remove soil

(so) land becomes desert

(so) land cannot produce

Here we have a semantic sequence realized in its congruent form—one clause after another with conjunctions construing the relation between one clause and the next (here, cause and effect).

But as we have seen, this text involves a number of technical terms: two were defined in the text (soil *erosion* and *desertification*), and three are assumed (*loss of vegetation, overgrazing, production*). Distilling whole activities as single terms makes it possible to draw on the explanatory resources of the clause (together with clause combining), and so use verbal groups and prepositional phrases to construe cause/effect relations within clauses, alongside conjunctions between clauses. So instead of saying that animals overgraze the land and so the land loses vegetation we can say *the loss of vegetation is due to overgrazing*, expressing the link between figures as a preposition (*due to*). And instead of saying that the land loses vegetation and so wind and water erode the soil we can say *the loss of vegetation has caused soil erosion*, expressing the link between figures this time as a verbal group (*has caused*). And if we want to make both overgrazing and loss of vegetation responsible for soil erosion, we can used grammatical metaphor to do so—simply by expanding the agentive (i.e. causer) nominal group. This is in fact what our original text has done: *The loss of vegetation due to overgrazing has caused soil erosion.*

Realizing more than one semantic figure inside a clause not only increases the explanatory power of specialized discourse, but opens up resources for evaluation and coherence as well. As far as evaluation is concerned, nominal groups afford grammar's most powerful resources for expressing attitude—targeting both people and things (Martin & White 2005). If for example we wanted to colour our account of the erosion of Australia's arid lands, inscribing an environmental stance (Martin 2002, Veel 1998), then the grammatical metaphors described above provide a comfortable host for greening: *the **distressing** loss of vegetation due to **irresponsible** overgrazing has caused **significant** soil erosion.* A milder version of this stance was in fact inscribed in our original text in relation to desertification—which is classified as *a major world problem.*

Grammatical metaphor is also a crucial resource for managing the flow of information in abstract written discourse. The passage we are working on here was in fact preceded by a paragraph on overgrazing, as reproduced below:

(3)   The arid lands of the world are being overgrazed. The United Nations has estimated that on 3.1 billion hectares 4 billion cattle, sheep, goats and camels graze. This is too many for the land to support.

The loss of vegetation due to overgrazing has caused soil erosion. Soil erosion is the loss of the soil and nutrients which make the grasses and trees grow. Wind and water remove the soil. Once the soil is eroded, the land cannot be used for production. These areas become 'deserts' of unusable land. Desertification, as the spread of deserts is called, is a major world problem. (Scott & Robinson 1993: 61)

In terms of information flow, *the loss of vegetation due to overgrazing* packages up all the information of the preceding paragraph as Theme of the clause, which is in turn expanded by *soil erosion* as its New information. *Soil erosion* is then made Theme in the next clause and expanded with *the loss of the soil and nutrients which make the grasses and trees grow* as New (its definition in fact). Later on in the paragraph, eroded land which cannot be used for production is made Theme (*these areas*) and expanded as *"deserts" of unusable land.* The expansion is then thematised as *desertification* and expanded as *a major world problem.* This particular rhythm of thematic orientation and news, from Theme to New to Theme to New, is outlined in Table 4 below (following Martin 1992, Martin and Rose 2003/2007). Without grammatical metaphor it would not be possible to package up just the information we need as Theme or New for this specialised field.

Table 4   Information flow—Theme (including marked Theme), and New (including extended New)[2]

(marked) Theme	(extended) New
the arid lands of the world	are being overgrazed
the United Nations	has estimated
that (on 3.1 billion hectares) 4 billion cattle, sheep, goats and camels	graze

(to be continued)

(marked) Theme	(extended) New
this	too many for the land to support
the loss of vegetation due to overgrazing	(has caused) soil erosion
soil erosion	the loss of the soil and nutrients which make the grasses and trees grow
wind and water	(remove) the soil
(once the soil is eroded), the land	(cannot be used) for production
these areas	(become) 'deserts' of unusable land
desertification…	a major world problem
<<as the spread of deserts	is called>>

Without grammatical metaphor we would in fact have to rely on a very spoken pattern of information flow, which I have caricatured in the following text.

(4) Too many animals can overgraze the land and if they do the land loses vegetation and if it does wind and water remove the soil and nutrients and if they do grasses and trees cannot grow and if they cannot farmers cannot use such areas to graze animals and they turn into deserts and if this keeps happening the deserts spread and we have a major world problem.

Scott and Robinson (1993: 51) in fact exemplify the contrast between spoken and written styles of explanation illustrated above in the captions for their figures 3.3 and 3.4. Figure 3.3 is a photo of desertified land and its caption is more spoken:

(5) Cattle and feral animals have eaten the vegetation.
    It has been overgrazed
    and blown away.
    The soil is then washed
    and blown away.

Figure 3.4 is a photo of wild horses grazing and has a more technical metaphorical caption:

(6) Domestic animals [[that have gone wild]], such as horses, goats, rabbits and donkeys, have also overgrazed the vegetation causing erosion

In our work with secondary school teachers (Macnaught et al. 2013) we have highlighted the crucial role played by grammatical metaphor as far as definition, explanation, evaluation and information flow are concerned by referring to it as **power grammar** (i.e. grammar that confers the authority of written discourse for the production and reproduction of specialized knowledge).

4.3 Power composition

Power grammar, along with power words, may also be involved in managing information flow beyond the clause. Scott and Robinson (1993: 50-51) for example discuss a number of issues involved in the management of arid lands. The headings organizing this discussion are outlined below.

(7)

The issues involved in managing the arid lands

Issue number 1 (SG+, SD-)

Changes to burning (SG-, SD+)

…

Issue number 2 (SG+, SD-)

Changing land ownership and responsibilities (SG-, SD+)

…

Issue number 3 (SG+, SD-)

Disappearing vegetation and soil (SG-, SD+)

…

Issue number 4 (SG+, SD-)

Changing animal life (SG-, SD+)

…

The main heading introduces the stages of the text as issues and specifies these as addressing land management. Subsequently, each sub-heading consists of two parts. The first is meta-textual, ordering the presentation of issues in relation to one another (e.g. *Issue number 1*), while the second is content oriented, specifying the particular issue to be addressed (e.g. *Changes to burning*). From the perspective of LCT the first headings have stronger semantic gravity than the second, since they refer directly to the sequence of the issues on the two-page spread readers are observing; conversely, the second headings have stronger semantic density than the first, since they flag specific entity and sequence relations relevant to managing arid lands. These relative values are notated below as SG+/- and SD+/-; indenting is used to show the move from higher layers of scaffolding to forecast ones. This scaffolding involves nominalizations (*changes, responsibilities*) and a number of technical terms (*land ownership, vegetation, animal life*). And there are 4 non-finite clauses[3] (acts)—*managing the arid lands, changing land ownership and responsibilities, disappearing vegetation and soil* and *changing animal life*; each of these could have been alternatively realized as a grammatical metaphor (on the model of the initial heading *changes to burning*)—*management of the arid lands, changes to land ownership and responsibilities, disappearance of vegetation and soil, changes to animal life*. The layout and formatting of the headings reinforces the scaffolding of the discussion here, with its macroTheme foregrounded at the top of the left-facing page and its four hyperThemes numbered below (each of which is then developed through a series of clause length waves of Theme and New). The general pattern we are looking at here is outlined in Figure 7 below, with layers of Theme potentially scaffolding a text's method of development in relation to its genre and layers of New potentially scaffolding a text's point in relation to its field (after Martin 1992, 1993, Martin and Rose 2003/2007). As indicated in the diagram, higher layers of Theme are prospective, predicting how a text will unfold; layers of News are retrospective, summing up where a text has gone. The more consciously planned and edited a text is, the more scaffolding of this kind is found.

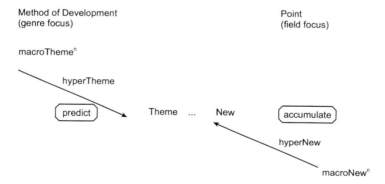

Figure 7   Layers of Theme and New (scaffolding genre and field respectively)

Abstract technical discourse featuring weak semantic gravity and strong semantic density relies heavily on scaffolding of this kind to organize information flow. Haire et al. (2004: 103) for example scaffold the text from which we took the cell membrane example above as outlined below (Text 8). Like Scott & Robinson they use headings to highlight this information flow; unlike Scott & Robinson they elaborate the first 5 of their headings with clauses spelling out the orientation of their macroTheme or hyperTheme (the *All wrapped up* heading is in fact elaborated 3 times).

(8)

In the five kingdoms

No matter how different an organism looks on the outside, its cells have the same basic structure.

Cells *of the* **five kingdoms**

Although the basic cell structure is the same, variations in the design are used to classify organisms into five main groups or kingdoms.

…

The brain *of the* **cell**

A largish round structure called the **nucleus** is the control centre of the cell. It contains chromosomes that contain information to keep the cell alive and working properly.

…

All *wrapped* **up**

Cells are wrapped in a **cell membrane**, which controls what goes into and comes out of the cell.

…

Cytoplasm is the part of the cell inside the cell membrane but outside the nucleus.

…

Some cells have another boundary around the cell membrane, called the **cell wall**.

…

Micro *factories* **and** *departments*

Structures called **organelles** are found in the cytoplasm of eukaryotes. They include mitochondria, chloroplasts, vacuoles and starch grains.

…

One cell *or* **more**

…

How big *is* **small**

…

The periodicity of their third section is spelled out in (8') below. Of special interest here is the use of metaphorical headings which draw analogies between the scientific field being developed and less technical concepts—between "wrapping presents" and cell membranes and cell walls here (*All wrapped up*); and between "brains" and the cell nucleus in the preceding section (*The brain of the cell*), and between "factories and departments" and organelles in the following one 76 (*Microfactories and departments*). We have more than a simple shift in semantic density at play here, since in each case an everyday field is being introduced as symbolizing a different uncommon sense one (a synergistic relation between what Bernstein 1996/2000, 1999 refers to as horizontal and vertical discourse).

(8')

macroTheme

All *wrapped* up

hyperTheme

Cells are wrapped in a **cell membrane**, which controls what goes into and comes out of the cell.

Material made of small particles moves in and out of cells through pores in the cell membrane. Sometimes this movement requires energy. This movement is necessary to supply substances needed by the cell and to remove wastes.

hyperTheme

Cytoplasm is the part of the cell inside the cell membrane but outside the nucleus.

In the cytoplasm hundreds of chemical reactions take place, transferring energy, storing food and making new substances. This activity within the cell is called its **metabolism**.

hyperTheme

Some cells have another boundary around the cell membrane, called the **cell wall**.

This gives protection, support and shape to a cell.

To this point the scaffolding discussed (Texts 7 and 8) has been prospective. An instance of retrospective scaffolding is illustrated in Text 9 below, from Scott and Robinson (1993: 21-22). The macroNew emphasizes the difficulty desert perennials have producing and reproducing from seed, evaluating the sequence flagged in the macroTheme (*Flowering and setting seed*) on the basis of the information provided in the conditional explanation.

(9)

macroTheme

Flowering and setting seed

hyperTheme

For many years geographers thought that our arid land shrubs and trees only flowered after rain. We now know this is not true.

The long living plants flower each year. Even in a dry time mulga will flower in spring and summer. The tree simply makes less flowers. If it rains in spring the tree makes more flowers.

hyperTheme

Even if a tree flowers it may not set seed.

Setting seeds uses a lot of energy, energy that may be needed to find water during a drought. If it has rained the tree does not have to use as much energy to find water. For the mulga to set seeds there must be rain in late summer and again in winter. When the seeds drop to the ground, rain is then needed if the seeds are to start growing.

What are the chances of the mulga tree being lucky enough to have these showers of rain when it needs them? The answer is very rarely—about once every ten years. So even if you see a desert plant flowering it may not mean that the plant will set seed.

hyperTheme

Other trees also grow in the mulga plain.

These desert perennials also need rain and sunshine at certain times to set seeds. These periods are called windows of opportunity.

macroNew

It is not easy for desert perennials to flower and set seed and for the seed to develop, drop and then grow. Only rarely are the conditions right for the plant to set seeds.

We can see here (Text 9) one of the ways in which SFL's approach to layers of Theme and New can be related to LCT's concept of semantic waves, as shifts in semantic gravity and semantic density correlate with layers of prospective and retrospective textual scaffolding. Technically speaking the organization of information flow in SFL is referred to as a text's periodicity (Martin 1992, Martin and Rose 2003/2007). In our work with secondary school teachers (Macnaught et al. 2013) we have highlighted the crucial role played by periodicity as far as managing layers of information flow is concerned as **power composition** (i.e. composition that confers the authority of discourse which has been textured to facilitate access to records of knowledge).

5. Knowledge building and pedagogy

5.1 Reading to Learn

For students at all levels, one of the major literacy challenges is the problem of having to read and harvest information from handouts, textbooks, web materials and model texts. The Reading to Learn (R2L) programs developed by Rose and his colleagues (Rose 2007, 2008, 2010, 2011, Rose and Martin 2012) have addressed these challenges by designing curriculum genres that provide teaching/learning activities for both reading and writing. This has involved both global and local design.

Globally, the R2L program takes learning a curriculum field through reading as its starting point, and writing for evaluation as its goal, via a flexible sequence of nine activities (Figure 8 below). Let's begin with the outer circle of these teaching/learning cycles. Preparing for Reading supports all students in a class to follow a text with general understanding as it is read aloud, identify its key information, and make notes. These notes may be used later on to support a Joint Construction, which involves the teacher and students constructing a comparable written text together (in the same genre, with the teacher in a mentoring role). Joint Construction may be followed by Individual Construction, with students writing comparable texts of their own using the same genre, again with the teacher's support, before independent writing for assessment. These activities directly embed literacy learning in curriculum teaching, as teachers select text from their curricula for reading and writing, plan their lessons around these texts, and evaluate students through the genres they have taught them to write.

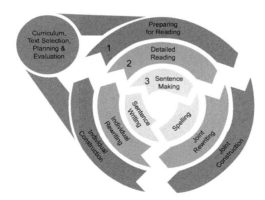

Figure 8   Reading to Learn teaching/learning cycles (Rose and Martin 2012: xx)

Turning to the middle circle, to ensure that all students can independently read curriculum texts with full comprehension, and use their language resources in their own writing, focus passages may be selected from the reading and model texts for Detailed Reading and Joint

Rewriting. Detailed Reading involves local design—carefully managed sentence-by-sentence guidance. Each sentence in the selected passage is first paraphrased for students, in terms that all can understand, and read aloud. Students are then guided to read each salient element of the sentence through interaction cycles of the kind outlined in Figure 9 (cf. Martin 2007, Martin and Rose 2005, 2007).

Figure 9   The local design of R2L teaching/learning interactions

In Detailed Reading, students' tasks are to identify elements of meaning in each sentence. Prepare moves give the meaning of the element to the class as a whole, in terms that all can understand. A Focus question is then addressed to a particular student, whose task is to identify the element and read it aloud. As a result of the preparation, the evaluation can always Affirm the chosen student (taking turns from task to task ensures that all students are successfully engaged in the interaction around the text). The teacher then directs the class to highlight the exact wording in the sentence (adding a Direct move to the generalized cycle for different teaching/learning tasks outlined as Figure 9). Their success in turn ensures that all students benefit from the Elaborate move, in which the meaning is further defined, explained or discussed (e.g. unpacking unfamiliar terms, abstract nominalizations and lexical metaphors) and related to students' experience. A micro-interaction of this kind might unfold as follows:

Note that just one or more paragraphs may be selected for Detailed Reading—ones that are particularly dense or technical for example. The Preparation moves illustrated above assume that the term "factor" has already been introduced, as the text's field and genre have been discussed previously in the Preparing for Reading stage. Through such guidance, key information in the passage is highlighted.

In the next stage of the middle cycle (Joint Rewriting), for factual genres students take turns scribing this highlighted information as notes on the class board, and the teacher guides them to rewrite these notes as a new text. Students can then use the same notes for Individual Rewriting of a text as different as possible from the joint text (holding genre and field constant), with the teacher circulating and providing as much guidance as needed. The focus here is on developing the grammatical resources for writing technical discourse, embedded in learning the curriculum. With stories and persuasive genres, Detailed Reading focuses on literary or evaluative language patterns of a selected passage, and Joint and Individual Rewriting follow the same language patterns but with different content.

(10)

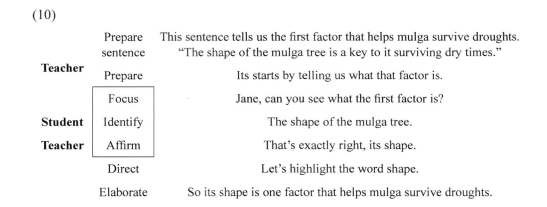

Teacher	Prepare sentence	This sentence tells us the first factor that helps mulga survive droughts. "The shape of the mulga tree is a key to it surviving dry times."
	Prepare	Its starts by telling us what that factor is.
	Focus	Jane, can you see what the first factor is?
Student	Identify	The shape of the mulga tree.
Teacher	Affirm	That's exactly right, its shape.
	Direct	Let's highlight the word shape.
	Elaborate	So its shape is one factor that helps mulga survive droughts.

Turning now to the inner circle of activities, further support may be provided through Sentence Making, Spelling and Sentence Writing. For this cycle, one or more sentences from the Detailed Reading passage are written on cardboard strips, which students are guided to cut up and re-arrange, strengthening their control over the grammatical patterns. Individual words are then cut up into their letter patterns, which students practise spelling on individual whiteboards. They then use this spelling knowledge to practise writing the whole sentences on their boards. The focus at this level is thus on foundation literacy skills, embedded in reading and writing curriculum texts. This level of intensive language activities can be especially helpful for students who are just beginning to read and write, who have been struggling with literacy, or are learning English as an additional language (these activities can be usefully supplemented in ESL/EFL contexts by drawing the text-based grammar building suggestions in Jones and Lock 2010). We should also keep in mind that even advanced students who are struggling with reading and writing dense passages of grammatical metaphor can benefit from well-designed inner circle activities (packing and unpacking metaphorical discourse for example, as exemplified in section 4.2 above).

These nine sets of strategies schematized in Figure 8 (Page 100), as three cycles, provide different levels of scaffolding support for reading and writing the curriculum. As with all Sydney School curriculum genres, movement around or between cycles is at the discretion of the teacher, depending on students' literacy levels in relation to the challenge of the genres in focus. Educators concerned about the relevance of the various cycles considered here for able students need to keep in mind that literacy learning is a lifelong process, and that in R2L classrooms texts are chosen which challenge the whole class, not just weaker students.

5.2. Scaffolding knowledge

5.2.1 Detailed reading (power words, power grammar)

A simplified annotated model of the teaching/learning cycle iterated in Detailed Reading activity is presented as Figure 10 below. The Prepare and Elaborate moves in this cycle offer important opportunities for developing students control of both power words and power grammar. Assuming a challenging passage of text has been chosen, the tendency in Prepare moves will be for the teacher to strengthen the semantic gravity (SG+) and weaken the semantic density (SD-) relative to the items students will have to identity and highlight in the text. For the Elaborate moves on the other hand, the teacher might choose to adjust semantic gravity and semantic density in different directions, at times "powering up" (SG-, SD+) into more academic language and at times "powering down" (SG+, SD-) to engage with more familiar understandings or experience; at times both powering up and powering down might prove useful (in an extended elaboration).

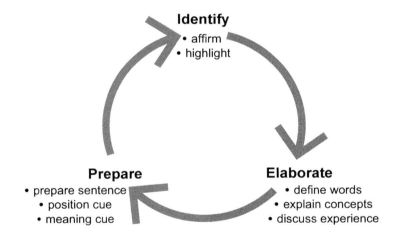

Figure 10   Teaching/learning cycle for Detailed Reading (simplified)

Let's focus at this point on one phase of Text 8' (Page 98), repeated as 8'' below:

(8'')   **Cytoplasm** is the part of the cell inside the cell membrane but outside the nucleus. In the cytoplasm hundreds of chemical reactions take place, transferring energy, storing food and making new substances. This activity within the cell is called its **metabolism**.

Interaction[4] around the second sentence of 8'' might involve prepare moves which gloss in general terms the meaning of the sentence after which the sentence in question is read aloud:

(11)

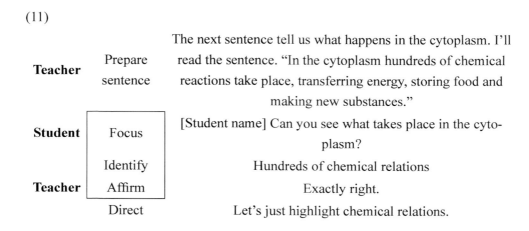

Teacher	Prepare sentence	The next sentence tell us what happens in the cytoplasm. I'll read the sentence. "In the cytoplasm hundreds of chemical reactions take place, transferring energy, storing food and making new substances."
Student	Focus	[Student name] Can you see what takes place in the cytoplasm?
	Identify	Hundreds of chemical relations
Teacher	Affirm	Exactly right.
	Direct	Let's just highlight chemical relations.

The Focus, Identify and Affirm sequence then zeros in on what happens in the cell, namely *hundreds of chemical reactions*. As far as power words and power grammar are concerned, the teaching/learning thus moves from lower semantic density (*what happens*) to higher semantic density (*hundreds of chemical reactions*). The sequence powers up into more challenging discourse (Figure 11 below).

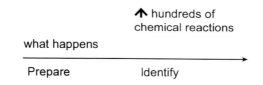

Figure 11   Powering up between Prepare and Identify moves

The teaching/learning then might move on to the functions of these chemical reactions, one at a time, with the Prepare Focus Identify Affirm sequence powering up again (from *three functions… the first one* function to *transferring energy*):

(12)

Teacher	Prepare	Then it says three things those chemical relations do, three functions.
Student	Focus	[Student name] What's the first one?
	Identify	Transferring energy
Teacher	Affirm	That's right.
	Direct	Just highlight energy.
	Elaborate	Transferring energy means taking energy from a chemical relation to do other work.

The Elaborate move then unpacks *transferring energy* as *taking energy from a chemical reaction to do other work*, powering down to make the concept of energy transfer more accessible to students.

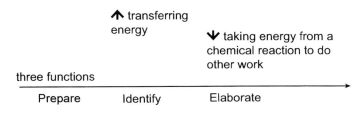

Figure 12   Powering down in an elaborating move

For the second function, the elaboration powers up, boosting the semantic density of *storing food* as *converting nutrients into glucose*:

(13)

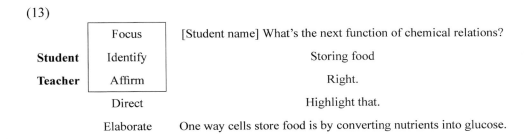

	Focus	[Student name] What's the next function of chemical relations?
Student	Identify	Storing food
Teacher	Affirm	Right.
	Direct	Highlight that.
	Elaborate	One way cells store food is by converting nutrients into glucose.

Note the field shift here, from the more familiar everyday activity of storing food for future consumption to the biological implication sequence which converts one type of chemical into another (i.e. nutrients into glucose).

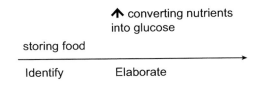

Figure 13   Powering up in an elaborating move

The third function, making new substances, is treated similarly, with the elaborating move specifying how many substances are made (*hundreds*) and what these substances are (*different chemicals*).

(14)

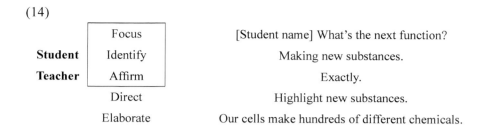

	Focus	[Student name] What's the next function?
Student	Identify	Making new substances.
Teacher	Affirm	Exactly.
	Direct	Highlight new substances.
	Elaborate	Our cells make hundreds of different chemicals.

The elaboration here doesn't strengthen semantic density as much as the elaboration in Figure 13; we haven't however attempted here to use the "y" axis to represent degrees of powering up and down.

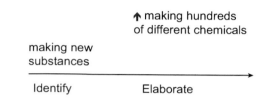

Figure 14　Powering up in an elaborating move

As we have illustrated, Detailed Reading provides powerful scaffolding as far as giving students access to uncommon sense knowledge is concerned, as teachers bridge from what students already know to what they are expected to learn. Typical manoeuvers are outlined in Figure 15 below. The Prepare moves will end to power down in relation to the challenging passages of discourse selected for Detailed Reading; Elaborate moves may move in either direction—either powering down where students still need support to understand the highlighted items and powering up to relate the terms in question to relevant classification, composition, array or implication sequencing relations in the field; movements in both directions may feature in extended elaborating moves, which may of course involve interaction with students.

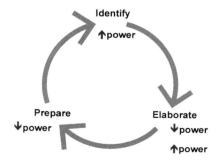

Figure 15　Typical direction of power moves in Prepare Task Elaborate cycle

5.2.2 Joint writing (power words, power grammar, power composition)

The second stage of both the outer and middle circles of R2L pedagogy involves students jointly constructing a text with their teachers. For Joint Construction (outer circle), the field shifts to a related topic (e.g. the function of the cell membrane after working on Text 8'' in Page 103); relevant information from various sources is gathered and annotated in note form on the board, and then a new text is co-constructed in the same genre. For Joint Rewriting of factual texts (middle circle) a student is selected to scribe the items highlighted in Detailed Reading on the board—with the class and teacher providing support with spelling, unfamiliar morphology and so on. The notes for Text 8'' would look something like the following:

cytoplasm

cell membrane

nucleus

chemical reactions

energy

storing food

new substances

metabolism

Such notes provide the basis for co-construction of a new text (same genre, same field), with students making suggestions orally and the teacher providing the scribe with support as required. This activity provides further opportunities for powering up and down in relation to power words and power grammar, including explicit discussion of the graphology, lexicogrammar, discourse semantics, register (field, tenor and mode) and genre where appropriate and where shared metalanguage allows. For longer texts it also provides opportunities for scaffolding power composition, as discussed in Macnaught et al. (2013). Space precludes further illustration of these activities here; for more detail see Rose and Martin (2012), and Rose's R2L website (www.readingtolearn.com.au).

6. Embedded literacy

In this paper, as in Martin (2013b), I have provided an SFL perspective on LCT's concepts of semantic gravity and semantic density and suggested that this functional linguistic perspective can be nurtured in teaching/learning activities through the "power trio"—power words, power grammar, power composition. I have also illustrated how these SFL and LCT concepts can be related to the designed curriculum genres associated with the so-called "Sydney School", the R2L teaching/learning cycles in particular. In doing so I have outlined in general terms an "embedded literacy" strategy which foregrounds high stakes reading and writing as the cornerstones of teaching and learning across the curriculum.

In doing so I am challenging the false opposition between learning language and learning content which currently cripples so much of what goes on in primary, secondary and tertiary sectors of education. Every educational linguist is familiar with the problem. Whenever the attention is drawn to the need to focus on teaching students to read and write uncommon sense discourse, content teachers invariably reply that they recognize the need and would like to do something about it, but they don't have time, because they are severely pressured by the demands of their prescribed curriculum and assessment procedures. Learning to read and write specialized discourse is seen as an activity which takes time away from content learning, and it is only in contexts where problems with academic literacy are severe that a little time is set aside to focus on literacy issues; and even here content teachers are typically given very little training or professional support as far as addressing literacy is concerned. In some classes we have observed, literacy activities may simply involve correcting a set of misspelled words, as if correct spelling magically enables students as far as power words, power grammar and power composition are concerned.

To overcome this impasse we have to get over the idea that learning language and learning content are two separate tasks. This means involving content teachers in curriculum genres such as the R2L teaching/learning cycles introduced above and letting them experience the power of such pedagogies to build knowledge through language—and see that learning power words, power grammar and power composition along these lines necessarily means learning content, and learning it many times more deeply and efficiently than what currently goes on in the classroom interactions content teachers are so keen to preserve. Over time this can lead to an appreciation of the ways in which the knowledge of their disciplines is conserved in writing—in the handouts, web material, textbooks and so on that they expect their students to read. And it can lead to a deeper appreciation of the ways in which the knowledge of their disciplines has to be reproduced by students in writing tasks, for both formative and summative assessment purposes.

Michael Halliday has written in many contexts (e.g. Halliday 2009) about his "learning trio" (learning language, learning through language, learning about language) as integral dimensions of a language-based theory of teaching/learning—a theory in which learning language and learning content are synthesized, not dualized. SFL, LCT and R2L have now provided us with the tools we need to enact this vision in classroom practice. We have the means; can we find the way?

Notes

1. The word "teaching" is tellingly absent from this list, since in these pedagogies knowledge blindness aligns with an excluding focus on student learning, sidelining the teacher—who is positioned as a facilitator (a "guide on the side").

2. In this table, Theme has been analyzed up to and including the Subject, whether a marked Theme is present or not; and New is extended to include process constituents to the left of the final constituent in the clause where these constituents contribute newsworthy information.

3. If we read the second sub-headings as elaborating the first, and render the relation as a finite negotiable clause, each would be embedded (e.g. Issue number 4 is [[changing animal life]]).

4. Texts 11-14 are taken from Rose and Martin (2012: 185-188).

References

Bednarek, M. and J. R. Martin (eds.) 2010. *New Discourse on Language: Functional Perspectives on Multimodality, Identity and Affiliation*. London: Continuum.

Bernstein, B. 1996. *Pedagogy, Symbolic Control and Identity: Theory, Research, Critique*. London: Taylor & Francis.

Bernstein, B. 1999. Vertical and horizontal discourse: an essay. *British Journal of Sociology of Education*. 20 (2), 157-173.

Christie, F. and J. R. Martin (eds.) 1997. *Genre and Institutions: Social Processes in the Workplace and School*. London: Cassell.

Christie, F. and J. R. Martin (eds.) 2007. *Language, Knowledge and Pedagogy: Functional Linguistic and Sociological Perspectives*. London: Continuum.

Christie, F. and K. Maton (eds.) 2011. *Disciplinarity: Functional Linguistic and Sociological Perspectives*. London: Continuum.

Derewianka, B. and P. Jones. 2012. *Teaching Language in Context*. Melbourne: Oxford University Press.

de Silva Joyce, H. and S. Feez. 2012. *Text-based Language & Literacy Education: Programming and Methodology*. Sydney: Phoenix Education.

Freebody, P, J. R. Martin and K. Maton. 2008. Talk, text and knowledge in cumulative, integrative learning: a response to "intellectual challenge". *The Australian Journal of Language and Literacy*. 31. 188-201.

Halliday, M. A. K. 1998. Things and relations: regrammaticising experience as technical knowledge. in Martin and Veel. 185-235.

Halliday, M. A. K. 2004. *The Language of Science*. Volume 5 in the Collected Works of M. A. K. Halliday. edited by Jonathan Webster. London: Conitnuum.

Halliday, M. A. K. 2009. *Language and Education*. Volume 9 in the Collected Works of M. A. K. Halliday. edited by Jonathan Webster. London: Conitnuum.

Halliday, M. A. K. and J. R. Martin. 1993. *Writing Science: Literacy and Discursive Power*. London: Falmer.

Haire, M., E. Kennedy, G. Lofts and M. J. Evergreen. 2004. Core Science 1: Stage 4. Sydney: Jacaranda.

Jones, R. and G. Lock. 2010. *Functional Grammar in the ESL Classroom: Noticing, Exploring and Practising.* London: Palrave Macmillan.

Macnaught, L., K. Maton, J. R. Martin and E. Matruglio. 2013. Jointly constructing semantic waves: implications for teaching. *Linguistics and Education,* 24, 50-63.

Martin, J. R. 1989. Technicality and abstraction: language for the creation of specialised texts. In F. Christie (ed.) *Writing in Schools: Reader.* Geelong: Deakin University Press. 36-44.

Martin, J. R. 1990. Literacy in science: learning to handle text as technology. In F. Christie (ed.) *Literacy for a Changing World.* 79-117. Melbourne: Australian Council for Educational Research.

Martin, J. R. 1991. Nominalisation in science and humanities: distilling knowledge and scaffolding text. E. Ventola (ed.) *Functional and Systemic Linguistics: Approaches and Uses.* 307-338. Berlin: Mouton de Gruyter.

Martin, J. R. 1992. *English Text: System and Structure.* Amsterdam: John Benjamins Publishing Company.

Martin, J. R. 1993. Life as a noun: arresting the universe in science and humanities. In M. A. K. Halliday and J. R. Martin (eds.), *Writing Science: Literacy and Discursive Power.* 221-267. London: Falmer.

Martin, J. R. 2002. From little things big things grow: ecogenesis in school geography. R. Coe, L. Lingard and T. Teslenko (eds.). *The Rhetoric and Ideology of Genre: Strategies for Stability and Change.* 243-271. Cresskill: Hampton Press. 2002.

Martin, J. R. 2007a. Genre and field: social processes and knowledge structures in systemic functional semiotics. L. Barbara and T. Berber Sardinha (eds.). *Proceedings of the 33rd International Systemic Functional Congress.* 1-35. São Paulo: PUCSP. Online publication available at http://www.pucsp.br/isfc.

Martin, J. R. 2007b. Construing knowledge: a functional linguistic perspective. In F. Christie and J. R. Martin (eds.). *Language, Knowledge & Pedagogy: Functional Linguistic and Sociological Perspectives.* 34-64. London: Continuum.

Martin, J. R. 2011. Bridging troubled waters: interdisciplinarity and what makes it stick. Christie and Maton 35-61.

Martin, J. R. 2012a. *Genre Studies.* Vol. 3: Collected Works of J. R. Martin (Wang Zhenhua Ed.). Shanghai: Shanghai Jiao Tong University Press.

Martin, J. R. 2012b. *Register Studies.* Vol. 4: Collected Works of J. R. Martin (Wang Zhenhua Ed.). Shanghai: Shanghai Jiao Tong University Press.

Martin, J. R. 2012c. *Language in Education.* Vol. 5: Collected Works of J. R. Martin (Wang Zhenhua Ed.). Shanghai: Shanghai Jiao Tong University Press.

Martin, J. R. 2013a. Modelling context: matter as meaning. In C. Gouveia and M. Alexandre (eds.), *Languages, Metalanguages, Modalities, Cultures: Functional and Socio-Discursive Perspectives.* 10-64. Lisbon: BonD & ILTEC.

Martin, J. R. 2013b. Embedded literacy: knowledge as meaning. *Linguistics and Education,* 24.1. 23-37.

Martin, J. R. and K. Maton (eds.). 2013. Cumulative knowledge-building in secondary schooling. *Special Issue of Linguistics and Education,* 24.1.

Martin, J. R., K. Maton and E. Matruglio. 2010. Historical cosmologies: epistemology and axiology in

Australian secondary school history. *Revista Signos* 43.74. 433-463.

Martin, J. R. and D. Rose. 2003. *Working with Discourse: Meaning beyond the Clause*. London: Continuum.

Martin, J. R. and D. Rose 2008 *Genre Relations: Mapping Culture*. London: Equinox.

Martin, J. R. and R. Veel. 1998. *Reading Science: Critical And Functional Perspectives on Discourses Of Science*. London: Routledge.

Martin, J. R. and P. R. R. White. 2005. *The Language of Evaluation: Appraisal in English*. London: Palgrave.

Maton, K. 2013. Making semantic waves: a key to cumulative knowledge-building. *Linguistics and Education,* 24.1, 8-22.

Maton, K. 2014. *Knowledge and Knowers: Towards a Realist Sociology of Education*. London: Routledge.

Maton, K. and J. Muller. 2007. A sociology for the transmission of knowledges. in Christie and Martin. 14-33.

Matruglio, E., K. Maton and J. R. Martin. 2013. Time travel: the role of temporality in semantic waves in secondary school teaching. *Linguistics and Education,* 24.1, 38-49.

Muller, J. 2000. *Reclaiming Knowledge: Social Theory, Curriculum and Education Policy*. London: Routledge.

Muller, J. 2007. On splitting hairs: hierarchy, knowledge and the school curriculum. In Christie and Martin. 64-86.

Rose, D. 1997. Science, technology and technical literacies. In F. Christie and J. R. Martin (eds.), *Genre and Institutions: Social Processes in the Workplace and School*. 40-72. London: Cassell.

Rose, D. 1998. Science discourse and industrial hierarchy. In J. R. Martin and R. Veel (eds.), *Reading Science: Critical And Functional Perspectives on Discourses Of Science*. 236-265. London: Routledge.

Rose, D. 2007. Towards a reading based theory of teaching. In L. Barbara and T. Berber Sardinha (eds.). *Proceedings of the 33rd International Systemic Functional Congress*. 36-77. São Paulo: PUCSP.

Rose, D. 2008. Writing as linguistic mastery: the development of genre-based literacy pedagogy. In R. Beard, D. Myhill, J. Riley and M. Nystrand (eds.), *Handbook of Writing Development*. 151-166. London: Sage.

Rose, D. 2010. Meaning beyond the margins: learning to interact with books. In J. R. Martin, S. Hood and S. Dreyfus. (eds.), *Semiotic Margins: Reclaiming Meaning*. London: Continuum.

Rose, D. 2011. Beyond literacy: building an integrated pedagogic genre. *Australian Journal of Language and Literacy*, 34 (1), 81-97.

Rose, D., D. McInnes and H. Korner. 1992. *Scientific Literacy (Write it Right Literacy in Industry Research Project—Stage 1)*. Sydney: Metropolitan East Disadvantaged Schools Program.

Scott, L. and S. Robinson. 1993. *Australian Journey: Environments and Communities*. Melbourne: Longman.

Unsworth, L. 1997a. Scaffolding reading of science explanations: accessing the grammatical and visual forms of specialised knowledge. *Reading,* 31.3. 30-42.

Unsworth, L. 1997b. Explaining explanations: enhancing scientific learning and literacy development. *Australian Science Teachers Journal,* 43.1, 34-49.

Unsworth, L. 1997c. "Sound" explanations in school science: a functional linguistics perspective on effective apprenticing texts. *Linguistics and Education,* 9.2, 199-226.

Veel, R. 1992. Engaging with scientific language: a functional approach to the language of school science. *Australian Science Teachers Journal,* 38.4, 31-35.

Veel, R. 1997. Learning how to mean—scientifically speaking. In F. Christie and J. R. Martin (eds.), *Genre and Institutions: Social Processes in the Workplace and School.* 161-195. London: Cassell.

Veel, R. 1998. The greening of school science: ecogenesis in secondary classrooms. In J. R. Martin and R. Veel (eds.), *Reading Science: Critical And Functional Perspectives on Discourses Of Science.* 114-151. London: Routledge.

White, P. 1998. Extended reality, proto-nouns and the vernacular: distinguishing the technological from the scientific. In J. R. Martin and R. Veel (eds.), *Reading Science: Critical And Functional Perspectives on Discourses Of Science.* 266-296. London: Routledge.

Wignell, P. 1998. Technicality and abstraction in social science. In J. R. Martin and R. Veel (eds.), *Reading Science: Critical and Functional Perspectives on Discourses Of Science.* 297-326. London: Routledge.

Wignell, P. 2007a. Vertical and horizontal discourse and the social sciences. In F. Christie and J. R. Martin (eds.), *Language, Knowledge and Pedagogy: Functional Linguistic and Sociological Perspectives.* 184-204. London: Continuum.

Wignell, P. 2007b. *On the Discourse of Social Science.* Darwin: Charles Darwin University Press.

Wignell, P., J. R. Martin and S. Eggins. 1990. The discourse of geography: ordering and explaining the experiential world. *Linguistics and Education,* 1.4, 359-392.

On the Formative Mechanisms of Semantic Waves

Yongsheng Zhu

Fudan University, China

1. Introduction

Wave, originally a technical term in physics, refers to the progressive transmission of energy by the vibration of a substance, e.g. sound waves, light waves and ultrasonic waves. Functional linguists like Halliday think that semantic flow is very much similar to energy flow so they coined the metaphorical term "semantic wave" by borrowing the concept of wave from physics. Halliday (1978, 1994, 2008) used this term to describe the information structure of the clause; Pike（1982: 12-13）found that the meaning of discourse flows like ripples, which merge into each other and become many different little waves and these little waves will merge into bigger ones. He used the term wave to depict the periodicity of information flow; Martin & Rose (2003: 175-186) held that Pike's idea is very important to the understanding of information flow and believed that semantic waves are closely related to the rhythm of discourse; Matruglio, Maton & Martin (2013) used the same concept to explore the information flow at discourse level. In their discussion about the formation of semantic waves, Martin, Maton and Coffin took different perspectives. Martin looked at this issue by analyzing Themes and News, Maton by examining Semantic Gravity and Semantic Density, and Coffin by dealing with Temporality. This paper attempts to make comment on their findings and bring into the picture the concept of Spatiality, which is believed to be another formative mechanism of semantic waves but is so far neglected.

2. Themes and news

2.1 Martin's points of view

Martin & Rose（2003）held that, like rhythms, semantic waves are hierarchical and that semantic waves fall into three types as far as the degree of their forces is concerned: little waves, bigger waves and tidal waves. They (2003: 179-186) examined the formative mechanisms of the three types of semantic wave and drew the following conclusion. The formation of little waves depends on the information flow of the clause. To be more specific, it depends on two kinds of semantic resources: 1) the Theme, which includes the selection of Theme of each clause and thematic progression of the whole discourse; and 2) the selection of New information. The formation of bigger waves is determined by the hyperThemes and hyperNews of the paragraph or the whole discourse. And the formation of tidal waves is made possible by the macroThemes and macroNews of the related discourses. These findings revealed the following two tendencies: 1) MacroThemes can predict hyperThemes and hyperThemes can predict Themes; and 2) macroNews can help accumulate hyperNews and hyperNews can accumulate News. This means, in my understanding, it is necessary to look at the formation of semantic waves not only at clause level, but at discourse level and interdiscursive level as well.

To follow Halliday, Martin explored discourse semantics from the perspective of textual function and took thematic structure and information structure as two separate but closely related semantic resources. To be more specific, Martin took the following two steps. The first step is to analyze the thematic structure of the clause by finding out which element functions as the Theme or the point of departure and which element functions as the Rheme and then looking at the hyperTheme of each paragraph or the whole discourse and finally examining the macroTheme by considering the hyperTheme in a larger context. The second step is to analyze the information structure of the clause by figuring out which element functions as the given information and which element functions as the New and then looking at the hyperNews of the paragragh or the whole discourse and finally examining the macroNews by considering the hyperNews in a larger context. Both these steps have one thing in common, i.e. they both look at the development and construal of textual meaning by going from smaller context into larger context so as to show how little waves merge into bigger waves and how bigger waves merge into tidal waves.

2.2 Comment

This two-step analysis makes it possible to construe the unfolding of discourse semantics from two perspectives, i.e. thematic structure and information structure. However, as I can see it, it is always the coming in of new information that pushes the semantic waves forward. This can be proved by the following analysis. First, from the perspective of information structure, the unfolding of discourse semantics depends on the introduction of new information, the turning of new information into old information and then the bringing in of more new information. When there is no more new information to bring in, the discourse will come to its end. Second, from the perspective of thematic structure, the unfolding of discourse semantics depends on which thematic progress pattern is chosen. Now let's look at the four most frequently used patterns of thematic progression (Zhu 1995).

Pattern One: The same Theme but different Rhemes, as in Example (1); Pattern Two: Different Themes but the same Theme, as in (2); Pattern Three: with the Rheme of the first clause functioning as the Theme of the second clause, as in (3); and Pattern Four: with one element of the first clause functioning as the Theme of the second clause and another element of the first clause functioning as the Theme of the third clause, as in (4) and (5):

(1) **I** have fought against white domination, and **I** have fought against black domination. **I** have cherished the ideal of a democratic and free society in which all persons live together in harmony and with equal opportunities. **It** is an ideal which I hope to live for and to achieve. But if needs be, **it** is an ideal for which I am prepared to die. (Nelson Mandela's speech on Feb. 11, 1990)

(2) The time for the healing of the wounds **has come**.
The moment to bridge the chasms that divide us **has come**. (Nelson Mandela's Inaugural Speech on May 10, 1994)

(3) His humility, his compassion, and his humanity earned him their love. Our thoughts and prayers are with **the Mandela family**. **To them** we owe a debt of gratitude.

(4) **Rotation** is different from **revolution**. **Rotation** is when something spins on its axis and **revolution** is when it moves around something. The earth revolves around the sun and rotates on its axis. (Mikipedia.ask.com, Q&A>science>astronomy)

(5) Just at this time last year in this gate,
I saw **her face** amid **peach blossoms** so great.
Now **her beautiful face** is no longer here in this place,
Only **the peach blossoms** are smiling in the gentle breeze.
(Cui Hu: **At the Southern Part of the Capital**)

These four patterns of thematic progression make semantic waves in different ways because they put new information in different positions. Specifically, new information is always carried by the Rheme in Pattern One but by the Theme in Pattern Two while new information is expressed by turning the Rheme of the previous clause into Theme in Pattern Three and two or more pieces of new information that have appeared in the former clause come in alternately in later clauses in Pattern Four. Therefore the analysis of information structure seems more important to the construal of semantic waves.

3 Semantic gravity and semantic density

3.1 Maton's points of view

Maton (2012) held in his Legitimation Code Theory that the formation of semantic waves is closely related to semantic gravity and semantic density.

Semantic gravity refers to the degree of dependence of meaning on the context and semantic density stands for the degree of contraction of meaning. These two concepts can be employed for various purposes, including tracing the changes of knowledge as time passes by. Maton (2012) termed these changes semantic profile and uses what he calls semantic scale to show how semantic gravity and semantic density move in opposite directions. Figure 1 below gives a description of the semantic profile of a single semantic wave, which shows how a semantic wave is formed by the way semantic gravity and semantic density move up and down the scale.

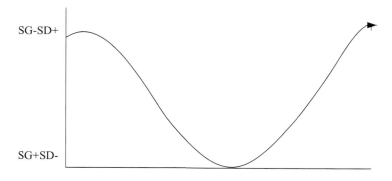

Figure 1   Semantic scale

Matruglio，Maton & Martin (2013) found that there are a lot of semantically contracted technical terms in textbooks and other teaching materials, which leads to high semantic density of the language and meanwhile the knowledge these materials intend to transmit does not depend on any specific context but on some abstract principles or general phenomena, which brings about a kind of weak semantic gravity in the language used in these materials. In this situation, teachers tend to use specific examples to increase semantic gravity and employ simple language to weaken semantic density so as to help the students to get a quicker and better understanding of what they are learning and acquire the knowledge they need by unpacking the meaning that is technicalized and very often nominalized. After they acquire the knowledge, the students will gradually learn how to abstract the knowledge and its context. In this way, the semantic gravity will be weakened and the semantic density will be strengthened. The process of repacking the knowledge will lead to the formation of a new semantic wave. Generally speaking, a learning process is a process from unpacking to repacking or from specification to abstraction.

3.2 Comment

Maton's points of view about semantic gravity and semantic density made a breakthrough both theoretically and practically.

Theoretically, he successfully demonstrated the unevenness and continuity of semantic waves. By unevenness is meant that every semantic wave has a peak and a valley, with the peak being formed by the elements with weak semantic gravity and strong semantic density and the valley being formed by the elements with strong semantic gravity and weak semantic density. By continuity is meant no disruption due to temporal reasons. In other words, discourse semantics unfolds itself gradually as time goes by and semantic waves follow one after another just like the waves in the ocean.

Practically, the analysis of semantic gravity and semantic density can help both teachers and students to see the regularities of the development of discourse semantics. Take foreign language teaching for example. When they come across knotty points during their lectures, teachers usually tackle them by paraphrasing. As a matter of fact, paraphrasing is a process of increasing semantic gravity and weakening semantic density. When all the paraphrases are linked together, a serial of semantic waves are formed. It is through this kind of process that students' understanding of what they are learning is deepened and their knowledge gets accumulated. For linguists and educators, it is now necessary to make a more thorough study on the similarities and differences in the formative mechanisms of semantic waves between natural sciences and human sciences. It would be even better to take a close look at the formative mechanisms of semantic waves in every field, so as to find out which elements have strong or weak semantic gravity and, which elements have strong or weak semantic density, how the teachers can change the degrees of semantic gravity and semantic density by unpacking, and how the teachers can cultivate in the students the ability to generalize and abstract the knowledge they have learned by repacking. I believe that this kind of research will play an important role in helping the teachers to know more about the knowledge structures of different fields, to make up a more appropriate curriculum, to design a better syllabus, to conduct their class more effectively, and to evaluate their teaching quality more accurately.

4. Temporality

4.1 Coffin's points of view

Coffin (1996, 1997, 2006), Martin (2002, 2003) and Matruglio, Maton and Martin (2013) held that temporality can also play an important role in the formation and progression of semantic waves and they put their focus on the field of history rather than natural sciences and have achieved fruitful results, the most influential of which is Coffin's research on the temporality in history teaching at secondary schools.

Coffin (2006) identified six types of construing temporality in the subject of history and provided examples for each category:

1) Sequencing: after coming to power in 1959, (Castro...)
2) Segmenting: the Great Depression
3) Setting: (25 million suffered malnutrition) in 1928
4) Duration: (he maintained his position) for 50 years
5) Phasing: the onset (of the Great Depression)
6) Organising: firstly... secondly... finally

Coffin found that the most frequently used type of temporality by secondary school students is segmenting and the least used ones are sequencing and setting. In the process of learning, the students gradually shift from their personal perspective to the more institutionalized or generally accepted perspective in construing temporality. And this finding is of great significance in describing the evolution and development of secondary school students' understanding of time.

Maton (2012; 2013) regarded temporality as one of the five principles of his Legitimation Code Theory and attached the same importance to it as to Autonomy, Density, Specialization and Semantics. All the five principles work together to generate all kinds of legitimation codes. Besides, Maton (2012: 18) held that Temporality also has two variables: temporal positioning and temporal orientation. The former refers to the fixing of the specific time of the occurrence of a certain event, which is very close to what Coffin calls Setting, whereas the latter stands for the direction of the development of the event, which is similar to what Coffin terms Sequencing.

4.2 Comment

It is true that the semantics of every discourse has the characteristic of linearity and the description of every event tends to follow the principle of temporality. However, there are at least two other aspects that should be taken into serious consideration: 1) explicitness and implicitness of temporality, and 2) complexity in the orientation of temporality.

4.2.1 Explicitness and implicitness of temporality

All the examples of Temporality given by Coffin are explicit. However, it is found that the realization of Temporality can be implicit as well. Just like explicit Temporality, implicit Temporality is a formative mechanism of Temporality. The ability to construe implicit Temporality should be taken as one of the parameters in judging the knowledge accumulating ability of the students.

Which type of Temporality is to choose is often determined by genre. Explicit Temporality tends to appear in narrative discourses like autobiography, manuals of product manufacturing, the instructions on work methods, the description of historical development, the evolution of human beings, and the growth of animals and plants. For example, Temporality is realized by the "first-then-then-after" chain in (5) and by "When I was a child—After I grow up" chain in (6):

(5) How to apply for a free mailbox? **First** you have to connect to the Internet and go to the homepage of the ICP providing free mailboxes. **Then** you will find an icon, an agreement about the rules for using the free mailbox will appear. If you want to go, click the icon "I agree". **Then** you have to fill in a form about your basic personal data, and the name and PIN of the mailbox. The PIN is the key to the mailbox. **After** finishing these, you will get a mailbox like this: your name @ mail server (for example: tvguide@mail.cctv.com. cn. "tvguide" is the name of the mailbox, and "mail.cctv.com.cn" is the name of the mail server.). The mailbox is separated into two parts by a separator "@", which is read as "at". The former part is the name of the mailbox. The latter is the domain name of the mail server. All mails to you will be received by the server and put into your mailbox. You can read these mails on any computer on the Internet in the world, if you have the name and PIN of the mailbox.

(6) **When I was a child** I thought you're very pretty
    Leading a flock of little birds flying everywhere
    When I was a child I thought you were very great
    Whatever you said made the heaven and the earth shake
    Not until I grew up and became a teacher like you
    Did I realize what you set flying out of the classroom was our hope
    But you stayed in the nestle without stop
    Not until I grew up and became a teacher like you
    Did I know what you wrote on the blackboard was truth
    And what you erased was fame and profit.
    (A Chinese song: *I Became A Teacher Like You When I Grew up*)

Implicit temporality, however, can be found in various genres, as shown in (7)-(9), which belong to the genres of conversation, poetry and short story respectively:

(7) I came. I saw. I conquered. (*Julius Caesar*)
(8) Before my bed there is bright moonlight,
    So that it seems like frost on the ground.

Lifting my head I watch the bright moon,

Lowering my head I dream I'm in my hometown.

(Li Bai: *Thoughts in the Silent Night*)

(9) Some men were shot. Some men were drowned. Some men were burned alive. Some men were blown to bits. Some men were only half blown to bits and came through with parts of their bodies missing. Hundreds of men were killed. And they were all real men, made of flesh and blood. They were not made of Tin or Iron.

(R. Briggs: *The Tin-Pot Foreign General and the Old Iron Woman*)

Implicit temporality rarely leads to hearer's misunderstanding because the writer usually follows the "first things first" principle unless there is a special temporal relationship that has to be made explicit.

Both implicit temporality and explicit temporality function as formative mechanisms of semantic waves. Just like explicit temporality, implicit temporality is a parameter in judging the knowledge accumulating ability of the students.

4.2.2 Complexity in the orientation of temporality

It is right for scholars like Coffin and Maton to attach a lot of importance to the positioning and orientation of temporality but it seems that they fail to see its complexity. In most cases, the speaker follows the narrative principle of "first things first", yet in other cases they can violate it by flashing back in the middle of discourse as in (10), or even at the very beginning of the whole discourse, which might sound abrupt to the reader, as in (11):

(10) This spring morning in bed I'm lying,

Not to awake till the birds are crying.

After one night of wind and showers,

How many are the fallen flowers?

(Meng Haoran: *Spring Morning*)

(11) Chapter 1

MANY YEARS LATER as he faced the firing squad, Colonel Aureliano Buendía was to remember that distant afternoon when his father took him to discover ice. At that time Macondo was a village of twenty adobe houses, built on the bank of a river of clear water that ran along a bed of polished stones, which were white and enormous, like prehistoric eggs....

(Gabriel Garcia Marquez: *One Hundred Years of Solitude*)

Apart from back flashes, teacher's digressions from the topic of the lecture in classrooms and writers' insertion in literary works can also affect the form, force and progression of semantic waves, as in (12):

(12) One dollar and eighty-seven cents. That was all. And sixty cents of it was in pennies. Pennies saved one and two at a time by bulldozing the grocer and the vegetable man and the butcher until one's cheeks burned with the silent imputation of parsimony that such close dealing implied. Three times Della counted it. One dollar and eighty-seven cents. And the next day would be Christmas.

There was clearly nothing to do but flop down on the shabby little couch and howl. So Della did it. Which instigates the moral reflection that life is made up of sobs, sniffles, and smiles, with sniffles predominating.

While the mistress of the home is gradually subsiding from the first stage to the second, take a look at the home. A furnished flat at $8 per week. It did not exactly beggar description, but it certainly had that word on the lookout for the mendicancy squad.

In the vestibule below was a letter-box into which no letter would go, and an electric button from which no mortal finger could coax a ring. Also appertaining thereunto was a card bearing the name "Mr. James Dillingham Young".

The "Dillingham" had been flung to the breeze during a former period of prosperity when its possessor was being paid $30 per week. Now, when the income was shrunk to $20, though, they were thinking seriously of contracting to a modest and unassuming D. But whenever Mr. James Dillingham Young came home and reached his flat above he was called "Jim" and greatly hugged by Mrs. James Dillingham Young, already introduced to you as Della. Which is all very good.

Della finished her cry and attended to her cheeks with the powder rag. …

(O. Henry: *The Gift of the Magi*)

If back flashes can be compared to the "turning back waves" in the famous Qiantang River in China in the mid-autumn period, it is appropriate to take the occasional insertions as cross waves, which do not come from your back or your front but from your left side or right side.

What I intend to say here in this section is that although back flashes and insertions do not occur in every discourse, their orienting function is not to be ignored.

5. Spatiality

Spatiality is another formative mechanism of semantic waves but it is largely ignored. In this section, I will discuss the definition and variables of spatiality before touching upon the relationship between spatiality and semantic waves.

5.1 Definition and variables of spatiality

Like time, space is a form of existence of the material movement. Any material movement has the characteristics of temporality and spatiality, which are different but closely related to each other.

Temporality means the continuity and sequencing of material movements, with continuity referring to the length of time to be taken by material movements, and with sequencing standing for the order in which different material movements happen one after another. Spatiality, however, means the expansion or extension of material movements, i.e. whether materials move from the outside to the inside, from the inside to the outside, from the top to the bottom, from the bottom to the top, from the center to the edges, or from the edges to the center.

Like temporality, spatiality has the two variables of positioning and orientation. Therefore, a distinction can be made between spatial positioning and spatial orientation. The former means the fixing of the specific location in which a certain event takes place and it is definite and static. And the latter refers to the fixing of the direction in which something or somebody moves on and it is movable and dynamic. Whether to choose spatial positioning or spatial orientation depends on the speaker's focus of attention.

5.2 The relationship between spatiality and semantic waves

Two kinds of phenomena deserve our attention. First, spatiality serves as the only formative mechanism of semantic waves, as in (13-14), and second, it functions as one of the formative mechanisms of semantic waves, as in (15-16):

(13) The Forbidden City grounds are divided into two main sections, the Front Palace to the south and the Inner Palace to the north. The long stone ramp carved with dragons sporting in clouds in bas-relief in the center of the staircase called the Imperial Way (or Dragon Pavement), which corresponded with the north-south axis of the city, was for the emperor's exclusive use; imperial family members and civil and military officials no matter how high their ranks had to climb the forty-four steps to either side.

In the center of the Front Palace stand the magnificent and imposing appearance of the Hall of Supreme Harmony, the Hall of Complete Harmony and the Hall of Preserving

Harmony. Commonly known as the "Three Great Halls" derivers from the broad, stately 7-meter-high terraces on which they stand.

(Baidu: Tour-China Guide/The Forbidden City)

(14) On your way **from Sichuan to Hunan**, there was an official road **on your left side. When you arrived at a small mountainous town called Chatong near the border of the west Hunan**, there was a stream. **By the stream** there was **a white pagoda.** And **at the foot of the pagoda**, there lived a family. This family had only an old man, a little girl, and a yellow dog.

(Shen Congwen: *The Border Town*)

Example (13) consists of three paragraphs. The first one divides the Forbidden City into two sections: the Front Palace and the Inner Palace. And the second and the third paragraphs describe the structures of these two parts respectively by leading our eyesight from the center to the wings and shows clearly that the semantic waves in this short passage move themselves from the whole to its specific parts, from the outside to the inside and from the center to the peripheral. This type of semantic progression tends to occur in narrative discourses like novels, travel notes and instructions for scenic spots. Example (14) not only contains spatial positioning like "official road", "near the border of Hunan", "a small mountainous town", "by the stream", "at the foot of the pagoda" but also employs spatial orientation like "from Sichuan to Hunan". By following the "spatial orientation—spatial positioning" pattern, the writer succeeded in bringing the reader's attention from far-away places to a nearby spot, and finally fixing on an old man and his daughter. The difference between example (13) and Example (14) lies in the fact that the former only uses spatial positioning whereas the latter employs both spatial positioning and spatial orientation.

Now let's look at the second type of phenomenon.

(15) *By the Red Sparrow Bridge* the wild flowers are spreading,

At the very ends of the Black Robe Alley the sun is setting.

Swallows used to nestle before the Wang and Xie's manors,

But they are now flying in and out of the houses of commoners.

(Liu Xiyu: *The Black Robe Lane*)

(16) *When I was a child,*

Nostalgia seemed a small stamp:

"Here am I

And yonder ... my mother."

Then I was a grown-up,
Nostalgia became a traveling ticket:
"<u>Here</u> am I
And <u>yonder</u> … my bride."

During the later years,
Nostalgia turned to be a graveyard:
"<u>Here</u> am I
And <u>yonder</u> … my mother."

And now at present,
Nostalgia looms large to be a channel:
"<u>Here</u> am I
And <u>yonder</u> … my continent."
(Yu Guangzhong: *Nostalgia*)

Example (15) is a traditional Chinese poem about the declining of two famous families. The major force that pushes semantic waves forward in this poem is the spatial chain of "By the Red Sparrow Bridge—At the ends of the Black Robe Alley—before Wang and Xie's manors—in and out of the houses of the commoners". Example (16) is a modern Chinese poem about the homesickness of a Taiwanese. Different from Example (15), this poem's semantic waves are formed by the interaction between temporality and spatiality. Let's look at temporality first. The first line of every stanza expresses a period of time, and if all the first lines of the four stanzas are singled out, it is not difficult to see that a temporal chain successfully describes the growing process of a human being and that four different periods of time start four different semantic waves. Now let's look at spatiality in this poem. At the end of each stanza there is a pair of antonyms indicating opposition of two places. In addition, there is another chain in this poem, which I would call an interpersonal chain: "I—my mother", "I—my bride", "I—my mother" and "I—the continent". The three chains of temporality, spatiality and interpersonal relationship develop in parallel and work together to create a semantic wave in each stanza. In this way this poem succeeds in depicting four different kinds of homesickness in the four different stages of the life of an old Chinese man who is looking forward to the reunification of Taiwan and the mainland of China.

It can be seen from the discussion above that there is a close relationship between spatiality and semantic waves and that spatiality can function as the only formative mechanism of semantic waves or work together with other mechanisms like temporality to push the progression of semantic waves.

6. Conclusion

Martin, Maton and Coffin have taken different approaches to explore the formation and progression of semantic waves and each of these approaches has its advantage. Martin's Theme/News approach can not only show the speaker's train of thought by examining the Theme of the clause, the hyperTheme of the paragraph or discourse, and then the macroTheme of a large context step by step, but also reveal the periodicity of the unfolding of discourse meaning by looking at which elements are given information, which elements carry new information, and how the given and the new interact with each other in the clause, in the paragraph or whole discourse, and then in a larger context. Maton's semantic gravity/semantic density approach vividly describes the ups and downs and continuity of semantic waves by analyzing which elements, e.g. technical terms and grammatical metaphors, need unpacking and repacking. Coffin's temporality approach clearly exhibits the formative stages of semantic waves by analyzing the beginning, development and ending of a social event or an invented story.

I have done roughly two things in this paper. First, I have made some comments on the strong points and weak points of each of the approaches mentioned above. And second, I have suggested that temporality is much more complicated than Coffin thought and time can move backward as well as forward and that spatiality should be taken into consideration as a driving force in the formation of semantic waves.

To conclude, each of the approaches that have been taken and the spatiality approach I have discussed in this paper has its own function, while the most important formative mechanism of semantic waves is nothing else but the new information. The unfolding of any discourse semantics is made possible by the coming in of new information, the turning of new information into the given, and the coming in of newer information. This process conforms to the cognitive process of human beings, i.e. probing into the unknown on the basis of what is already known, and accumulating knowledge and experience step by step.

References

Coffin, C. 1996. Exploring literacy in school history. Sydney: Metropolitan East Disadvantaged Schools Program.

Coffin, C. 1997. Constructing and giving value to the past: An investigation into secondary school history. In F. Christie and J. R. Martin (eds.), *Genre and Institutions: Social Processes in the Workplace and School*. 196-230. London: Cassel.

Coffin, C. 2006. Reconstruing "personal time" as "collective time": learning the discourse of history. In R. Whittaker, M. O'Donnell and A. McCabe (eds.), *Language and Literacy*. 207-230. London: Continuum.

Halliday, M. A. K. 1978. *Language as Social Semiotic: The Social Interpretation of Language and Meaning*. London: Arnold.

Halliday, M. A. K. 1994. *An Introduction to Functional Grammar*. London: Edward Arnold.

Halliday, M. A. K. 2008. *Complementarities in Language*. Beijing: The Commercial Press.

Martin, J. R. 2002. Writing history: Construing time and value in discourses of the past. In M. Schleppegrell and M. C. Columbi (eds.), *Developing Advanced Literacy in First and Second Languages: Meaning with Power*. 87-118. Mahwah, NJ: Lawrence Erlbaum Associates.

Martin, J. R. 2003. Making history: grammar for interpretation. In J. R. Martin, & R. Wodak (eds.), *Re/reading the Past: Critical and Functional Perspectives on Time and Value*. 19-57. Amsterdam, Philadelphia: John Benjamins Publishing Company.

Martin, J. R. and D. Rose. 2003. *Working with Discourse*. London: Continuum.

Martin, J. R. 2013. Embedded literacy: Knowledge as meaning. *Linguistics and Education*, 24 (1), 23-27.

Martin, J. R., K. Maton and E. Matruglio. 2010. Historical cosmologies: Epistemology and axiology in Australian secondary school history discourse. *Revista Signos*, 43 (74), 433-463.

Maton, K. 2012. *Knowledge and Knowers: Towards a Realist Sociology of Education*. London: Routledge.

Maton, K. 2013. Making semantic waves: A key to cumulative knowledge-building. *Linguistics and Education*, 24, 8-22.

Matruglio, E., K. Maton, and J. R. Martin. 2013. Time travel: The role of temporality in enabling semantic waves in secondary school teaching. *Linguistics and Education*, 24 (1), 38-49.

Pike, K. L. 1982. *Linguistic Concepts: An Introduction to Tagmemics*. Lincoln: University of Nebraska Press.

Zhu, Yongsheng. 1995, Thematic progression and discourse analysis. *Foreign Language Teaching and Research*, 1, 6-12.

An Analysis of the Redistribution of Literacy Resources: Motivation and Efficiency

Bin Tang

Southeast University, China

1. Introduction

The research projects conducted by the Sydney School during the 1980s and 1990s aimed at equipping disadvantaged learners with literacy resources through redistributing literacy resources of the culture to learners so that they can improve their literacy and renegotiate their position in society (Martin 2011: 38). Literacy resources refer to linguistic resources which can contribute to improvement of literacy standard. The control of literacy resources varies among individuals, which results in the achievement of different literacy levels by different individuals. The unbalanced distribution of literacy resources reinforces the unbalanced distribution of power among individuals. The purpose of redistributing literacy resources is to promote a balanced distribution of power in society through bridging the literacy gap among individuals. Although the unbalanced distribution of literacy resources was already recognized by linguists such as Martin early in the 1980s, there has been no adequate explanation of this fact on the basis of SFL. Since 2008 Martin (2008, 2009a, 2010) has put forward a new theory within SFL— "individuation", which throws light upon literacy resource distribution among social groups and individuals (Martin and Wang 2008). This paper centers on three questions: (1) In the process of individuation, how are social semiotic resources distributed to individuals? (2) What is the motivation for the redistribution of literacy resources? (3) How can the efficiency of the redistribution be raised?

2. Models of social semiotic resources distribution in process of individuation

Martin (2009a: 564) analyzed the distribution of semantic resources among individuals from the respective angles of "allocation" and "affiliation". The former is a process of individuation, focusing on how social semiotic resources are distributed among language users so as to enable the construction of their individual identities; the latter is a process of socialization, focusing on how individuals establish social relation with other social members through the use of the allocated social semiotic resources (Zhu 2012). An individual's control of social semiotic resources is the precondition for the formation of his socio-cultural identity and the guarantee for his affiliation with others. As Figure 1 shows, the allocation of social semiotic resources is realized through a hierarchical distribution. Moving from the most general level to the most specific, the semiotic resources are distributed hierarchically to each individual, contributing to the ultimate construction of his identity. The hierarchy of literacy resource distribution corresponds to the hierarchy of socio-cultural identities. The individual's socio-cultural identity (persona) falls under a certain sub-culture. This sub-culture is a part of a certain master culture, which, in turn, constitutes a part of the culture.

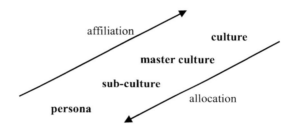

Figure 1   Individuation as a hierarchy of affiliation and allocation (Martin 2009a: 565)

Martin (2009a) mainly approached the process of semiotic resource distribution from the perspective of socio-cultural identity. Building on the theory of individuation, we are going to discuss the distribution process from another two angles: features of social semiotic resources and manners of semiotic resource distribution. This extension aims at revealing the allocation models through which semiotic resources are distributed to individuals in the process of individuation. To explore the features of social semiotic resources, it is helpful to draw on Bernstein's concepts of "reservoir" and "repertoire" (Bernstein 1999). Reservoir refers to the total of semantic resources possessed by a social community as a whole; repertoire refers to the total of semantic resources possessed by an individual. The distribution of social semiotic resources is a process whereby the individual acquires semantic resources from the reservoir of meanings in a culture and forms his own repertoire of meanings. Individuals' repertoires share a common nucleus but differences also exist in between (Bernstein 1999: 159). In other words, some semantic resources are shared, whereas others are unshared among individuals. The unshared semantic resources explain the differences between repertoires. The manner of semiotic resource distribution can be "acquisition" or "transmission". According to Bernstein (1990: 214), acquisition emphasizes the individual acquirer's active role in regulating an implicit facilitating practice in learning; transmission emphasizes the explicit ordering of learning by the transmitter. Learners act as an active agent in the acquisition of semiotic resources, whereas teachers act as an active agent in the transmission of semiotic resources.

Combining the features of social semiotic resources and the manners of semiotic resource distribution, we propose a framework for analyzing the models of semiotic resource distribution in Figure 2, where the two poles of the vertical line represent shared resources and unshared resources respectively; the two ends of the horizontal line represent acquisition and transmission. The four regions cut up by the two crossing lines correspond to four models of semiotic resource distribution: acquisition of shared resources, acquisition of unshared resources, transmission of shared resources and transmission of unshared resources.

An individual's literacy is often developed in both the context of mundane or quotidian activities and the official pedagogic context (Hasan 1996a: 384). Our models of social semiotic resources distribution are in line with Hasan's view. Specifically, in both natural quotidian context and official pedagogic context, the individual gains social semiotic resources through acquisition and transmission respectively, which contributes to his literacy development. Generally speaking, a normal child can acquire the semiotic resources of his mother tongue in a natural quotidian context. This process embodies the acquisition of shared resources. Acquisition of mother tongue is a part of the process of learning how to mean, which is a life-long process (Hasan 1996a: 384). After the successful acquisition of his mother tongue, the individual continues to be engaged in learning how to mean in a natural quotidian context. An individual's literacy development in the natural every-day context is dependent to a large extent on his social positioning (Hasan 1996a: 385). Different social positioning will orient individuals to participate in different socializations, leading individuals to form different ways of meaning and acquire different social semiotic resources. An example of the acquisition of unshared resources is individuals' formation of different coding orientations. Individuals in families with different social positions acquire different semantic resources, which contribute to the formation of "restricted code" and "elaborated code". Language of those with a restricted coding orientation is heavily context-dependent, features simple syntax and a narrow range of lexical choices, and is not suitable for the expression of abstract ideas; language of those with an elaborated coding orientation, however, is less context-dependent, features more complex and exact syntactic structures, and is suitable for analysis, inference and the expression of abstract ideas (Zhu 2011). These coding orientations are capable of both facilitating and hindering literacy development of the individuals. This explains why the acquisition of mother tongue does not mean that everyone has acquired the same level of literacy.

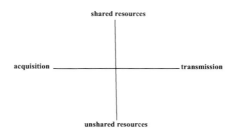

Figure 2   Models of social semiotic resources distribution

The literacy development within the official pedagogic context chronologically postdates but logically relies on the literacy development in the natural quotidian context (Hasan 1996a: 385). In other words, prior to his or her entry into school education, an individual has already acquired a certain way of meaning. When this way of meaning is compatible with the pedagogic discourse, school education will facilitate the individual's literacy development; otherwise, it will hinder his or her development. Both facilitation and hindrance here embody the transmission of unshared resources, which strengthens the differences in social positioning between individuals. Similar to the natural every-day context, individuals' literacy development within formal school education can also be affected by their social positioning. If school education disregards individuals' differential social positioning and adopts the same pedagogic goals and methods, it will augment the differences of literacy development between individuals. If school education, however, pays attention to the effect of differential social positioning on individuals' different ways of meaning and manages to bridge the gap through redistribution of pedagogically significant literacy resources, more balanced literacy development can be achieved. This process embodies the transmission of shared resources.

3. Motivation for redistribution of literacy resources

An individual's literacy development in either natural quotidian context or official pedagogic context can be affected by his social positioning. One's social positioning is crucially linked to both his development of higher mental functions (Vygotsky 1978) and his ontogenesis of ideology (Hasan 2005), both of which underpin his social-cultural identity. Different social-cultural identities correspond to different habitual ways of meaning, which makes it possible for different literacy resources to be allocated to the individuals in the formation of their own respective ways of meaning. As Figure 2 shows, individuals in the natural quotidian context can acquire both shared and unshared resources. The acquisition of unshared resources results in uneven distribution of literacy resources. And the differences between socio-cultural identities are directly responsible for the unbalanced distribution of literacy resources. This has been proved by the studies of Hasan (2005, 2009). Through a careful analysis of dialogues between mothers and children from various social classes, she discovers a strong bond between speakers' socio-cultural identities and their ways of semantic expression. From the perspective of affiliation, as the literacy resources used specifically by an individual shows his or her identity, the social identity of the individual will be strengthened when he applies the literacy resources to building affiliation with other members of the same cultural community. Differences between identities contribute to uneven distribution of literacy resources, which will, in turn, reinforce identity differences when individuals use the allocated literacy resources to affiliate with others.

In the transmission of social semiotic resources, socio-cultural identities can also influence the distribution of literacy resources because the habitual ways of meaning corresponding to different socio-cultural identities show varying degrees of compatibility with pedagogical discourse. As mentioned above, individuals have mastered a certain way of meaning prior to their entry into school education. Different socio-cultural identities enable the individuals to acquire different literacy resources in the natural quotidian context and form different ways of meaning. If classroom language teaching fails to take into account the differences between individuals' cultural identities and ways of meaning, the way of meaning which is compatible with pedagogic discourse will promote the individual's literacy development. Otherwise, it will hinder his or her literacy development. Such classroom language teaching will result in the transmission of unshared resources, which, in turn, will strengthen disparities between socio-cultural identities.

The stronger the isolation or the exclusion between social members is, the weaker the social base is for the development of reservoir and repertoire (Bernstein 1999: 160). The greater the differences between socio-cultural identities are, the more unbalanced the distribution of literacy resources is and the more necessary the redistribution of literacy resources becomes. The process of individuation is a process of allocating specific literacy resources to the individual so that his or her socio-cultural identity can be constructed; the process of affiliation is a process of using the same literacy resources to associate with others sharing the same socio-cultural identity. Martin's theory of individuation thus reveals a co-constructive bond between one's socio-cultural identity and repertoire of literacy resources, which gives rise to mutual reinforcement between differences of individuals' identities and uneven distribution of literacy resources and furnishes the motivation for the redistribution of literacy resources. The purpose of literacy resource redistribution is to realize a balanced distribution of power in society (Martin 2011), for the uneven distribution of power is a major cause behind the formation of individuals' different socio-cultural identities.

4. How to raise the efficiency of literacy resource redistribution

Allocation of literacy resources is conditioned by the individual's socio-cultural identity. Differences between identities make it unavoidable for the individuals to acquire unshared resources in a natural quotidian context. In a formal pedagogic context these differences can also lead to the transmission of unshared resources. Both processes solidify the disparities of social positioning between individuals. The transmission of unshared resources in formal pedagogic contexts is closely related to the acquisition of unshared resources in natural quotidian contexts, for the latter has already oriented individuals to different ways of meaning which vary in terms of compatibility with the pedagogic discourse. The acquisition of unshared resources, therefore, constitutes the key problem in the redistribution of literacy resources. After being internalized by the individual, the unshared resources will develop into different coding orientations— restricted code and elaborated code, which will subliminally affect the individual's literacy development and hinder the redistribution of the literacy resources featuring elaborated code. The transmission of shared resources offers an efficient mode of literacy resource redistribution, for it gives due attention to the effect of socio-cultural identities on the individual's way of meaning and adopts visible pedagogy to redistribute literacy resources to the individuals so as to bridge the gap between different coding orientations and enable individuals of various socio-cultural backgrounds to master the elaborated code which is compatible with the pedagogic discourse.

4.1 Inhibiting negative effect of restricted code in literacy resource redistribution

The acquisition of unshared resources enables individuals to form different coding orientations, which however does not imply a difference of intelligence among the children of different social classes (Bernstein 1958, 1960; Halliday 1988). The coding orientations have already been internalized by the individuals. If there is no intervention and prevention, differences in coding orientations will hinder the individuals' learning at school, which will result in different educational achievements even if no sharp contrast in intelligence exists among them. Since pedagogic discourse is more in line with the elaborated code, school education will become symbolic and social development for the individuals oriented toward the elaborated code; for those oriented toward the restricted code, school education will become a symbolic and social change (Bernstein 1971: 143-144). Cultural discontinuity caused by different coding orientations places in a disadvantaged position in school education the individuals oriented already toward the restricted code, depriving them of equal educational opportunities. Clearly, what should be redistributed to the disadvantaged individuals are the literacy resources featuring an elaborated code.

Learning is a process of construing resources for meaning; individuals simultaneously engage in learning through language and learning language (Halliday 1993). The more literacy resources one possesses, the higher efficiency of knowledge learning one can achieve. Meanwhile, the individual's literacy resources can be further solidified and enriched, contributing to a virtuous circle between literacy development and knowledge learning. On the contrary, deficiency of literacy resources will prevent individuals from effectively acquiring knowledge. Failure of knowledge learning will, in turn, limit the individual's literacy development. The disparities between the restricted code of some individuals and the elaborated code underlying pedagogic discourse in school education make those individuals with a restricted code unable to gain successful education. The real cause of this is the individual's lack of literacy resources. Compared with the restricted code, the elaborated code brings richer literacy resources to the individual. In our view, to inhibit the negative effect of the restricted code is to shorten the distance between the restricted code and elaborated code and thereby reduce its impeditive effect on knowledge learning and promote redistribution of the literacy resources featuring the elaborated code among individuals. Inhibiting the negative effect of the restricted code, therefore, becomes the core link in the process of literacy resource redistribution.

4.2 Transmission of shared resources as an efficient way of inhibiting negative effect of restricted code

As shown in Figure 2, the transmission of shared resources is one of the ways in which social semiotic resources are allocated to the individual. The transmission of shared resources aims at achieving balanced allocation of social semiotic resources to the individuals of different socio-cultural identities. Coding orientation is the result of distributing social semiotic resources to the individuals in accordance with their respective socio-cultural identities. During this process the individual acquires the social semiotic resources which correspond to his or her identity. To inhibit the negative effect of the restricted code through the transmission of shared resources is to regard the literacy resources featuring the elaborated code as the shared resources and transmit them in classroom language teaching to the individuals who have already been oriented toward the restricted code in the natural every-day context. The process of transmitting these specific literacy resources, however, is not easy, for the learning of them can still be affected by the individual's restricted code. The choice of a proper language teaching pedagogy and a correct target for language teaching bears directly upon effective transmission of these literacy resources, which ultimately affects the efficiency of literacy resource redistribution. We hold that the gap between coding orientations can be effectively bridged through raising the visibility of pedagogy and the degree of sharing of semantic resources.

4.2.1 Raising the visibility of pedagogy

Bernstein (1975: 116-117) makes a distinction between invisible pedagogy and visible pedagogy: the more implicit the manner of transmission and the vaguer the teaching criteria, the more invisible the pedagogy; the more explicit the manner of the transmission and the more specific the criteria, the more visible the pedagogy. Invisible pedagogy preconditions a longer educational life[1] and a child's early orientation toward the elaborated code[2], emphasizing either that the child's specific educational competencies can be postponed, or that the child will achieve these competencies early because of his orientation toward the elaborated code (Bernstein 1975: 124). Invisible pedagogy deemphasizes transmission and acquisition of educational competencies and literacy resources, resulting in reinforcement of learner's already established coding orientations. It models the classroom language teaching on a process of allocating social semiotic resources to the individuals according to their respective socio-cultural identities, drastically diminishing the efficiency of redistributing pedagogically meaningful literacy resources.

Constructivist pedagogy is a typical invisible pedagogy. It draws on the developmental psychology of Piaget, which maintains that all children go through biologically fixed stages of cognitive and emotional development. According to this pedagogy, learning is to emerge from within the child, the criteria for assessment are not visible and the pedagogic focus is on implicit acquisition of cognitive and emotional dispositions (Rose and Martin 2012: 16). In fact, the constructivist pedagogy has ruled out any serious intervention from the teacher. And it explains why in Australia the progressive pedagogy, the precursor of constructivism, had banished explicit teaching of knowledge about language (KAL) from classroom teaching (Martin 2009b). Rose and Martin (2012: 3) point out that constructivism was designed to serve the interests of middle-class professional families and cannot provide marginalized social groups with access to successful education. Since students from middle-class families have already acquired the elaborated code which is compatible with pedagogic discourse, it is quite likely for them to adapt successfully from home context to school education and achieve success in knowledge learning. As students from socially marginalized families are usually oriented toward the restricted code, the code differences between home and school context make it difficult for them to quickly adapt to school education and achieve success in knowledge learning. If those students are not made aware of the contents, methodology, and objectives of teaching and the evaluative criteria, they will be confined to the home context and their restricted code acquired in home life will be solidified, which will lead to failure of their knowledge learning (Rothery 1996; Martin 1999). Invisible pedagogy, therefore, strengthens individuals' acquisition of unshared resources in natural quotidian context and is a reproduction and fortification of the existent power structure, which runs counter to the motivation for literacy resource redistribution. Given this, a visible rather than invisible pedagogy should be adopted for the redistribution of literacy resources.

During the allocation of social semiotic resources to the individuals, visible pedagogy is an intervention from outside. Although it cannot change the fact that social semiotic resources are allocated to the individuals according to their respective socio-cultural identities, it can make explicit the differences between the coding orientations and make the individuals aware of the existence of new social semiotic resources. And to raise the visibility of the pedagogy is to raise the visibility of the literacy resource redistribution itself.

4.2.2 Raising the degree of sharing of semantic resources

In addition to raising the visibility of our pedagogy, we should also pay attention to the effect of social positioning on the individuals' ways of meaning, namely, the effect of the disparities between restricted and elaborated coding orientations. Raising the pedagogic visibility without considering the differences between coding orientations can also lead to the transmission of unshared resources, which will hinder the redistribution of literacy resources. Compared with the constructivist pedagogy, the traditional formal language pedagogy attaches greater importance to the accuracy of grammatical forms and features stronger visibility. This pedagogy, however, ignores the fact that language is also a social semiotic practice and ultimately transforms into a process of teachers' attempt to inculcate in their students the linguistic standards (Hasan 1996a: 338-389). These standards are prescriptive in nature, governing the grammatical correctness of language use. Grammar is a resource for meaning and the learning of language is a process of construing resources for meaning (Halliday 1975, 1993, 1994). The denial of language as a resource for meaning will deprive us of an important perspective in the interpretation of the differences between individuals' ways of meaning. Transmission of these standards alone in language teaching will strengthen the differences between individuals' ways of meaning and run the risk of keeping some individuals from accessing the pedagogically significant discourse, for some people may have already acquired in the natural quotidian context the ways of meaning which is compatible with the linguistic standards while others have failed to do so. In order to raise the efficiency for redistributing pedagogically significant literacy resources, the use of language should be treated as a social semiotic behavior, i.e. the individuals make use of the semantic resources for meaning. Only in this way can we explain the differences between individuals' ways of meaning and the cause behind the formation of different coding orientations.

The purpose of raising the degree of sharing of semantic resources is to bridge the gap between the elaborated code underlying pedagogic discourse and the restricted code held by the disadvantaged children. For this reason, in the choice of language teaching contents we need to consider which semantic resources can effectively shorten the gap. Based on the definitions of the restricted code and the elaborated code (Bernstein 1971), it is found that context-independency is one key parameter for the differentiation of these two codes. The elaborated code leads the child early to become aware of the significance of relatively context-independent meanings (Bernstein 1975: 124). Compared with the restricted code, the syntactic features of the elaborated code are more difficult to predict from the context (Bernstein 1990: 96). Certain caution is deserved when we use the term *context-independency*. Any use of language is dependent on context. Drawing on Halliday's (1978: 144-145) distinction between first-order and second-order features of context, we define the *context* in the term context-independency as a first-order context which refers to a concrete world of actions where language mainly serves an ancillary function. When meaning becomes independent of its first-order context, it may gradually depend on its second-order context where language serves a constitutive role and meaning has to be encapsulated within a coherent and textually-constructed organization. This may motivate the child to step out the immediate control of the concrete context and organize his meaning in a coherent text, which can contribute to the formation of the elaborated code.

Another key indicator for differentiating restricted and elaborated codes is semantic density (Maton 2014). Semantic density refers to the degree of meaning condensation within semiotic symbols of culture (Maton 2011: 65-66). In terms of the use of language, semantic density concerns the meaning condensation within various linguistic expressions in a text. Raising semantic density can contribute to the construction of logical relationship between units of meaning. This contribution to the symbolic organization of the text is conducive to the cultivation of the elaborated code. Compared with the elaborated code, language use featuring the restricted code contains lower semantic density and can relieve the language user of the need to construct a symbolic organization for the meaning.

We believe that the transmission of the semantic resources featuring context-independency and a higher degree of semantic density should become the objective of classroom language teaching for the redistribution of literacy resources. A case in point is the teaching of grammatical metaphor, which is a linguistic device for raising both context-independency (Martin & Matruglio 2013) and semantic density (Martin 2013). Compare the following two sentences:

Wealthy families *manufactured* garum in Pompei.
Wealthy families controlled *the manufacture of garum* in Pompei.
(Martin & Matruglio 2013: 85)

In the first sentence, the construal of experience is similar to the real world experience; in the second sentence, however, the process of *manufacturing* is metaphorically construed as a thing (*the manufacture*). Although the nominalization has construed the same experience, the construal is somehow different from the real world experience. The ideational grammatical metaphor as such is a typical illustration of the elaborated code. The experiential construal realized by this resource shows a lower degree of contextual dependency as well as a higher degree of semantic density. The context-independent discourse with higher semantic density, which characterizes the elaborated code, can make it convenient for students to set up logical connections between various definitions and lay the groundwork for the formation of hierarchical knowledge structures (Maton 2013; Tang 2014). If students fail to gain control of the context-independent discourse in secondary school, their access to relevant technical knowledge will be severely limited, for the construction of specialized knowledge in textbooks, handouts and on the web are largely dependent on this discourse; they will also be unable to demonstrate their control of knowledge for assessment purposes(Martin 2013; Martin and Matruglio 2013), for the code underlying such assessment is based on the elaborated code and demands a good command of the context independent discourse. Compared with the individuals oriented toward the restricted code, the individuals oriented toward the elaborated code will excel in both knowledge learning and assessments. Bridging the gap between coding orientations can be effectively facilitated by redistributing the context-independent semantic resources to the individuals already oriented toward the restricted code.

5. Implications of literacy resource redistribution to China's language education policy

According to Bernstein (1971), the child's success in school education is to a large extent dependent on his coding orientation. Because the elaborated code is more compatible with the pedagogic discourse of the school, it will be very hard for the children oriented toward the restricted code to gain equal educational opportunities. Those oriented toward the elaborated code are more likely to get good education at school. Hasan (1996b: 164) points out that different levels of educational success correlate typically with students' social positioning. Different social positioning leads to the acquisition of different coding orientations. The children born in working-class families are more likely to master the restricted code, whereas those born in middle-class families are more likely to master the elaborated code. The studies by Hasan (2005, 2009) have attested to the influence of social positioning on the child's mode of communication, showing that children from middle-class families have already familiarized themselves with the elaborated code underlying educational discourse prior to school education. As discussed above, the differences between coding orientations are in fact the differences of literacy resource distribution. Students oriented toward the elaborated code possess those literacy resources required for school education, those oriented toward the restricted code do not. Consequently, the former's literacy ability is better than the latter's and the former can usually get successful education while the latter may be deprived of equal educational opportunities. In order to realize educational justice to the largest extent, it is very important to regard the redistribution of pedagogically significant literacy resources as a key part in the formulation of our national language education policies.

As the theory of individuation shows, if the differences between socio-cultural identities continue to exist, the unbalanced distribution of social semiotic resources will continue to exist and the necessity for redistributing the pedagogically significant literacy resources will continue to exist. In the 21st century, literacy education in China is confronted with both opportunities and challenges. Over recent years, many children in the countryside have moved with their parents to large cities. While their parents work as migrant workers, the children attend local urban schools. The difficulties experienced by these children in urban school education might be related to their coding orientations (Zhu 2011). These children usually live in poor families. As bread-winners, their parents either ignore them in order to focus on work, or they involve their children in the daily management of small businesses. These children have been locked in a context-dependent semiotic environment and seldom get an opportunity to step out the restriction of immediate and everyday context, a crucial step in forming the elaborated code. In response, China has enacted many protective policies in order to ensure that the disadvantaged groups get good education. At the same time, we should also consider how to improve their literacy ability for this ability bears directly upon the efficiency of knowledge learning. Our view is that proper management of the differences between socio-cultural identities and the improvement of literacy resource redistribution efficiency can effectively ensure a steady progression of literacy education in our country.

Linguistic instances are the result of the instantiation of language semiotic systems in specific contexts. It is from these instances that individuals learn and finally master the semantic resources. As instances are produced by individuals possessing certain socio-cultural identities and materialize as a result of instantiation of their respective social semiotic repertoire, the instances are specific to various socio-cultural identities, thus enabling learners not only to master specific semantic resources, but also to acquire corresponding specific socio-cultural identities. When the semantic resources acquired beforehand in natural quotidian contexts are in conflict with the pedagogic discourse, students' knowledge learning will be negatively affected. While the conflict between natural quotidian and formal pedagogic discourses appears to be a discord between different coding orientations of meaning making, it is, in essence, a conflict between two different socio-cultural identities for the coding orientations grow out of differential distribution of literacy resources in accordance with learners' specific socio-cultural identities. According to Halliday (1995: 128), when the children oriented toward a restricted code receive school education featuring the use of an elaborated code, their new experiences cannot be referred back to their coding orientation, which creates a cultural discontinuity and motivates teacher and these students to "disvalue one another". As a result, proper management of the interrelationship across various socio-cultural identities at school is conducive to shortening the social distance between teachers and students, strengthening their solidarity and making the disadvantaged learners more willing to take in new social semiotic resources in classroom language teaching.

The earlier the intervention in the coding orientations is in language education, the more efficient the literacy resource redistribution is. Classroom language teaching is an efficient approach to inhibiting the negative effect of the restricted code and realizing the redistribution of pedagogically significant literacy resources. The formation of coding orientations requires a certain period of time. If classroom language teaching can help overcome the coding orientation mismatch during the early stage of school education, the distribution of overall literacy resources across different social strata will become more balanced.

6. Conclusion

Literacy resource redistribution is a process of reallocating pedagogically significant social semiotic resources to the individuals disadvantaged by their restricted coding orientation. The process of individuation emphasizes the effect of different socio-cultural identities on the distribution of social semiotic resources, while literacy resource redistribution aims at mitigating this effect. In the process of individuation, the unbalanced distribution of social semiotic resources strengthens the uneven distribution of semiotic power across social strata while the process of redistribution aims at promoting a balanced distribution of semiotic power by balancing the distribution of pedagogically significant literacy resources. The theory of individuation reveals that social semiotic resources are allocated to the individuals according to their respective socio-cultural identities, thus furnishing the motivation for the redistribution of pedagogically significant literacy resources. Effectively inhibiting the negative effect of the restricted code constitutes the key link in the process of literacy resource redistribution. Raising the pedagogic visibility and the degree of sharing of semantic resources can reduce the negative effect of the restricted code in classroom language teaching and raise the efficiency for redistributing pedagogically significant literacy resources.

Notes

1. According to Bernstein (1975: 123), the invisible pedagogy had its origins within a fraction of the middle class. This pedagogy provides more advantages for the middle class

than for the working class. It presupposes a relatively long educational life for the middle class (Bernstein 1975: 124). The reasons are as follows. First of all, play is a basic concept in the invisible pedagogy (Bernstein 1975: 117). For the working class, work and play are very strongly classified and framed, whereas work and play are weakly classified and framed for the middle class (Bernstein 1975: 118). In other words, learning through working has provided the middle class with more opportunities and a longer time for education. Secondly, compared with the children from the working class, those from the middle class will experience fewer cultural discontinuities in both elementary and secondary school education. Invisible pedagogy deemphasizes the early attainment of basic competencies like reading and writing. The children from the working class families will experience a discontinuity between home education stressing the acquisition of the basic competencies and the elementary school education featuring invisible pedagogy. For the children from both the middle class and the working class, secondary education features a visible pedagogy (Bernstein 1975: 134). The shift from invisible to visible pedagogies poses fewer difficulties for the middle-class children, because the home education in the middle-class families has prepared them for the visible pedagogy in secondary education which features strong classification and framing of knowledge and teaching. Nurtured in the invisible pedagogy of the elementary school, unaided by their home education, the working-class children will experience a cultural discontinuity in secondary schools which might seriously impair their education. To sum up, learning through working and an easy transition to visible pedagogy offer the middle-class children a longer educational life in comparison with the working-class children.

2. The socialization within middle-class families is characterized by the elaborated code. This coding orientation can help the child achieve some basic educational competencies early in family life. This can explain why the failure of a middle-class child to obtain the basic competencies in elementary education can be compensated by private coaching or by the mother's own efforts in family education (Bernstein 1975: 129). This can also explain why the middle-class children are more likely to adapt to the visible pedagogy in secondary education than the working-class children although both have received the same elementary education featuring the invisible pedagogy.

References

Bernstein, B. 1958. Some sociological determinants of perception: An enquiry into sub-cultural differences. *The British Journal of Sociology*, 9 (2), 159-174.

Bernstein, B. 1960. Language and social class. *The British Journal of Sociology,* 11(3), 271-276.

Bernstein, B. 1971. *Class, Codes and Control: Theoretical Studies Towards a Sociology of Language, Volume 1*. London: Routledge and Kegan Paul.

Bernstein, B. 1975. *Class, Codes and Control: Towards a Theory of Educational Transmission, Volume 3*. London: Routledge and Kegan Paul.

Bernstein, B. 1990. *The Structuring of Pedagogic Discourse: Class, Codes and Control, Volume 4*. London and New York: Routledge.

Bernstein, B. 1999. Vertical and horizontal discourse: An essay. *British Journal of Sociology of Education*, 20 (2), 266-279.

Halliday, M. A. K. 1994. *Introduction to Functional Grammar* (2nd edition). London: Edward Arnold.

Halliday, M. A. K. 1975. *Learning How to Mean: Explorations in the Development of Language*. London: Edward Arnold.

Halliday, M. A. K. 1988. Language and socialization: Home and school. In L. Gerot, J. Oldenburg and T.van Leeuwen (eds.), *Language and Socialisation, Home and School: Proceedings from the Working Conference on Language in Education*. 1-14. North Ryde, N.S.W: Macquarie University.

Halliday, M. A. K. 1993. Towards a language-based theory of learning. *Linguistics and Education*, 5, 93-116.

Halliday, M. A. K. 1995. Language and the theory of codes. In A. R. Sadovnik (ed.), *Knowledge and Pedagogy: The Sociology of Basil Bernstein*. 127-143. Norwood: Ablex.

Hasan, R. 1996a. Literacy, everyday talk and society. In R. Hasan and G. Williams (eds.), *Literacy in Society*. 377-424. London: Longman.

Hasan, R. 1996b. Speech genre, semiotic mediation and the development of higher mental functions. In C. B. Cloran, D. G. Butt and G. Williams (eds.), *Ways of Saying, Ways of Meaning: Selected Papers of Ruqaiya Hasan*. 152-190. London: Cassell.

Hasan, R. 2005. *Language, Society and Consciousness*. London: Equinox.

Hasan, R. 2009. *Semantic Variation: Meaning in Society and Sociolinguistics*. London: Equinox.

Martin, J. R. 1999. Mentoring semogenesis: "genre-based" literacy pedagogy. In F. Christie (ed.), *Pedagogy and the Shaping of consciousness: Linguistic and Social Processes*. 123-155. London: Cassell.

Martin, J. R. 2008. Innocence: Realisation, instantiation and individuation in a Botswanan town. In N. Knight and A. Mahboob (eds.), *Questioning Linguistics*. 32-61. Cambridge: Cambridge Scholars Publishing.

Martin, J. R. 2009a. Realisation, instantiation and individuation: Some thoughts on identity in youth justice conferencing. *DELTA-Documentação de Estudos em Linguistica Teorica e Aplicada*, 25, 549-583.

Martin, J. R. 2009b. Genre and language learning: A social semiotic perspective. *Linguistics and Education*, 20, 10-21.

Martin, J. R. 2010. Semantic variation: Modelling realisation, instantiation and individuation in social semiosis. In M. Bednarek and J. R. Martin (eds.), *New Discourse on Language: Functional Perspectives on Multimodality, Identity and Affiliation*. 1-34. London: Continuum.

Martin, J. R. 2011. Bridging troubled waters: Interdisciplinarity and what makes it stick. In F. Christie and K. Maton (eds.), *Disciplinarity: Functional Linguistic and Sociological Perspectives*. 35-61. London: Continuum.

Martin, J. R. 2013. Embedded literacy: Knowledge as meaning. *Linguistics and Education*, 24 (1), 23-37.

Martin, J. R. and Z. Wang. 2008. Realization, instantiation and individuation: A systemic-functional linguistic perspective. *Journal of SJTU (Philosophy and Social Sciences)*, (5), 73-81.

Martin, J. R. & E. Matruglio. 2013. Revisiting mode: Context in/dependency in ancient history classroom discourse. In Z. Li and D. Lu (eds.), *Studies in Functional Linguistics and Discourse Analysis, Volume 5.* 72-95. Beijing: Higher Education Press.

Maton, K. 2011. Theories and things: The semantics of disciplinarity. In F. Christie and K. Maton (eds.), *Disciplinarity: Functional Linguistic and Sociological Perspectives.* 62-84. London: Continuum.

Maton, K. 2013. Making semantic waves: A key to cumulative knowledge-building. *Linguistics and Education,* 24 (1), 8-22.

Maton, K. 2014. *Knowledge and Knowers: Towards a Realist Sociology of Education.* London and New York: Routledge.

Rose, D. and J. R. Martin. 2012. *Learning to Write, Reading to Learn: Genre, Knowledge and Pedagogy in the Sydney School.* Sheffield: Equinox.

Rothery, J. 1996. Making changes: Developing an educational linguistics. In R. Hasan and G. Williams (eds.), *Literacy in Society.* 86-123. London: Longman.

Tang, B. 2014. On the cooperation between Maton's Legitimation Code Theory and Systemic Functional Linguistics. *Modern Foreign Languages (Bimonthly),* 1, 52-61.

Vygotsky, L. S. 1978. *Mind in Society: The Development of Higher Psychological Processes.* Cambridge, MA: Harvard University Press.

Zhu, Y. 2011. Impact of Bernstein's theory of pedagogic sociology on Systemic Functional Linguistics. *Foreign Language Education,* 4, 6-12.

Zhu, Y. 2012. The study of individuation in SFL: Motivation and philosophy. *Modern Foreign Languages (Quarterly),* 4, 331-337.

A Functional Approach to Content Literacy in a TESOL Teacher Training Program

Wei Zhang

The University of Akron, USA

1. Introduction

English language learners (ELLs) are the fastest growing student body in the United States. Between 1998 and 2008, the number of ELLs increased by 51.01% nation-wide to 5,346,673 with a growth of more than 200% in 11 states (The National Clearinghouse for English Language Acquisition and Language Instruction Educational Programs 2011). By 2030, ELLs enrolled in U.S. public schools are projected to account for approximately 40% of the entire student population (Roseberry-McKibbin and Brice 2013). Such a rapid increase of ELLs challenges the existing educational infrastructure and resources in many cities across the country, including teacher training, teaching materials, and curriculum development (Short and Fitzsimmons 2007).

To meet the challenges, the U.S. Department of Education put forth a number of initiatives to train in-service teachers to improve the teaching efficacy of ELLs through grant funding and program development. One of the initiatives, the National Professional Development Grant, supports "professional development activities that are designed to improve classroom instruction for English Learners (ELs) and will assist educational personnel working with such children to meet high professional standards, including standards for certification and licensure as teachers who work in language instruction educational programs or serve ELs" (The Department of Education 2011: 14954). The TESOL teacher training program reported in this paper is one of the awardees of the National Professional Development Grant. It offers training for a TESOL Endorsement to four cohorts of in-service content and special education teachers in Northeast Ohio. As one of the linguistic faculty teaching in this program, I incorporated Systemic Functional Linguistics (SFL), originally proposed by M. A. K. Halliday, into two of the courses in the TESOL Endorsement to help the trainee teachers identify content text complexity and design activities to teach academic language and develop content literacy in ELLs.

2. Curriculum design

The curriculum of our TESOL Endorsement program recognizes the current research findings of ELLs, how they learn, and how to teach them. First, ELLs come from very different and diverse backgrounds and face unique challenges linguistically and academically. Cummins (1984) differentiates two levels of language development of language learners: Basic Interpersonal Communicative Skills (BICS) or social language, and Cognitive/Academic Language Proficiency (CALP) or academic language. Depending on the onset of English acquisition and other factors, ELLs might exhibit a whole gamut of rates in acquiring English for social interaction and academic functions, but academic language generally takes a considerably longer time to develop than social language (e.g., Baker 2011; Cummins 1984; Haynes 2007; Zwiers 2008). Explicit teaching of academic language is thus necessary for ELLs' academic language development.

Second, academic language is the pathway to academic literacy. Academic literacy is the language for "reading, writing, and oral discourse for school" that "varies from subject to subject and requires knowledge of multiple genres of text, purposes for text use, and text media" (Short and Fitzsimmons 2007: 8). The content specific nature of academic literacy requires content teachers to explicitly teach academic language in the content area to ELLs.

Third, a lack of proficiency in English and academic language can delay ELLs' acquisition of knowledge and mastery of key skills in content areas necessary to be college and career ready. In the Common Core State Standards (CCSS), a set of high-quality academic standards developed in 2009 and adopted by a majority of states in the United States, language plays a pivotal role in student achievement in all subject areas, including English language arts, math, social studies, and science. These standards are demanding enough for native-speaking students and present extra challenges for ELLs. Currently, ELLs lag behind their peers in all measures of academic achievement (e.g., National Education Association 2008; Short and Fitzsimmons 2007). To complicate the matter, classroom teachers, content teachers in particular, are not usually trained or prepared to teach academic language and develop academic literacy for ELLs (Schleppegrell 2004; Short 2002; Short and Fitzsimmons 2007). For instance, Short and Fitzsimmons (2007) identified "[i]nadequate educator capacity for improving literacy in ELLs" and "[i]nadequate use of research-based instructional practices" as two of the six major challenges to improving ELL's academic literacy (14).

Based upon these research findings, our TESOL Endorsement program concentrates on linguistics, language acquisition, language pedagogy, and culture in the selection and configuration of courses. It has 22 credit hours, including six three-credit courses in linguistics, second language acquisition, and second language pedagogy, a two-credit course in differentiated instruction, and a two-credit practicum. All these courses were designed to support the implementation of the Sheltered Instruction Observation Protocol (SIOP) model, a content-based approach to language teaching and content instruction that has thus far been proven to be effective with empirical data in concurrently teaching grade-level academic content and academic language (Echevarria et al. 2011; Short et al. 2011; Short et al. 2012). This model systematically synthesizes the best practices in language teaching and content instruction in eight components and 30 features to guide the preparation, delivery, and assessment of each lesson. Figure 1 below provides an overview of the SIOP model.

The SIOP model, as stated in its eight components, places a double emphasis on content instruction and language teaching, especially the teaching of content-specific academic language. While the trainee teachers in our TESOL Endorsement program are experienced content teachers, they are not trained to teach the language used in specific content areas. It thus becomes one of the goals of the TESOL Endorsement program to help the trainee teachers recognize and identify the linguistic features of content texts that constitute linguistic complexity and derive effective teaching strategies to develop content literacy in ELLs.

3. SFL course projects

The two courses with SFL integration in our TESOL Endorsement program are Linguistics and Language Arts, a foundation course in linguistics, and Theoretical Foundations and Principles of ESL, a course in second language acquisition theory and language teaching methods. The former introduces the grammatical aspects of language, including morphology, syntax, phonetics, phonology, and semantics; and the latter covers theories of first and second language acquisition and language teaching methods with a focus on the communicative approach, including Communicative Language Teaching, Task-based Language Teaching, and Content-based Instruction or SIOP. These two courses are taught in two consecutive semesters to the same cohort of trainee teachers. This schedule offers an opportunity to plan for course projects that build upon each other to deepen the trainee teachers' understanding of content text complexity by applying an SFL analysis to content texts from different angles and design effective teaching strategies. Table 1 is a summary of the courses and integrated SFL projects.

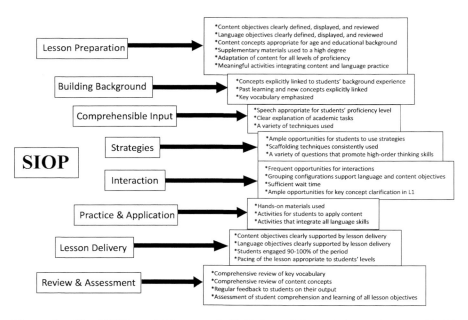

Figure 1   The SIOP model in a nutshell (Adapted from Echevarria et al. 2012)

Table 1   Course and SFL Project Overview

Courses	SFL Projects		
	Name	Purpose	Description
Linguistics and Language Arts -Morphology -Syntax -Phonetics -Phonology -Semantics	1. Content Text Analysis	-Get to know SFL framework of content text analysis -Apply the SFL framework to analyze a content text	This project introduces the framework of SFL content text analysis in two rounds of reading and requires the trainee teachers to select one content text with examples to illustrate all SFL linguistic features to gain an understanding of content text complexity
Theoretical Foundations and Principles of ESL -1st Language acquisition -2nd Language acquisition -Language teaching methods	2. Text Complexity and Teaching Strategies	-Apply SFL linguistic features to analyze multiple content texts -Design teaching activities and strategies based on the SFL analysis	This project requires the trainee teachers to apply one or two SFL linguistic features to analyze multiple content texts from different sources and/or from different grade levels and design teaching activities and strategies to teach the selected SFL linguistic features

3.1 Content text analysis

Text analysis in the SFL framework is an approach for reading "closely and critically" to "develop an understanding of how language works in different subjects" (Fang and Schleppegrell

2008: 1). In *Content Text Analysis*, the trainee teachers are first assigned to read a selection of chapters in their respective content areas from *Reading in Secondary Content Areas: A Language-Based Pedagogy* (Fang and Schleppegrell 2008) (See Appendix I SFL Reading Selections for a complete list of readings). Second, they are assigned to summarize the principles of SFL and the linguistic features of the texts in their content areas in two graphic organizers. Third, they select a text from the textbooks they use and conduct an SFL analysis of the text in small groups of two or three people.

As summarized in Figure 2, SFL takes the clause as the base unit to construct three kinds of meaning simultaneously: experiential (what the text is about), interpersonal (what the relationships between the author and the reader and among the characters are), and textual (how the text is organized into a coherent message). Analyzing a clause into participants (nominal groups), processes (verbal groups), and circumstances (adverbial groups and prepositional phrases) helps to understand experiential meaning; classifying a clause into declarative (statements), interrogative (questions), and imperative (commands) and the presence of modal verbs helps to show interpersonal meaning; and analyzing the Theme-Rheme structure among clauses helps to present the textual meaning.

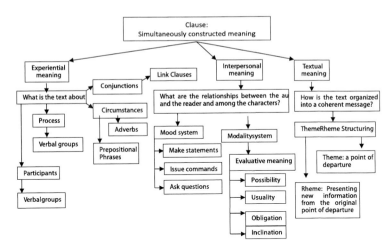

Figure 2　Principles of SFL (Based on Fang and Schleppegrell 2008: 10-11)

These SFL principles can be applied to analyzing texts in specific content areas to reveal the linguistic features of the texts. As shown in Figure 3, scientific discourse is simultaneously technical, abstract, dense, and tightly knit. The following text on plant science, suitable for a high school science class, illustrates these features.

The researchers determined that the light-sensitive substance in plants is a soluble protein, which they named phytochrome. This protein is an enzyme. It is the biological catalyst that controls many kinds of plant responses in different plant tissues. For example, stem elongation and leaf growth seem to be by phytochrome. Mature apples turn red in light having a wavelength of 600 nm. The light causes the production of the red pigment anthocyanin. The same red light that promotes the germination of some seeds also controls the production of anthocyanin in a number of seedling plants. Seed germination is inhibited by exposure to far-red light at a wavelength of 730 nm.

The germination response is also controlled by the radiation exposure given last. If the seeds are last exposed to red energy, germination occurs. If the energy is far-red, germination does not occur, regardless of the number of cycles of red and far-red energy.

(From *Effects of Environmental Factors on Plant Growth* by J. Boodley and S. Newman)

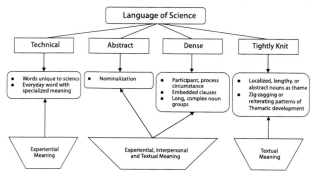

Figure 3   Linguistic features of science texts (based on Fang and Schleppegrell 2008: 20-34)

1) Technical: The technicality of science texts comes from technical words unique to the discipline, such as *phytochrome, anthocyanin, catalyst, enzyme, germination,* and *nanometer (nm)*, and everyday words with special scientific meanings, such as *light, soluble, tissues, responses, red,* and *protein*.

2) Abstract: Science texts are abstract due to high frequency use of nominalization, which is a process of turning verbal or adjectival groups into nominal groups. For instance, *the germination response* at the beginning of the second paragraph refers to the last two sentences in the previous paragraph in the sample text.

3) Dense: Science texts are densely packed with clauses that involve long nominal groups with pre-and-post modifiers and embedded clauses. The first three sentences of the sample texts include three long nominal groups (underlined) and two of them also include an embedded attributive clause (shaded):

The researchers determined that the light-sensitive substance in plants is a soluble protein, which they named phytochrome. This protein is an enzyme. It is a biological catalyst that controls many kinds of plant responses in different plant tissues.

A close analysis of one of the nominal groups demonstrates the complex nature of long nominal groups:

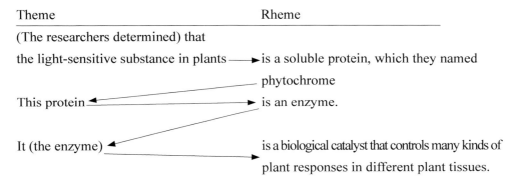

4) Tightly knit: Science texts are tightly knit with reiterating patterns of thematic development, or a zigzagging Theme-Rheme structure as illustrated by the first three sentences:

Theme	Rheme
(The researchers determined) that	
the light-sensitive substance in plants ⟶	is a soluble protein, which they named phytochrome
This protein ◂	⟶ is an enzyme.
It (the enzyme) ◂	is a biological catalyst that controls many kinds of plant responses in different plant tissues.

3.2 Text complexity and teaching strategies

After the trainer teachers complete a comprehensive survey of the SFL linguistic features of the texts in their respective content areas in *Content Text Analysis*, *Text Complexity and Teaching Strategies* requires them to identify one or two difficult SFL linguistic features of the texts in a content area and draw on their knowledge in linguistics, second language acquisition, and language teaching methods and strategies to recommend teaching strategies to target the difficult linguistic features. The project should include the following content: 1) a description of the SFL linguistic feature or features in the texts of the content area and justify why it is difficult to ELLs; 2) a selection of text samples across lessons, textbooks, or grade levels to illustrate the SFL linguistic feature or features; and 3) teaching strategies to target the SFL linguistic feature or features based on literature and teaching experience.

The purpose of the project is to deepen the teachers' understanding of the SFL linguistic features and transform their knowledge in text analysis into practical applications in the classroom. For instance, the zigzagging thematic organization scheme is typical of science texts at high school level, but also applicable to science texts in lower grades as illustrated in the paragraph below:

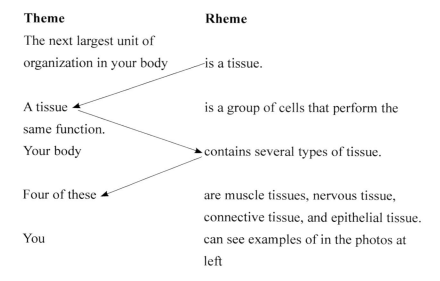

Theme	Rheme
The next largest unit of organization in your body	is a tissue.
A tissue	is a group of cells that perform the same function.
Your body	contains several types of tissue.
Four of these	are muscle tissues, nervous tissue, connective tissue, and epithelial tissue.
You	can see examples of in the photos at left

Interestingly, the zigzagging pattern of the Theme-Rheme structure is by no means unique to science texts. It is also found in readings used in other content areas as illustrated in the nursery rhyme *Ten Little Monkeys*:

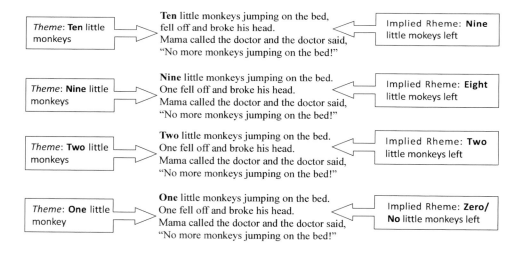

Teaching the zigzagging Theme-Rheme organization will help students recognize the inner structure of a text and increase their comprehension and retention of a text. The following strategies can be used in the instruction of this linguistic feature to the students:

1) Rename the technical terms "Theme" and "Rheme" as "beginning ideas" and "ending ideas" .

2) Demonstrate dividing a clause/sentence into "beginning ideas" and "ending ideas" and provide a few sentences from the target text for practice.

3) Ask students to underline the "beginning ideas" in each clause in an easy-to-understand practice text of the same or similar topic to the target text.

4) Ask students to rearrange the clauses in the practice text into two columns and put the "beginning ideas" into Column A and "ending ideas" into Column B.

5) Demonstrate the zigzagging pattern in the practice text.

6) Introduce the target text and ask students to underline the "beginning ideas" in each clause.

7) Ask students to rearrange the clauses in the target text into two columns and "beginning ideas" into Column A and "ending ideas" into Column B.

8) Ask students to link the same "ending ideas" with the following "beginning ideas" to reveal the zig-zapping organization scheme of the target text.

9) Check students' comprehension with questions; if the "beginning" and "ending" ideas in the clauses in the target text can be represented in pictures, ask students to replace the text with the pictures and retell the text.

4. Conclusion

SFL is a practical linguistic tool that can be incorporated into TESOL teacher training to enhance TESOL teachers' capacity to teach academic language and content-specific literacy to ELLs. With the ever growing number of ELLs, if classroom teachers do not have ELLs in their classroom now, they will in the foreseeable near future. The SIOP model offers a systematic guidance for simultaneous teaching content and language to ELLs with its eight components and 30 features. SFL text analysis, as demonstrated in the course projects in this paper, could be a well-matched approach to support the implementation of the SIOP model to its full potential.

References

Baker, C. 2011. *Foundations of Bilingual Education and Bilingualism* (5th edition). Clevedon, England: Multilingual Matters.

Boodley, J. and S. Newman. 2009. Effects of environmental factors on plant growth. In J. Boodley and S. Newman (eds.), *The Commercial Greenhouse* (3rd edition). 154. USA: Delmar/Cengage Learning.

Cummins, J. 1984. Wanted: A theoretical framework for relating language proficiency to academic achievement among bilingual students. In C. Rivera (ed.), *Language Proficiency and Academic Achievement*. 2-19. Clevedon, England: Multilingual Matters.

Echevarria, J., C. Richards-Tutor, R. Canges, and D. Francis. 2011. Using the SIOP Model to promote the acquisition of language and science concepts with English learners. *Bilingual Research Journal*, 34, 334-351.

Echevarria, J., M. Vogt and D. J. Short. 2012. *Making Content Comprehensible for English Learners: The SIOP Model (4th edition)*. New Jersey: Pearson Education, Inc.

Fang, Z. and M. J. Schleppegrell. 2008. *Reading in Secondary Content Areas: A Language-Based Pedagogy*. Ann Arbor, MI: The University of Michigan Press.

Haynes, J. 2007. *Getting Started with English Language Learners: How Educators Can Meet the Challenge*. Alexandria, VA: Association for Supervision and Curriculum Development.

National Education Association. 2008. *English Language Learners Face Unique Challenges*. Retrieved from http://www.nea.org/assets/docs/HE/ELL_Policy_Brief_Fall_08_(2).pdf.

Roseberry-McKibbin, C. and A. Brice. 2013. *What's "normal," What's not: Acquiring English as a Second language*. Retrieved from http://www.readingrockets.org/article/5126.

Schleppegrell, M. J. 2004. *The Language of Schooling: A Functional Linguistic Perspective*. Mahwah, New Jersey: Lawrence Erlbaum Associates, Publishers.

Short, D. J. 2002. Language learning in a sheltered social studies class, *TESOL Journal*, 11, 18-28.

Short, D. J., C. G. Fidelman and M. Louguit. 2012. Developing academic language in English language learners through Sheltered Instruction. *TESOL Quarterly*, 48 (2), 334-361.

Short, D. J., J. Echevarria and C. Richards-Tutor. 2011. Research on academic literacy development in sheltered instruction classrooms. *Language Teaching Research*, 15 (3), 363-380.

Short, D. J. and S. Fitzsimmons. 2007. *Double the Work: Challenges and Solutions to Acquiring Language and Academic Literacy for Adolescent English Language Learners*. Retrieved from http://carnegie.org/fileadmin/Media/Publications/PDF/DoubletheWork.pdf.

The Department of Education. 2011. National professional development grant. *Federal Register*, 75 (53), 14954-14959.

The National Clearinghouse for English Language Acquisition and Language Instruction Educational Programs. 2011. *The Growing Numbers of English Learner Students 1998/99-2008/08* [Data file]. Retrieved from http://www.ncela.gwu.edu/files/uploads/9/growingLEP_0809.pdf.

Thomas, W. P. and V. P. Collier. 1997. *School Effectiveness for Language Minority Students*. Washington, D.C.: National Clearinghouse for English Language Acquisition.

Zwiers, J. 2008. *Building Academic Language: Essential Practices for Content Classrooms, Grades 5-12*. San Francisco, CA: Jossey-Bass.

Longitudinal Changes in Use of Engagement in University History Writing: A Case Study

Thomas. D. Mitchell[a], Ryan T. Miller[b] and Silvia Pessoa[c]

[a]Carnegie Mellon University in Qatar; [b]Kent State University;
[c]Carnegie Mellon University in Qatar

1. Introduction

In this study we track the writing development of a first-year student by examining her use of engagement[1] (Martin and White 2005) resources in argumentative writing during a one-semester history course. We focus our analysis on her use of several engagement moves that were found to be valued in argumentative writing in that course (see Miller, Mitchell, and Pessoa 2014). The engagement moves we examine allow authors to strategically incorporate their own perspectives in relation to other perspectives. Academic arguers must make claims against a background of already-existing perspectives (Martin 1989), and successful academic writers create a balance between introducing their own perspective, acknowledging the existence of other perspectives, and effectively estimating what their audience's assumed perspective will be.

Martin and White's (2005) system of engagement resources from their appraisal framework provides a useful tool for analyzing how authors manage this balance. Using engagement resources, authors position themselves in relation to prior voices about a particular subject. Following Bakhtin (1981), Martin and White (2005) describe the construal of voice in text as either monoglossic (single-voiced) or heteroglossic (multi-voiced). With monoglossic propositions, such as bare assertions or presuppositions, writers allow no room for alternative voices, projecting complete agreement onto the audience. With heteroglossic resources, writers acknowledge the existence of differing perspectives (expanding the dialogic space) or refute opponents while still keeping their viewpoint in play (contracting the dialogic space).

Previous research has found that engagement resources are important in argumentative writing (e.g., Wu and Allison 2005; Lee 2008; Ryshina-Pankova 2014), specifically argumentative history writing (e.g., Coffin 1997, 2006; de Oliveira 2011). Coffin (2006) noted that as students progress toward writing analytical history genres, there is increased negotiation of alternative voices and acknowledgement of similar and opposing perspectives. Most of the studies of engagement in history writing, however, have focused only on discrete linguistic forms used to enact singular engagement resources. De Oliveira (2011) found that engagement resources used in expository history writing included projection using mental processes, concession using conjunctions (e.g., *but, even though, although*), and acknowledgement of alternative voices using modality. Similarly, Coffin (1997, 2006) found that persuasion in argumentative history genres is assisted through positioning alternative voices using modality (e.g., *X does not necessarily*) or by making categorical statements (e.g., *X clearly demonstrates*). These studies have concluded that integrating other's voices and perspectives with the author's own is a difficult skill to acquire.

Building on these studies, our previous research investigated how students make strategic and purposeful use of engagement resources for argumentation in history writing, finding that especially valued were the combined use of *Attribute* and *Endorse* moves, and *Concede* and *Counter* moves (Miller, Mitchell, and Pessoa 2014). Attribute is used to acknowledge another's voice (e.g., *according to X*), such as referring to a source text, and Endorse (e.g., *X shows, demonstrates*) to construe external voices as "correct, valid, undeniable or otherwise maximally warrantable" (Martin and White 2005: 126). Concede (signaled by *although, whereas, while,* etc.) and Counter (signaled by *even, only, still*, etc.) are used in conjunction to align a resistant reader to the author's position, as the concession "validates the reader's contrary viewpoint by acknowledging that it is understandable… [before showing that] the usual or expected implications do not arise from the conceded proposition" (Martin and White 2005: 125-126).

In our previous study of argumentative history writing (Miller, Mitchell, and Pessoa 2014), we found that more successful student writers (i.e., higher-graded essays) used these two sets of moves to construct an argument in relation to others' perspectives. These students used the expanding Attribute move to set up a direct textual reference, followed by the Endorse move to contract the dialogic space by telling the reader how to interpret the source text as support for the student's central claim. We also found that while most students used paired Concede + Counter moves, successful students used this move to project a consistent alternative position and strengthen their argument, whereas less successful students incorporated this move in ways that did not support, or often even undermined, their argument.

Building on our previous work, in this paper we investigate whether there is longitudinal development in the use of these engagement resources over time. We do this by analyzing a series of argumentative history essays by one student over a one-semester course, examining changes in her use of these engagement resources for supporting her argument. While there have been studies that have focused on undergraduate writing development from an ethnographic perspective (see, for example, the work of Leki 2007; Sommers 2008; Sternglass 1997), fewer studies have been text-based tracing students' literacy development longitudinally (see Gardner 2008; Hewings 2004; Mahboob and Devrim 2013; Nesi 2009; Pessoa, Miller, and Gatti 2014 forthcoming; Woodward-Kron 2008). In the following section, we describe our methodology, followed by the results of our text analysis.

2. Methods

Our data are drawn from a larger four-year longitudinal study of academic literacy development at an English-medium university in the Middle East. The larger study focused largely on the academic literacy development of a group of 92 students during their undergraduate education, 15 of which were case studies who participated in extensive interviews throughout the four years. In their first year at the university, students took a writing-intensive world history course that emphasized, in addition to the subject matter, helping students develop academic reading, writing, and research skills. The data we analyzed in this paper is drawn from this course.

In the world history course, students wrote a series of six short (approximately 300-800 words in length) argumentative essays based on historical and academic readings, responding to one of several prompts supplied by the professor. Some source texts were primary sources while others were secondary sources. The source text titles and authors are included in the Appendix. The assignment rubric showed that students were expected to write argumentatively by having a clearly stated thesis statement and supporting this thesis statement with appropriate evidence from source texts, by making links between historical events or sources, and by being sensitive to biases and limitations in the sources. According to the history professor, many students experienced difficulty writing these essays, with many relying on narration and description rather than argument and analysis, particularly at the beginning of the semester (History professor, personal communication, January 26, 2010).

As a follow-up to our previous research described earlier, we report here the longitudinal writing development of one student, Karida[2], during this course. We selected Karida because she was one of the focal case studies in the larger study, providing us with interview data as well as her writing. We also chose Karida because her essay grades generally improved over the semester, which, based on our previous research, we thought might indicate improvement in her use of engagement resources. The prompts that Karida selected are in the Appendix.

Karida grew up in the Middle East, and spoke Arabic, English, and Swahili at home, although she considered English her native language. She attended English-medium primary and secondary schools, and had high TOEFL scores when she entered the university. Nevertheless, she was not confident in her argumentative writing, saying that it was very different from writing in high school, which focused more on writing for tests.

Using the engagement system from Martin and White's (2005) appraisal framework, two of the authors coded the five[3] short essays Karida wrote in the world history course, focusing in particular on her moves for inclusion of voices from source texts and management of alternative and opposing voices. Additionally, we include data from a one-hour interview with Karida, conducted by one of the authors. This interview focused on Karida's academic literacy development during her first year at the university, including her writing in the history course.

3. Results and discussion

We report here the findings of our longitudinal analysis of Karida's use of engagement resources. We first discuss her use of engagement resources to bring in and interpret voices from source texts, followed by a discussion of her use of engagement for managing alternative voices.

3.1 Inclusion and interpretation of the source text

Our analysis found that Karida showed considerable development in her incorporation of source texts into her essays over the course of the semester, particularly in her use of the valuable combination of Attribute and Endorse moves to introduce and interpret direct textual references.

Early in the semester, Karida referred very little to the source text. In the earliest essays that we analyzed (Essays 1 and 3), there is a complete absence of reference to either the source text or the source author. For example, she begins Essay 1 with the following paragraph:

> Around 7 million years ago everyone used to nourish themselves by hunting and gathering wild plants. In Today's era people eat food that was produced for them. They specialize in other jobs while farmers produce food to sustain the rest of the non-producing society. Individual hunting and gathering as done in the past is dying out and within a couple of decades it will be completely gone soon.

Here, Karida obviously draws on a source text for the information she writes, which was about the transition of human societies from hunting and gathering to agriculture, but neglects to make any direct reference to where this information came from. As a result, it is difficult to distinguish what claim she is making based on the source text, and how the source text is being used to support her claim. Similar to this excerpt, in Essay 3 she also re-presents information from a source text, but with no mention of the source and without any Attribute or Endorse moves to show where the information came from and how it supports her argument.

In Essay 4, the prompt asks for a comparison between two texts by Chinese philosophers, one by Confucius and the other by Han Fei. In this essay, Karida makes references to both source text authors, most often through Attribute moves such as *Confucius believes* and *According to Han Fei*. Though the use of these references may be affected by the task (i.e. the need to differentiate between the two authors being compared), it is still an improvement over the previous essays. While Karida does not ever directly quote or cite the source text, she does bring these authors' voices into her essay in the majority of her sentences, in some cases dedicating a following sentence to explaining the idea attributed to the author, such as in the following:

Confucius believed in an idea called Confucianism. <u>This is a concept</u> where people are governed my morals and virtue. That way they feel guilty with the wrongs and sins they have committed.

Here, Karida attributes a concept (Confucianism) to Confucius, and then goes on to explain this concept in the next sentence. In the third sentence, she then explains how this is relevant to her thesis (that a difference between Confucius and Han Fei was in *how they convince people to follow government*), although without an Endorse move to explicitly link the evidence from the source text with the thesis. Compared to her previous essays, which were almost entirely monoglossic, this essay shows considerable improvement in terms of use of engagement resources to incorporate and interpret sources, as she brings in outside voices in nearly every sentence, and she makes use of Attribute resources.

In the final two essays, Karida begins to anchor her claims with integrated citations. In Essay 5, she mentions the author of the source text in the topic sentence of her first body paragraph, includes direct quotations, and even uses the combination of Attribute and Endorse, albeit with mixed success. For example, in Essay 5, she executes the moves well in combination once:

Equiano and his sister were kidnapped... by Africans **as described in the quote** "[...] Here they tied our hands, and continued to carry us as far as they could, till night came on" (para.3). <u>This is to prove</u> that the cruelty began by those other than white people.

Though the Attribute move (*as described in the quote*) is somewhat ungainly, she effectively uses the source text to support her claim about it, followed by the Endorse move (*this is to prove that...*) that instructs the reader how to interpret the quotation as evidence for her overall claim that whites do not hold complete blame for slavery.

Later in Essay 5, however, she uses the Attribute move, but does not follow it with a quotation or an Endorse move:

> **Equiano explains** that on the ship they were flogged anytime slaves supposedly didn't behave, they went without food, and they were kept below deck where they were usually suffocated in sewage.

The attribution to the author, Equiano, is useful here; however, this sentence is the last in the paragraph, without any contraction of the dialogic space to impose her own meaning on the Attribution's significance to her central claim. In another instance, she incorporates both Attribute and Endorse moves, but with an infelicitous placement of the Endorse move:

> **Equiano notes** that he would have rather have stayed a slave with his former African masters <u>as illustrated</u> "... and I even wished for my former slavery in preference to my present situation, which was filled with horrors of every kind, still heightened by my ignorance of what I was to undergo" (para.14) .

Rather than first incorporating the quotation and then explaining how the quotation supports her thesis by following it with *This illustrates*..., she uses a version of the Endorse move early, as further set up for the quotation. Thus, even before readers understand the quote, they are already being told how to interpret it, creating confusion about the quote's role in the development of the paragraph's claim.

In Essay 6, Karida demonstrates similar mixed success with her reference to and incorporation of the source texts. She does not mention the author's name until the first sentence of the final body paragraph. Previous to that moment, she experiments with a different style of referencing the text, merely including parenthetical citations to indicate the source of her paraphrases (which may be considered a type of Attribution move), followed by Endorse moves:

> Although this did not contribute to the disasters within China, it still caused harm such as deforestation in other countries providing the timber. **(p. 370-371)**. <u>This shows</u> that through trade, China's problems have become everyone else's problems as well.

Once again, Karida's Endorse move strengthens the argument by emphasizing the relevance of the quotation to her central claim. By the end of the semester, although she decidedly had not mastered how to weave expanding and contracting moves together (Ryshina-Pankova 2014), we did see substantial improvement from the early essays, where she did not incorporate these resources at all.

3.2 Management of alternative voices

In our analysis of Karida's use of engagement resources to manage alternative voices, we also saw considerable development over the semester, particularly in her strategic incorporation of outside and alternative voices to advance her argument. As stated earlier, Essay 1 is nearly entirely monoglossic, although there are two instances of contrastive transitions (*on the other hand*; *in contrast*). With these exceptions, however, the rest of the essay merely reports information from the source text with a list of bare assertions, and includes no Concede + Counter moves or other management of alternative voices.

Essay 3 is similar in that it is dominated by the use of monoglossic resources that list information. However, it incorporates a few more heteroglossic moves, including four instances of Entertain (via modality), one instance of Deny, and two instances of Counter, including one concurring Concede + Counter[4] move, seen in the following:

> **Although** natural fires are helpful, <u>agrarian fires will cause</u> more fire-resistant plants to appear and other plants will not be able to reestablish themselves, like a forest cover that can prevent erosion.

This move is consistent with how Karida positions the reader in the previous paragraph, where she explains the benefits of agrarian fires. However, it does not advance her (rather unclear) central argument, and the move is not well integrated into the paragraph where it appears (the previous sentence is about lack of floods and soil depth, the following one about the disadvantage of mild winters).

In Essay 4, Karida includes one Concede + Counter move. This is done more effectively than before, especially given the constraints of the comparison-contrast rhetorical mode inherent in the assigned writing task. In this essay, Karida embeds the Concede + Counter move in an Attribution: "Han believes that **although** people may have morals, they may overcome these morals and act wrongly." Given that the previous paragraph explains how Confucianism relied on people's morals for a strong society, this Concede + Counter move is an effective way of comparing the two authors, and is especially strong given her thesis that the two authors' disagreement was based on their view of the power of morals. Karida uses the Concede + Counter move to place the source texts in conversation with each other, showing how Han Fei would counter Confucius's position.

In the final two essays, Karida uses Concede + Counter moves to position her reader consistently in a way that strengthens her argument. For example, in Essay 5:

Although white men **did** own many of the African slaves and they had ill-treated the slaves much more as compared to how an African would treat the African slave they owns. Thus since slavery was accustomed [gloss: already customary] it is only a small degree that which white people can be blamed for their slavery.

Though she does not transition between these moves with complete fluidity, she positions her reader as someone who would expect whites to be blamed for slavery by conceding this as an understandable position, and counters by explaining that slavery's prior existence in Africa indicates otherwise. She effectively addresses the question of the prompt and follows through in her essay to support the counter-expectational claim that whites *only* hold a small degree of blame.

In Essay 6, Karida includes three successful Concede + Counter moves, all of which demonstrate consistency between the positions she establishes for herself and her reader in the introduction. In the first body paragraph, she argues: "China **did** realize the danger it was in, thus many things were banned in China, for instance logging and fishing in certain areas. However, China still needed other material such as timber, so they had to import it instead." Her concurring concession demonstrates her sensitivity to a reader who might think China's problems are not global problems, and her counter explains why this is not the case.

3.3 Interview data

In the interview (conducted after the end of the course), Karida commented on the importance in history writing of incorporating evidence from the source text, stating that "We know how to find evidence, if we say this happened [...], you need the evidence." This was reflected in her writing in her transition from near complete monoglossia and lack of reference to the source texts in her early essays, to inclusion of direct and indirect quotations and citations of page numbers in her later essays.

Karida also spoke about not only referencing, but also interpreting the source text, another area where we saw development. She stated, "In history when you are writing a paper, you are not repeating what it said. For our class it is not only history, these are the facts, [...] It is more our interpretation." Just as Karida's comments indicate that history writing should go beyond reporting "facts" to interpreting them, her writing increasingly used Endorse moves to interpret the source texts to support her argument.

4. Conclusion

From the analysis presented, we see that Karida did improve in her use of engagement resources to strategically incorporate and interpret the source text and manage alternative and opposing voices. This study builds on previous work (e.g., Miller, Mitchell, and Pessoa 2014; Ryshina-Pankova 2014) which has stressed the importance of looking not only at the simple presence or absence of individual engagement resources, but rather at the purposeful and strategic ways in which these resources are used in combination. Extending our previous research (Miller, Mitchell, and Pessoa 2014), which focused on valued strategic combinations of engagement resources, this study shows that not only are these valued, but students can improve in their use of these resources, even during a one-semester course. From the interview data, we also see that Karida seems to have had, at least retrospectively, an awareness of the rhetorical significance of the moves that these engagement resources enact.

Although Karida's developing awareness and use of these moves was achieved without explicit instruction, we note that in the absence of instruction, it took an entire semester for Karida to successfully implement these moves in her writing, and even then with limited success. Thus, we emphasize the important role of explicit instruction in use of engagement resources for including and interpreting source texts and managing alternative voices. With explicit instruction, many of the uses of engagement resources in Karida's writing that took an entire semester may have been achieved much earlier.

Acknowledgement

This publication was made possible by NPRP grant #5-1320-6-040 from the Qatar National Research Fund (a member of Qatar Foundation). The statements made herein are solely the responsibility of the authors.

Notes

1. Consistent with notation in Systemic Functional Linguistics research, small capital letters are used to distinguish appraisal systems as semantic systems.

2. A pseudonym.

3. We analyzed essays one, three, four, five, and six; essay two was missing from our data.

4. Karida used will in some Counters, which, according to Martin and White (2005: 98), is expanding rather than contracting, as it is "grounded in its own contingent, individual subjectivity" representing a proposition as "one of a range of possible positions". However, here, it functions pragmatically as a Counter in relation to the preceding Concede.

References

Bakhtin, M. M. 1981. *The Dialogic Imagination* (translated by C. Emerson and M. Holquist). Austin: University of Texas Press.

Coffin, C. 1997. Constructing and giving value to the past: An investigation into secondary school history. In F. Christie and J. R. Martin (eds.), *Genre and Institutions: Social Processes in the Workplace and School.* 196-230. New York: Continuum.

Coffin, C. 2006. *Historical Discourse: The Language of Time, Cause and Evaluation.* New York: Continuum.

de Oliveira, L. C. 2011. *Knowing and Writing School History: The Language of Students' Expository Writing and Teachers' Expectations.* Charlotte, NC: Information Age Publishing.

Gardner, S. 2008. Integrating ethnographic, multidimensional, corpus linguistics and systemic functional approaches to genre description: An illustration through university history and engineering assignments. In E. Steiner and S. Neumann (eds.), *Data and Interpretation in Linguistic Analysis: 19th European SFL Conference July 2007.* Saarbrücken, Germany.

Hewings, A. 2004. Developing discipline-specific writing: An analysis of undergraduate geography essays. In L. J. Ravelli and R. A. Ellis (eds.), *Analysing Academic Writing: Contextualised Frameworks.* 104-130. London: Continuum.

Lee, S. H. 2008. An integrative framework for the analyses of argumentative/persuasive essays from an interpersonal perspective. *Text & Talk, 28*, 239-270.

Leki, I. 2007. *Undergraduates in a Second Language: Challenges and Complexities of Academic Literacy Development.* New York: Routledge.

Mahboob, A. and D. Y. Devrim 2013. Supporting independent construction online: Feedback in the slate project. *Linguistics and the Human Sciences, 7*, 101-123.

Martin, J. R. 1989. *Factual Writing: Exploring and Challenging Social Reality.* New York: Oxford University Press.

Martin, J. R. and P. R. R. White. 2005. *The Language of Evaluation.* London: Palgrave Macmillan.

Miller, R. T., T. D. Mitchell, and S. Pessoa 2014. *Valued Voices: Students' Use of Engagement in Argumentative History Writing.* Manuscript submitted for publication.

Nesi, H. 2009. Extended abstract: A multidimensional analysis of student writing across levels and disciplines. In M. Edwardes (ed.), *Taking the Measure of Applied Linguistics: Proceedings of the BAAL Annual Conference.* University of Swansea, 11-13 September 2008. London: BAAL/Scitsiugnil Press.

Pessoa, S., R. T. Miller, and N. Gatti 2014. *Academic Literacy Development Trajectories: Student Experiences and Texts.* Manuscript submitted for publication.

Ryshina-Pankova, M. 2014. Exploring academic argumentation in course-related blogs through Engagement. In G. Thompson and L. Alba-Juez (eds.), *Evaluation in Context.* 281-302. Amsterdam: John Benjamins Publishing Company.

Sommers, N. 2008. The call for research: A longitudinal view of writing development. *College Composition and Communication, 60.* 152-164.

Sternglass, M. S. 1997. *Time to Know Them: A Longitudinal Study of Writing and Learning at the College Level*. Mahwah: Lawrence Erlbaum.

Woodward-Kron, R. 2008. More than just jargon–the nature and role of specialist language in learning disciplinary knowledge. *Journal of English for Academic Purposes, 7*, 234-249.

Wu, S. M. and D. Allison 2005. Evaluative expressions in analytical arguments: Aspects of Appraisal in assigned English language essays. *Journal of Applied Linguistics, 2*, 105-127.

Would "pinyinising" English Help Chinese Students Speak English Better?

Michael Youles

University of Nottingham, Ningbo

1. Introduction

1.1 General background

According to Shaw (1948), the alphabet of the English language "is reduced to absurdity by a foolish orthography based on the notion that the business of spelling is to represent the origin and history of a word instead of its sound and meaning"; Shaw's words identify what is surely the Achilles heel of English, that is the problem that far too much of its vocabulary is written in ways that confuse (not just) second language learners. In making this statement, Shaw was of course referring to the English language as a whole. This paper, however, has a far narrower focus, attempting as it does to seek ways in which to help Mother-tongue Mandarin speakers entering an English-medium university such as the University of Nottingham Ningbo China (UNNC) to overcome the confusion caused by the complex relationship between English spelling and pronunciation, a factor that tends to impede the progress of the vast majority of Mother-tongue Mandarin speakers learning English.

1.2 Practicalities

At this point, I should highlight an assumption underpinning the whole of this paper: it is assumed that Chinese learners of English, particularly in the early stages of studying the language, need an accessible written point of reference in order to improve their spoken English. Of course, standard written English is not the only resource already available to them for this purpose; there is also the IPA, a system taught throughout China right through the three years of Middle School; in many, though by no means all, regions of China, the IPA is also taught in the last two years of Primary School; however, expecting students who have not formally studied the

IPA through the three years of High School to recall and apply their knowledge of this system to deal with all the problems presented by "weak forms" and "linking" on entering university would be impracticable. It would therefore seem logical to use instead a more readily accessible phonemic script for this purpose: the use of a phonemic script based on a combination of both "Hanyu Pinyin", the system used throughout China in order to teach all students the sounds of Mandarin, as well as the IPA could help such students develop fluency in speaking English. This system, which I call "pinyinising", in fact uses standard written English as far as possible; it also uses the IPA, whilst additionally drawing on the principles underpinning "Hanyu Pinyin".

2. Parameters

What follows needs to be prefaced by a delineation of parameters: the idea outlined here deals exclusively with a method of teaching the pronunciation of English in connected speech, focusing first on that area of "stress" known as "weak forms"; in practice, the focus of this aspect of this paper is on those monosyllabic words for each of which there is an alternative pronunciation throughout the English-speaking world; apart from this, as the focus of the whole of this paper is on helping students from China to develop (two) aspects of (their) pronunciation of English in the flow of speech, some attention is also given to an area that is tricky for most students of English as a second language in many parts of the world, namely "linking". One final point concerning the delineation of parameters: this paper does not deal with intonation; this is because the successful teaching of "weak forms" and "linking" is seen as a prerequisite to the successful teaching of intonation.

3. Aims

Given the enormous difference between Mandarin and (spoken) English, not to mention the challenges presented by the vagaries of the English spelling system, it would seem reasonable to investigate the value of providing China's students with a new means to develop their confidence and also their sense of control when speaking English. The idea analysed here is inspired largely by "Hanyu Pinyin", the phonemic system used in order to teach people from China (and from much of the rest of the world) the pronunciation of Mandarin in the flow of speech. This paper focuses on the needs of Chinese students throughout their preliminary year at an English-medium university, specifically UNNC, arguing that an extended use of the IPA, a system that all Chinese students currently learn for several years prior to entering university, combined with an adaptation of "Hanyu Pinyin", the system that all Chinese students are taught while learning Mandarin, could be made an integral part of the whole of UNNC's two-semester preliminary year course. If this idea were put into practice, something that of course could only be done after extensive tests were carried out to evaluate the viability of incorporating such a system into classroom practice, the aim would be to adapt a combination of the IPA and "Hanyu Pinyin" in conjunction with standard written English, the amalgam which I call "pinyinising", in order to bridge the gaps, in terms of pronunciation, between all the words for which there already exists a broadly agreed pronunciation (the last point being dependent on the region of the English-speaking world, say, the UK or the US, that is the preferred point of reference for this purpose).

4. Methodology

Whilst native speakers of English are able to deal intuitively with the challenges of using "weak forms" appropriately without needing to learn any part of the IPA, non-native speakers clearly do not have this advantage. It is for this reason that this paper proposes the introduction of a method, "pinyinising", aimed at helping Chinese learners to develop an awareness of how to use "weak forms" appropriately in the flow of speech; this method draws heavily on the rationale underpinning China's "Hanyu Pinyin", a system that corresponds to the phonemes used in English (such as the English language's most frequently used sound represented as /ə/ by the IPA) but one that goes one crucial step further than the IPA system in that it sets out to bridge all the gaps (between all those phonemes containing "weak forms" or involving "linking"), thereby stitching together what can otherwise be a bafflingly fragmented patchwork from the point of view of many students learning English as a second language. Admittedly, one of the reasons that "Hanyu Pinyin" seems to have bridged all the gaps and stitched together the patchwork of the vocabulary of Mandarin so successfully can probably be explained by the fact that Mandarin seems to have only one word, the word for "no" or "not", which can be pronounced in more than one way, namely bú or bù; English, though, has many more words that are systematically pronounced in one of two ways. Given the widespread occurrence of this phenomenon in spoken English, one question that should be asked is how, say, the Chinese learner can be expected to know whether the following words should be pronounced in one way or the other:

	Strong form	Weak form
to	/tuː/	/tə/
at	/æt/	/ət/
for	/fɔː/	/fə/
from	/frɒm/	/frəm/
of	/ɒv/	/əv/

	Strong form	**Weak form**
and	/ænd/	/ən(d)/
but	/bʌt/	/bət/
be	/biː/	/bɪ/
was	/wɒz/	/wəz/
were	/wɜː/	/wə/
have (main verb)	/hæv/	(auxiliary verb)/həv/
can	/kæn/	/kən/
could	/kʊd/	/kəd/
must	/mʌst/	/məs(t)/
shall	/ʃæl/	/ʃəl/
should	/ʃʊd/	/ʃəd/
would	/wʊd/	/wəd/
the	/ðɪ/	/ðə/
you	/juː/	/jə/
your	/jɔː(r)/	/jə(r)/

(*Cambridge Advanced Learner's Dictionary* 2008)

In fact, this list is far from being exhaustive. It does, though, cover almost half of all such examples and as such can be seen as being fairly comprehensive. In order to try and facilitate the task of China's students of English, this paper investigates the practicability of attempting to create a system as foolproof as the Chinese "sound" system, "Hanyu Pinyin", for the teaching of "weak forms" and "linking". Of course, before this can be done, (some) clear guidelines have to be established, indicating when the "strong" or "weak form" can be used in instances where the option is clearly a matter of individual choice. For example, in the following dialogue, in the case of those words that can be pronounced using either the "weak form" or the "strong form" (c.f. the list above as well as the claim made in the previous sentence), it is implied that, whilst native speakers would generally base their choice of which form to use on issues such as (an individual speaker's) perceived need to provide emphasis in any given context, there is nonetheless a tendency amongst all native speakers to opt systematically for the "weak" or "strong form" in such cases and according to a set of implicit rules when using any of the prepositions in the list except where these words are used at the end of the sentence:

A: Where *are you* going *to*?

        W S/**WS**

B: Home, once I've *been to* the bank. What about *you*?

S/W W   S

A: I'm going *to* the opera.

                  W

B: *But* I thought *you* said *you* didn't like classical music.

S/W   S/W   S/**W**

A: That *was* before I heard an extract *from* it.

         W   W

(N.B. The use of "bold" here indicates where the writer believes he would pronounce these problematic words either strong **S** or weak **W**, when the use of one of the two forms is deemed optional.)

Of course, this dialogue includes only a few of the words listed above. However, the dialogue probably does enough to demonstrate the potential value of at least attempting to "pinyinise" English comprehensively in that it would surely help Chinese students, whose first language is in virtually every particular profoundly different from English, to develop their confidence in speaking English, using "weak forms" (more) appropriately, particularly in situations such as those where students are expected to give presentations in seminars and such like. If the same dialogue is reproduced, using the IPA phonemic script, whilst also drawing on Hanyu Pinyin's systematic highlighting of what Roach (2004) calls "syllable division" to represent "linking" (in addition to "weak forms"), the end product would, following this UK speaker's speech patterns, look like this in "pinyinised" form:

A: weə rə jə going tuː?

B: Home, wʌn saɪ(v) biːn tə the bank. what about juː?

A: I'm going tə the opera.

B: bu taɪ thought juː said jə didn't like classical music.

A: That wəz bɪˈfɔː raɪ hear də ˈnexstract frə mit.

This transcription illustrates the essence and scope of "pinyinising": this system uses standard written English as far as possible, but uses features of the IPA as well, and it also uses an adaptation of "Hanyu Pinyin" to highlight examples of "linking", emphasising in some instances the integrity of the syllable at the expense of the word; the purpose of doing this is simply to indicate where syllables start and finish in those cases where reference solely to the standard written form leaves this issue open to interpretation: hence the transcription of phrases such as, "where are you…?", transcribed here as /weə rə jə/, and "what about…?", transcribed (in pinyinised English) as /what about/ and where, in both cases, the final consonant sound of the first word is attached to the beginning of the second syllable. According to Ramsey (1987: 59), a "native speaker of Chinese instinctively divides an utterance up into as many units as it has syllables". Given that Chinese students often fail to become fluent English speakers in part because of their many difficulties in dealing with "linking", it would seem that applying the process of "pinyinising" English in the classroom could equip (China's) students with the comprehensive system they need to compensate for the lack of phonetic indicators in the standard written form of English.

If it can be assumed that "linking" does not exist in Mandarin, or that, if it does exist, is used only extremely rarely, then given the entirely separate point that in Mandarin "every syllable usually means something" (Ramsey 1987: 60), all this, when taken together, is likely to reinforce the (Chinese) student's expectation that, in spoken English, syllables should be separated from each other. In practice, this means that, for Chinese students, it usually requires a special effort to pronounce English words such as "start-up" appropriately, since there is the (student's) expectation that each part of this compound noun should be pronounced separately, whereas native speakers would most probably divide up the syllables of this noun as follows: /startup/ with the /t/ in "start" not being articulated until the beginning of the second syllable. In the following example, there are two issues for the student: the "weak form" /jə/, in the first instance, and "linking" as in /boot sən/ in both instances. It is in the light of such phenomena that it is recommended that speaking be taught with reference to the full range of devices that can be used to "pinyinise" speech.

Put *your* boots on
/put jə boot sɒn/
　　W
/put jɔ: boot sɒn/
　　S

5. Anticipated problems

The question now would seem to be how this idea could be turned into a usable program where any text could be typed into the program with the problematic bits then being converted automatically into "pinyinised" form; c.f. Artifical Intelligence (AI) in the context of automatic translation (Stanford University Natural Language Processing Group (n.d.); The Writing Code 2007). Given factors such as the alternatives imposed by the existence of "weak" (and "strong") "forms", not to mention the problems posed by the complexities of "linking", the program devised would then have to be made systematic in order to be viable, which in the case of the definite (and indefinite) articles, both of which have two "weak forms", should present no problem to any IPA-savvy Chinese student. The speaker's choice of /ðə/ (c.f. /ə/) or/ðɪ/ (c.f. /ən/) is determined solely by whether the sound used immediately after the article is a consonant sound or a vowel sound; in the former case, speakers use /ðə/, whilst, in the latter case, they normally, though not always (Ladefoged 2006), use /ðɪ/ : the MP /ðɪ em pi:/ should record the one-off payment / ðə wʌ nɒf ˈpayment in his income tax return. The point is that, in order to choose the correct form of the definite (or indefinite) article in any given context, the speaker needs to be aware of what the next sound is (i.e. the sound articulated immediately after the article). The university /ðə ˌjuːnɪˈvɜːsətɪ/ offers the undergraduate /ðɪ ˌʌndəˈgrædjʊət/ many opportunities. Then there is the problem posed by the existence of alternatives (c.f. "weak" and "strong forms"), and it should be noted that all other examples of "weak forms" are harder to use appropriately than the definite (or indefinite) article is; this problem could be dealt with by signalling the fact that there are options and that it is the student's responsibility to decide which option should be used in any given context; given the support that the student would derive from the "pinyinising" of dialogue, the student should, through exposure and experience, gradually develop the ability and confidence to make appropriate choices in this key area of spoken English.

6. Conclusion

This paper appraises the potential value of "pinyinising" as a teaching and learning strategy only in relation to the teaching of speaking. It focuses on just two areas of the rhythm of spoken English: "weak forms" and "linking". It is my belief that, in the teaching of English as a second language, certain aspects of the rhythm of spoken English need to be taught, before intonation, the music of the language, can be taught successfully. Whether this idea should be implemented on any teaching programme is of course open to debate. Arguments against trying out this idea in order to see whether it might make a positive contribution to teaching methodology must include the fact that it would initially involve extra work for teachers, although it can be seen from the examples used above that, in the pinyinising of speech, every effort has been made to use the IPA as minimally as possible. Set against this point, though, are the arguments in favour of following through with this idea; these have already been explained, particularly the fact that the spelling of English is often a misleading guide when it comes to pronunciation, hampering students' progress with speaking; there is also the fact that all students from the mainland of China go to university already knowing the IPA reasonably well, indicating that the IPA is a resource that is there to be exploited for the long-term benefit of all concerned. Although some students from China may well manage to make progress in this tricky area of pronunciation without recourse to any written point of reference, it is my contention that the majority of these students would need such a point of reference for this purpose, given the enormous differences between the prosodic features of Mandarin and those of (spoken) English.

References

Cambridge Advanced Learner's Dictionary (3rd edition). 2008. Cambridge: Cambridge University Press.

Ladefoged, P. 2006. *A Course in Phonetics*. Boston: Wadsworth, Cengage Learning.

Ramsey, S. R. 1987. *The Languages of China*. Princeton: Princeton University Press.

Roach P. 2004. *English Phonetics and Phonology.* Cambridge: Cambridge University Press.

Shaw, G. B. 1948. Preface to R.A. Wilson, *The Miraculous Birth of Language*. Available at http://homepage.ntlworld.com/vivian.c/EnglishSpellingSystem/ShawPreface.htm (retrieved on 2/07/2013).

Stanford University Natural Language Processing Group (n.d.). *Machine Translation*. Available at http://nlp.stanford.edu/projects/mt.shtml (retrieved on 31/05/2013).

The Writing Code (2007): How to apply for patenting of new teaching method in university. Available at http://www.thewritingcode.com/pages/image%20targets/gbs.html (retrieved on 1/06/2013).

Part Three
Social Linguistic Studies

English as a Global Lingua Franca: A Threat to Multilingualism and Translation?

Juliane House

Hamburg University, Germany;

Hellenic American University, Greece

1. What is English as a lingua franca

A lingua franca—the term is often said to derive from Arabic LISAN AL FARANG—in its original meaning was simply an intermediary or contact language used, for instance, by speakers of Arabic with travellers from Western Europe. In this original meaning, a lingua franca was a contact or vehicular language that consisted of elements and structures of diverse origins. Its meaning was later extended to describe a language of commerce in general, a rather stable variety with little room for individual variation. As a mixed contact language, a lingua franca would be more or less neutral, since it does not belong to any national language, any national language community or any national territory—concepts that arose much later.

More recently, lingua francas were also based on certain territories or speech communities, but from these they tended to be locally adapted according once their radius of influence expanded. One of the historically most important lingua francas is of course Latin during the Roman Empire, which also survived for a long time afterwards as a language of Science and Religion. In more modern times, it was French that was elevated to lingua franca status as the language of European royalty, aristocracy and diplomacy. Other kinds of lingua francas are artificially constructed systems, the most well-known being Esperanto.

English is without doubt the currently most wide-spread and most widely used lingua franca in the world—a truly global phenomenon that cuts right across the well-known Kachruvian circles: it can occur anywhere and in any constellation of speakers, and can also integrate native speakers of English, though they tend to play a minor role. ELF is characterized by a great variability, it is *not* a fixed code, and it cannot be defined by certain formal characteristics. Rather, it is an open-source phenomenon, a resource available for whoever wants to take advantage of the virtual English language. ELF is negotiated *ad hoc* varying according to context, speaker constellation and communicative purpose. It is individually shaped by its users and can fulfil many different functions ranging from simple small talk to sophisticated arguments. While of course based on English, ELF is also full of interlingual and intercultural adaptations, such that it typically contains elements from different linguacultures.

Since the major aim of any lingua franca communication from the time of the crusades to the present day has been mutual intelligibility and efficient communication, correctness tends to be not overly important. Equally unimportant for ELF is what generations of learners of English have dreaded and often unsuccessfully imitated: typically English forms such as idioms or other phrases referring to insider cultural phenomena.

Taken together, we can say that the most important features of ELF are its enormous functional flexibility, its variability and spread across many different linguistic, geographical and cultural areas, as well as its openness to foreign forms. Internationally and intra-nationally, ELF can thus be regarded as a special type of intercultural communication. Since the number of non-native speakers of English is now substantially larger than its native speakers, English in its role as a global lingua franca can be said to be no longer owned by its native speakers.

ELF is not as a language for specific purposes, or a sort of pidgin or creole. Nor is it some species of "foreigner talk" or learner language. And it is certainly not "Globish" or BSE—Bad Simple English. The interlanguage paradigm with its focus on deficits of learners' competence in a foreign or second language measured against a native norm is also clearly no longer valid here. Instead of comparing ELF speakers' competence with a hypothetical native speaker competence, it is rather the multilingual individual and his or her "multicompetence" (Cook 1992) that should be taken as a norm for describing and explaining what ELF speakers typically do when they are engaged in ELF communication. Here we can look for support from the rich literature on bilingualism and multilingualism, where proficiency in more than one language is generally seen as beneficial and enriching.

ELF Speakers are per se multilingual speakers, and ELF is a language for communication, i.e. a medium which can be given substance with different national, regional, local and individual cultural identities. ELF does not carry these identities; it is not a language for identification. (House 2003) When English is used as a language for communication, it is in principle neutral with regard to the different socio-cultural backgrounds of its users. It has thus a great potential for international understanding—precisely because there is no pre-fixed norm, and because ELF speakers must always work out anew—in different communities of practice—a joint linguistic, intercultural and behavioural basis for their communication.

It may be legitimate to ask why it should be English, and not for instance Spanish or Arabic or any other widely spoken language that has developed into today's major lingua franca. The answer is simple: this is due to the former world-spanning British Empire, which was seamlessly replaced after the Second World War by the United States and its current dominant political and economic status. Another facilitating factor is contemporary technological progress propelling a demand for fast and efficient international communication—preferably in one language. Other explanatory suggestions point to the supposed simplicity of the English language—a rather dubious explanation. There may also be another banal reason for the continuous growth of ELF: once a language has reached such a global spread and such a high degree of availability and frequency of use, it will simply keep growing. This growth, however, may well come to a halt, once the support by the current world power is waning—but I do not want to speculate about this at the present time.

The dominant role of ELF as a means for worldwide communication has of course not been welcomed unanimously. On the contrary, there has been a lot of controversy surrounding the use of ELF. This will be discussed in the next section.

2. ELF: A threat or a blessing for global communication?

One of the strongest oppositional stances vis-à-vis the use of ELF is the propagation of "Linguistic Human Rights" coupled with the idea that, if these rights are denied, many languages are doomed to die (cf. Phillipson 2009). The widespread use of ELF—seen as embodying "linguistic imperialism"—is considered a severe threat to linguistic human rights and to people's unfettered use of their mother tongues.

However, one may also simply view ELF as a useful language for communication, not a language for affective and emotional identification (House 2003), and the difference between a language for communication and a language for identification is subjectively felt by many language users. Languages for communication and languages for identification are not in competition, rather they supplement each other. This does not mean, however, that ELF users cannot develop an affective identification with ELF, but the point I am trying to make here is that this must not necessarily be the case.

The opposition against the use of English in multilingual contexts has recently found a now voice propagating the use of a "lingua receptiva" or "parallel talk", promoting what has been called "receptive bilingualism" (cf. ten Thije and Zeevaert 2007). The idea is that in multilingual constellations each speaker uses his or her native language. Interactants will then infer the meanings of others' talk and understand what has been said. While this is an interesting attempt to avoid ELF, it is obviously meant to function first and foremost with groups of people who speak typologically close languages, such as languages belonging to the Scandinavian, Romance or Slavic language families. In the case of typologically distant languages, however, communication following this model will be rather difficult to put into practice.

That English will sweep away other languages is unlikely. In fact, one can often observe that widespread use of English tends to also strengthen the use of indigenous languages for identification purposes, and that these languages can then also be employed as vehicles of protest against English. In the Internet, long thought to be the prime killer of languages other than English, a profusion of many different languages has come to be used. So we have here a healthy co-existence of English and native languages, which has, in some cases, stimulated the emergence of new "mixed" varieties.

Following these general ideas about the use of ELF in the world today, I will now look at several more specific arguments against its use. I will discuss these arguments and try to relativize them by drawing on the results of empirical research.

3. A compromise position argued from different perspectives
3.1 The linguistic perspective

From a linguistic perspective, one often hears statements such as the following: The use of ELF in multilingual constellations is unfair to all those who are non-native speakers of English, because however advanced their command of English may be, it will never be as differentiated and sophisticated as their L1 competence. Anecdotally, one can refute this argument by pointing to the numerous cases where users of an L2 successfully overcame the putative "non-native handicap", and turned out to be perfectly happy in their use of a new language. Recent approaches to second or third language acquisition no longer focus on its shortcomings; they emphasize instead the positive sides of multilingualism for individual speakers (cf. e.g. Kramsch 2009). With regard to the way users of ELF are affected by the fact that English is not their L1, much recent research has shown that interactions in the medium of ELF clearly work, thus contradicting the claim that they are inherently problematic and precarious (cf. e.g. Cogo and Dewey 2006; Firth 2009; House 2009a; Baumgarten and House 2010; House 2009a; 2010, 2011; Seidlhofer 2011). ELF use seems to work surprisingly well, not least thanks to the "Let it pass" principle, an interpretive procedure where interactants tolerantly wait for problematic utterances to become clearer as the discourse proceeds (Firth 2009). Further, many studies of ELF talk found that few misunderstandings, corrections or other-repairs occur in ELF talk – a stark contrast to non-native-native talk examined in classic interlanguage studies.

Evidence of this comes from my own work on the pragmatics of ELF interactions in the framework of the project "Multilingualism and Multiculturalism in German Universities" funded by the Volkswagen Foundation at Hamburg University. The project features a corpus of institutional and every-day interactions between ELF users complemented by retrospective interviews with these users about "rich points" in the interaction as these emerged from our analyses. The four most interesting findings are:

(1) Recourse to interactants' L1

Such recourse was, for instance, found to occur in this data in the form of transfer of discourse norms holding in speakers' mother tongues. An example is transfer from Asian ELF users' tendency to engage in a kind of cyclical topic management, which leads to a number of non-sequitur turns. These often puzzling non-sequiturs are however consistently ignored by other participants, such that the discourse remains "normal" and "robust". Another form of taking recourse to a speaker's L1 is of course code-switching. Analyses of how speakers use code-switching in our Hamburg ELF office-hour interactions show that this device is not necessarily a sign of incompetence, but can also be taken as an indication of speakers' subjective identification with their linguistic origins.

This example shows the ease with which one of the interactants, P, switches into his German L1. We can assume that his L1 is always present in his mind and can thus be effortlessly accessed amidst the flow of ELF talk in this interaction. Clearly, this switch shows that ELF users are multilingual speakers, who do not lose their loyalty to their L1. The normality of code-switching in ELF discourse, whenever this is possible given the constellation of speakers on hand, has also been amply documented by other ELF researchers using different data (cf. e.g. Pölzl and Seidlhofer 2006).

(2) Accommodation: Frequency of the multi-functional gambit Represent

In the Hamburg data we found a high incidence of speakers' deliberate accommodation to other participants' ELF competence via the use of a 'certain gambit, which Edmondson (1981) called a "Represent". A Represent is a meta-communicative procedure and a useful and versatile discourse marker with which a speaker re-presents (parts of) a previous speaker's move in order to: 1. strategically support his own and his interactants' working memory, 2. create coherence by constructing lexical-paradigmatic clusters, 3. signal receipt and confirm understanding, and 4. strengthen awareness of the ongoing talk and monitor its progress. Other researchers have confirmed such uses of Represents albeit using different terms. (cf. e.g. Cogo and Dewey 2006).

Represents—also referred to in the literature as echo-signals, mirror elements or shadow-elements—are typical of psycho-therapeutic interviews, instructional discourse ("teacher talk") and aircraft control discourse—genres where information is deliberately and routinely re-stated to ensure understanding. That ELF users frequently resort to this procedure can be taken as proof of their well-developed strategic competence and their meta-communicative awareness.

(3) Solidarity and consensus via the co-construction of utterances

In the face of manifold cultural and linguistic differences, ELF users demonstrate their solidarity with each other by co-constructing utterances whenever necessary—a clear sign of a feeling of group identity that develops in the community of practice in which ELF speakers find themselves. One might say that ELF users view ELF as an egalitarian tool ("We're all in the same boot"), and there seems to be an underlying determination and consensus about making the discourse work.

(4) Re-interpretation of gambits: *You know, yes/yeah; so, okay, I think, I don't think, I mean*

The analyses of the Hamburg data show that ELF users tend to use certain gambits in a way which systematically differs from the way native English usage is described in the literature. For instance, the analysis of the behaviour of the gambit *you know* in our data shows that *you know* is predominantly used in this ELF data as a routinized self-supportive strategy whenever speakers want to make salient coherence relations or bridge word-finding difficulties ("fumbling"). *You know* in ELF discourse is thus *not* used primarily as a polite hedge or an interpersonal expression appealing toknowledge shared with addressees, as it has often been described in the literature on native English usage. And in its function as a routinized fumble, *you know* was found to help ELF users structure their output and monitor the progression of their talk. So *you know* in ELF talk is clearly a speaker strategy, *not* a sign of a "restricted code" or proof of some underdeveloped competence in English. When employing the gambit *you know*, a speaker primarily demonstrates that her strategic competence is intact, and that she is capable of exploiting the resources of the English language.

Analyses of other discourse markers such as *I think, I don't think* and *I mean* (see Baumgarten and House 2010) show that ELF speakers prefer using these gambits in their prototypical semantic meanings rather than as routinized de-semantized phrases common in native English speakers' usage. And ELF users' employment of the gambits *yes/yeah, so,* and *okay* (House 2011) seems to also deviate from native speaker usage in that in ELF, speakers tend to creatively modify their L1 employment for self-support, monitoring and coherence-creation. When using the gambits *yes/yeah/ja,* for instance, ELF speakers formally and functionally vary their usage preferring the token *yes* for agreement, *yeah* for signalling comprehension and the equivalent German token *ja* for back-channelling.

Taken together, the results of analyses of ELF interactions in our Hamburg data show that ELF talk does work surprisingly well because ELF speakers are able to make good use of the English language for their very own purposes exploiting its potential to suit their own particular needs.

Another often heard argument against the widespread use of ELF is that ELF "contaminates" other languages. Purists and prescriptivists have long worried about English as the world's foremost language invading other languages in the form of Anglicism, more often than not compiling "black lists" of those foreign bodies and providing readers with native alternatives. Such an argument against ELF can be relativized on the basis of another research project—a project that went beyond examining those rather obvious and, I believe, essentially harmless lexical importations from English. I am referring to the project "Covert translation" which I directed at the German Science Foundation's Research Center on Multilingualism from 1999 to 2011. The initial assumption of this project was that ELF changes the communicative norms in other languages via massive unidirectional translations from English into these languages. In this study, we mainly examined whether and how translations change the German language—German being the most popular target language for the translation of English texts, but we also considered some translations into French and Spanish.

The project work is based on my previous extensive German-English contrastive research (cf. e.g. House 2006) on communicative conventions, which were hypothesized to vary along a number of parameters in German and English. German texts in many genres were found to be more direct, more explicit, more oriented towards the content of the message and thus generally more transactional and detached than comparable English texts that tend to be more interactional and involved. In the past, translations of texts from English into German were routinely subjected to a "cultural filter" in order to adjust them to the new audience's expectation norms (House 1997). Given the dominance of ELF, we assumed that these differences in communicative conventions would no longer be heeded such that English communicative conventions would now be superimposed on German texts.

These considerations led to the formulation of two hypotheses: 1. In translations from English into German, a cultural filter will be less consistently applied over time such that English-German translations increasingly follow Anglophone text conventions and 2. Anglophone text conventions will spread from English-German translations to German original texts. These hypotheses were operationalized as follows: the frequency and usage patterns of certain linguistic items (resulting from detailed qualitative analyses of some 80 textual exemplars) change over time. Two time frames were examined: 1978-1982 and 1999-2002 (2006 for economic texts). The hypotheses were tested using a multilingual, one million word corpus that contained texts from two genres: popular science and business texts—genres which we assumed to be particularly vulnerable to Anglophone influence. The texts were drawn from popular science magazines (*Scientific American* and *Spektrum der Wissenschaft*), and letters to shareholders in globalized companies' annual reports. The corpus holds English texts, their German translations (parallel texts), German originals (comparable texts), some translations and original texts into French and Spanish as well as translations into the opposite direction (i.e. into English). The method used in this project combines qualitative and quantitative approaches progressing from detailed text analyses and comparisons on the basis of a translation evaluation model (House 1997; 2009b; 2014) to a quantitative phase involving frequency counts, and finally to a re-contextualized qualitative phase, where we investigated how certain linguistic items and pattern were translated, and how these compared with original texts. The qualitative analyses revealed differences in the linguistic realization of subjectivity and addressee-orientation, i.e. the expression of author identity and addressee-orientation in simulated author-reader interaction in written discourse.

The project's quantitative studies focused on the use of linguistic items associated with author-reader interaction. They include investigations of personal pronouns *we-wir*, conjunctions, additive *and-und* and concessive *but-aber/doch* linking constructions as well as expressions of epistemic modality.

The results of these studies show that there is indeed an English influence in the translations for all phenomena investigated, but the hypothesized influence on original German texts is only documented for *but-aber/doch*. Over time, the frequency of all other phenomena associated with interactionality in written discourse was found to remain consistently higher in the English originals than in the German originals, i.e. the English texts remain more personal, more dialogic and more interactional than the indigenous German texts. In other words, Anglophone influence via translation seems to be a marginal phenomenon: it does not affect original mainstream text production. The influence of English on other languages is probably more indirect: it may have to do with a current trend towards colloquiality fuelled by general contemporary processes such as the democratization of knowledge and the growing acceptance of informality not only in oral, but also in written interaction, particularly in the social media, e-mail, SMS, blogs, Wikis, etc.

So the hypotheses underlying this project were essentially not confirmed. No wonder, you might think, since these hypotheses are typically mono-causal ones of the kind: "the bigger the prestige of a language—ELF in this case—the bigger its influence". Such a simplistic assumption, you might say, needs to be rejected. Instead we should assume a complex interaction of many different factors in language change, such as linguistic economy and intelligibility, standardization of genres in the target language (both popular science texts and letters to shareholders were new genres in German in the seventies of the last century!), as well as jargonisation and popularization. We might therefore conclude that German translations do not simply take over Anglophone text conventions, rather translators may have set out to creatively achieve their own communicative goals responding to a new need in German for expressing interpersonality, addressee orientation, and jargonisation by exploiting the existing interpersonal and interactive Anglophone model for their own benefit.

3.2 Psycholinguistic and neurolinguistic perspectives

Here I refer to the popular claim that massive importation of English lexis into another language influences thinking and concept formation in that language, and that the onslaught of English words and phrases damages a person's L1-mediated knowledge. Such a claim is, in my opinion, compatible with the strong version of the Humboldt-Sapir-Whorf hypothesis—a version which was refuted a long time ago and was subsequently replaced by a weak version for at least the following three reasons: 1. the universal possibility of translation, 2. the fact that all languages in use are in a sense "anachronisms", i.e., linguistic forms in the flow of natural language use rarely rise to a speaker's consciousness (at least in the case of ordinary language users, not linguists!) (Ortega y Gasset 1960), and 3. the converging evidence that multilinguals—such as ELF users—possess a "deep" common conceptual store to which "lower level" language-specific systems come to be attached (cf. Paradis 2004). With expert multilinguals, which many ELF speakers are, processing often remains "shallow", i.e., there is no semantic-conceptual processing at all (Sanford and Graesser 2006). And neurolinguistic studies of translation and language switching (e.g. Price et al. 1999) show that multilinguals move flexibly and smoothly between their languages, the two systems being distinct but permeable. There is thus no proof of a direct link of only one particular language to thinking and conceptualizing.

In other words: speakers' increased use of ELF worldwide need not necessarily inhibit concept formation in their mother tongues.

4. Is ELF a threat to translation?

Not really! The very same phenomena that have caused ELF use to surge have also influenced translation, i.e. globalization processes that boosted ELF use have also led to a continuing increase in translations worldwide. Alongside the impact of globalization on the world economy, on international communication and politics, translation has also become more important than ever before.

Information distribution via translation today relies heavily on new technologies that promote a worldwide translation industry. Translation plays a crucial and ever-growing role in multilingual news writing for international press networks, television channels, the Internet, the World Wide Web, Social media, blogs, Wikis, etc. Whenever information input needs to be quickly disseminated across the world in different languages, translations are indispensible. Translation is for instance essential for tourist information worldwide and for information flows in globalized companies, where ELF is now often replaced by native languages to improve sales potentials.

Further, there is a growing demand for translation in localization industries. Software localization covers diverse industrial, commercial and scientific activities ranging from CD productions, engineering, testing software applications to managing complex team projects simultaneously in many countries and languages. Translations are needed in all of these. Indeed, translation is part and parcel of all localization and glocalization processes. In order to make a product available in many different languages it must be localized via translation. This process is of course similar to what was described above as "cultural filtering". Producing a localized, i.e. culturally filtered and translated, version of a product is essential for opening up new markets, since immediate access to information about a product in a local language increases its demand. An important off-shoot is the design localized advertising, again involving massive translation activity.

Translation is also propelled by the World Wide Web, the development of which has spread the needs for translation into e-commerce globalization. And the steady increase of non-English speaking Web users also boosts translation.

Another factor contributing to the growing importance of translation is e-learning. The expansion of digital industries centered around e-learning and other education forms spread over the Web in many different languages again shows the intimate link between translation and today's global economy.

In sum, we can say that globalization has led to an explosion of demand for translation. And translation is not simply a by-product of globalization, but an integral part of it. Without it, the global capitalist, consumer-oriented and growth-fixated economy would not be possible. ELF has not threatened translation.

5. Conclusion

ELF is a useful tool for communication, an additional language, but never a substitute for other languages, as these fulfil different, often affective and identificatory functions. When using ELF in multilingual constellations, speakers frequently take recourse to their L1s via the use of transfer and code-switching, thus documenting that other languages are well and alive underneath the English surface. ELF users also creatively appropriate the English language for their own strategic purposes. The influence of ELF on communicative conventions of other languages via massive translations from English turns out to be marginal in the case of German. Psycho-and neurolinguistic studies of bilingualism and translation disconfirm the view that the heavy use of one particular language inhibits conceptualization in another. Finally, translation is not at all threatened by ELF. Globalization which boosts ELF, has also led to an explosion of demands for translation. In fact, translation lies at the heart of the global economy. English as a global lingua franca is therefore not a threat to multilingual communication and translation.

References

Baumgarten, N. and J. House. 2010. Stancetaking through high-frequency I plus verb collations in native and non-native English. *Journal of Pragmatics*, 42, 1183-2001.

Cogo, A. and M. Dewey. 2006. Efficiency in ELF communication: From pragmatic motive to lexico-grammatical innovation. *Nordic Journal of English Studies*, 5.2, 59-93.

Cook, V. 1992. *Linguistics and Second Language Acquisition*. New York: St. Martin's Press.

Edmondson, W. J. 1981. *Spoken Discourse: A Model for Analysis*. London: Longman.

Firth, A. 2009. The lingua franca factor. *Intercultural Pragmatics*, 6.2, 147-170.

House, J. 1997. *Translation Quality Assessment. A Model Revisited*. Tübingen: Narr.

House, J. 2003. English as a lingua franca: A threat to multilingualism? *Journal of Sociolinguistics,* 7.4, 556-578.

House, J. 2006. Communicative styles in English and German. *European Journal of English Studies,* 10, 249-267.

House, J. 2009a. Subjectivity in English as lingua franca discourse: The case of *you know. Intercultural Pragmatics,* 6.2, 171-193.

House, J. 2009b. *Translation*. Oxford: Oxford University Press.

House, J. 2010. The pragmatics of English as a lingua franca. In A. Trosborg (ed.), *Handbook of Pragmatics* (vol. 7). 363-387. Berlin: Mouton de Gruyter.

House, J. 2011. Global and intercultural communication. In K. Aijmer & G. Andersen (eds.), *Handbook of Pragmatics* (vol. 5). 363-390. Berlin: Mouton de Gruyter.

House, J. 2014. *Translation Quality Assessment: Past and Present*. London: Routledge.

Kramsch, C. 2009. *The Multilingual Subject*. Oxford: Oxford University Press.

Ortega Y Gasset, J. 1960. *Miseria y Esplendor de la Traducción.* München: Langewiesche-Brandt.

Paradis, M. 2004. *A Neurolingustic Theory of Bilingualism*. Amsterdam: John Benjamins Publishing Company.

Phillipson, R. 2009. *Linguistic Imperialism Continued*. London: Routledge.

Pölzl, U. and B. Seidlhofer. 2006. In and on their own terms: the "habitat factor" in English as a lingua franca interactions. *International Journal of the Sociology of Language,* 177, 151-176.

Price, C., D. Green and R. v. Studnitz. 1999. A functional imaging study of translation and language switching. *Brain,* 122: 2221-2235.

Sanford, A. and A. Graesser. 2006. Shallow processing and underspecification. *Discourse Processes,* 42.2, 99-108.

Seidlhofer, B. 2011. *Understanding English as a Lingua Franca*. Oxford: Oxford University Press.

ten Thije, J. and L Zeevaert. 2007. *Receptive Multilingualism*. Amsterdam: John Benjamins Publishing Company.

The Self-representation of Old-generation Chinese Migrant Workers

Qingye Tang

Shanghai University, China

1. Introduction

This article, based on the spoken narratives of 15 old-generation Chinese migrant workers, draws upon the social identity theory and van Leeuwen's system of social actors representation to explore how the old generation migrant workers represent their self, how they view others and what social reality the self-representation reveals.

"Migrant workers", in Chinese " 农民工 " (*nongmingong*), are the most typical vulnerable group in China. They were born in rural areas but live and work in cities. Either they or their forefathers are farmers, but leave their lands and family, engaging in non-agricultural work in China's booming cities. This term was first used in the 1980s, when with the policy of reform and opening up in China farmers flooded into the cities to seek work and fortune. Other labels for this group are "farmer/peasant/rural workers", "peasant/rural labors", "peasant employees", "moving civil workers" or "blind flow".

Due to the strict household registration system in China, migrant workers cannot enjoy equal rights with the local urban residents, and can hardly merge into the local society. They face the identity trouble, the dilemma to identify themselves. They are not urban residents, nor farmers, often cast as marginal members of the society. Although their population is large, the social resources distributed to them are limited. Meanwhile, they confront all kinds of predicament when they work in big cities, such as lack of accident and unemployment insurance, medical care, and fair chances for their children to go to the public schools.

Migrant workers draw the attention of the society. Media reports on them have increased by years. Negatively slanted news items about out-group members are better recalled by in-group members than items with a positive slant (van Dijk 1989: 203). Naturally, the image and representation of migrant workers is distorted. Using the out-group concept to frame an issue is likely to result in an increase in public opposition (Azrout et al. 2011). In addition, because they have few accesses to social resources and few chances to speak on their behalf, they are not understood and recognized by the public, and their voices are hard to be heard. Some urban residents regard migrant workers as the root of disorder, ugliness and violence, and therefore represent them as threatening, and demonized flooding. Their images are stereotyped. The positive sides of migrant workers like diligence, honesty, optimism and tolerance are often ignored. Therefore, there is a great necessity to reveal the authentic self of this group. It is also crucial for us to uncover the actual facts of their life and experience that have been hidden, inaccessible, suppressed, distorted, misunderstood, and ignored (DuBois 1985, cited in Liamputtong 2007).

2. Data collection

The data for the present study are in-depth interviews, collected during the winter holiday in 2011 when the migrant workers went back to their hometowns for the traditional Chinese Spring Festival. The subjects were told that the recordings would be used for academic purpose only and they all consented. We gathered about 13 hours of spoken narratives of 15 Chinese migrant workers. The interview was conducted by the second author, and the interviewees are the relatives or neighbors of the second author. They are from County Huaining of Anqing, Anhui Province, China, whose ages vary from 40 to 67, often officially called the old generation migrant workers. This group were chosen because they have experienced a lot of hardship in life and work and have their tradition and uniqueness, while the new generation, despite a larger population, is quite different in their worldview and values. Every interview lasted 40 to 60 minutes. All the data were transcribed into written Chinese texts. The sum of the transcription is about 81,383 Chinese characters.

The interviewees work in large cities like Beijing, Shanghai, Guangzhou, Tianjin, Shenyang, etc. Nine are male and six female. The male workers are engaged in construction work such as painting, interior decoration and furniture manufacture. Female workers often do cleaning work. Twelve of them received primary school education, two graduated from junior middle school and only one had ever received education in a senior middle school. To protect their privacy, we refer to them by the acronyms of their names in Chinese phonetic alphabet.

3. Research questions

This study, based on the analytical framework, addresses the following questions:
(1) What are the discursive strategies migrant workers adopt to represent their self?

(2) How do migrant workers represent the identities of in-group and out-group members when representing their self?

(3) What social reality does the self-representation reveal?

4. A review on the study of identity and the representation of the vulnerable group

Identity is the social positioning of self and other (Bucholtz and Hall 2005: 586), a series of relations and interrelations (Dobly and Cornbleth 2001), and a part of an individual's self-concept which derives from his membership of a group with the value and emotional significance attached to that membership (Tajfel 1978: 61).

First of all, identity is not static but dynamic, which is always negotiated and under construction (Reed 2001: 328). Different times and circumstances may elicit different responses to identity recognition because identity is relational, contested, contingent, negotiated, and multiple (Rohrer 1997). When the circumstance and context alter, one's conceptual realization on self and others will change as well.

Secondly, identity representation is related with power, ideology, and culture. Martin and Rose (2003: 15) put forward that people are positioned within social context as having more or less power. Ideology and power run through language and culture to open or narrow people's access to resources for meaning. Although every speaker shares an equal range of meaning-making potentials, there exists a variety of meanings which are not equally distributed. Edwards (2009) claims that adjusting the use of language can enhance the sense of belonging and identification of a group. The best way to identify a person is to identify his language. Cultural factors should also be taken into consideration when it comes to identities. Reed (2001) finds that when individuals meet, they employ identity filters like look, dialect, acceptable discourse and affiliation that integrate each other into one category or the other. More importantly, identity is discursively constructed in that various text genres contribute to the construction of different types of identities (de Fina et al. 2006).

Lastly, identity is a kind of cognition on self and others. One's self is represented in contrast with others' identity because others are the mirror of self (Hayati and Maniati 2010). The individual represents his identity by understanding others' attitude toward him, and re-realizes and re-evaluates himself according to others' opinion. That is to say, one's identity is his self-identification relative to his social group. Social identification is gained by comparing US group (in-group) and THEM group (out-group). US group includes the target group and similar groups who have equal status and stance with the target group. THEM group refers to the opposite group or the enemy group. Studies on self and others' identities and in-group and out-group identities have been carried out from cognitive, social and linguistic perspectives (Duszak 2002; Myers-Scotton 1993; Richards 2006).

Previous studies on the vulnerable group have shed some lights on this study. The research shows that the vulnerable tend to maintain their positive social identity by beautifying their own images and derogating those of others following underlying strategy of "positive self-presentation and negative other-presentation" (van Dijk 2001: 103). The researched specific group involves poverty-stricken people (Mieroop 2011), beggars (Hayati and Maniati 2010), refugees, asylum seekers (Gabrielatos and Baker 2008), immigrants (de Fina and King 2011) and construction workers (Baxter and Wallace 2009), etc. To be more specific, Hayati & Maniati (2010) analyze beggars' speech based on Labov's model of personal narrative, which shows how the beggars shape the formulation of the relations between self and others while recounting their experiences. Baxter and Wallace (2009) examine the professional and workplace discourse of a group of British construction workers in an ethnographic way, which shows that they are highly collaborative in constructing narratives of in-group and out-group identities. de Fina and King (2011) investigate how immigrant women position themselves relative to language obstacles and ideologies through narratives. Gabrielatos and Baker (2008) examine the discursive construction of refugees and asylum seekers from a corpus-based approach. Liamputtong (2007) proposes ethical, practical and methodological researches on the vulnerable and marginalized people.

In China, the research on the vulnerable group and migrant workers involves such perspectives as politics, economics, law, management, journalism, education and mass communication. Also, some research is done from the linguistic and discursive perspectives. Tang (2008, 2012) studies the identity representation of the vulnerable group by the mass media in China from the perspective of positive and multimodal discourse analysis. Tang (2010) combines critical discourse analysis, corpus linguistics and cognitive linguistics to explore the diachronic discursive representation of migrant workers in *People's Daily* (1987-2007). He points out that the migrant workers are constructed as nameless, voiceless, marginalized, rootless and wandering people.

Migrant workers are the silent group, who seldom have the chances to voice their opinions. To have a better understanding of Chinese migrant workers and get their voice heard, this study conducts an in-depth interview on them. The stories they tell, the images they produce, and the emotions they reveal enable us to know who they are and move close to their inner self.

5. The analytical framework

Social identity theory is based on the idea that society is hierarchically structured into different social groups that stand in power and status relations to one another. Generally, people hold favorable ideas about the group to which they belong, and frequently represent the social world in terms of US and THEM (Oktar 2001). Tajfel and Turner (1979) propose that there are three mental processes involved in evaluating others as US or THEM, i.e. social categorization, social identification and social comparison. Social identities are the products of categorization processes, through which the world is divided into WE/US and THEY/THEM through a process of social categorization. US is generally self-evaluated as holding better values that are particularly relevant to us, whereas THEM is perceived as bad in the process of social comparison. Narrating or storytelling is a good way to present a person's self-identity because people can position themselves by recounting the differences between self and others, thus showing "who they are". Narrative is part of discursive ideology, which reflects and shapes social realities and relationships. Narrative analysis based on detailed textual examination can help reveal how socially shared group representations are managed and replayed by members of particular groups and what kinds of conflicts and acts of resistance are associated with them (de Fina 2006: 352). People are who they are because of the way they talk, and their identity is represented in the recounting of their lives which can be linguistically indexed through labels, stances, styles or linguistic structures and systems (Bucholtz and Hall 2005: 585). This paper works within van Leeuwen's (1996) social actor representation theory. Both qualitative and quantitative methods are employed.

Different ways of representing social actors and social actions encode different interpretation of and different attitudes to the social actors represented (Fairclough 2003; van Leeuwen 1995). Based on a generically diverse corpus of texts, van Leeuwen (1996) draws upon a socio-semantic inventory of the ways in which social actors can be represented, and posits that representations include or exclude social actors to suit their interests and purposes in relation to the readers for whom they are intended, thus creating the difference between self and other, or between US and THEM. His network embraces two main categories: exclusion and inclusion, which refer to the absence or presence of social actors. Inclusion involves role allocation, personalization and impersonalization. Exclusion is the phenomenon that the agent of the action is excluded from the representation. It can be further divided into suppression and backgrounding, each having subcategories. Suppression is the exclusion of social actors which leaves no traces in the text so that we are not sure who the social actors are. However, for backgrounding, the actors are mentioned somewhere else in the text, realized by non-finite clauses with -ing/-ed participles, infinitival clauses and paratactic clauses in English.

Van Leeuwen's network system is extremely complicated, and not all the subsystems are suitable for the present data, therefore only part of the system is employed in the present study.

6. Analysis and discussions

Self-representation is the process of differentiation, a differentiation of others, heavily dependent on the representation of others. The social actor represents and re-evaluates self by understanding others' attitude or opinion. In their narratives, the migrant workers draw borders in their mind, as a result of which other group of people become THEM as different from US. They represent not only the self, and their own group, i.e. the in-group or US group, but also other group such as the boss group and the intellectual group, i.e. the out-group or THEM group. In the light of this, the social actors in the data are divided into four subgroups, namely, the old generation migrant workers group, the new generation migrant workers group, the boss group and the intellectual group which are respectively labeled by US_1, US_2, TM_1 and TM_2.

6.1 Representation by suppression and backgrounding

Suppression and backgrounding are very important discursive features in the data. If the excluded social actors can be inferred through the context, they are backgrounded. If not, they are suppressed. Some of the exclusions in the data are "innocent" because both the interviewee and the interviewer know the excluded actors. However, in most cases the narrators deliberately exclude the social actors. Table 1 shows how US and THEM groups are represented in the data.

Table 1　Exclusion and inclusion of US and THEM groups in the data

Social Groups		Excluded		Included
		Backgrounded	Suppressed	
US (Total: 891)	US1 (Total: 737)	15 (2.04%)	217 (29.44%)	505 (68.52%)
	US2 (Total: 154)	8 (3.25%)	38 (24.68%)	108 (70.13%)
THEM (Total: 514)	TM1 (Total: 274)	3 (1.09%)	42 (15.33%)	229 (83.58%)
	TM2 (Total: 240)	2 (0.83%)	39 (16.25%)	199 (82.91%)

The linguistic representation of self and others and the discursive strategies as shown in Table 1 are elaborated as follows.

First, in the data the social actors include colleagues, children, bosses and intellectuals. US group is more often represented than THEM group. The old generation migrant workers, i.e. the narrators themselves are represented as the main social actors while the new generation migrant workers have the lowest frequency. The boss group (TM_1 group) is represented most frequently and the intellectual group (TM_2 group) also occurs frequently. These two typical THEM sub-groups form a sharp contrast with the US_1 group. The self-representation of migrant workers is combined with the indirect representation of in-group and out-group members. Their vulnerable self is indirectly realized with the comparison of the advantaged group.

Second, all the four groups are much more included than excluded. The migrant workers try to construct their self-image by narrating all aspects of their life. However, the percentage of the inclusions of US_1 group is lower than that in the other three groups, while the percentage of the exclusions is higher than that in the other groups. This demonstrates that migrant workers avoid representing themselves as the agents, even though they are given the right to speak for themselves. They intentionally exclude themselves by suppression and backgrounding, which shows their uncertainties of identity and fear of speaking out their voices. This discursive strategy may distance themselves from any possible charge and is also the evidence for their lack of confidence in self to avoid being responsible for the negative appraisal on other groups since they are in a vulnerable social status. Their lack of social power leads to the lack of discursive power as well.

Third, in addition to the four sub-groups, migrant workers involve other social actors in the narratives for 36 times in total. These include "国家" (country), which occurs 6 times, "本地人" (local people) like "北方人" (northern people), "大西南人" (southwestern people) and "天津人" (Tianjin people), which occur 13 times, and social institutions like "社会劳保局" (Social Labor and Security Bureau) and "劳动力保障单位" (Labor and Security Unit), which occur 9 times, and other social actors like "律师" (lawyer) and "劳务警察" (labor police), which occur 8 times. Such social actors are mentioned because they are strongly associated with power, interests and hot issues such as delayed salaries or related dominant out-groups. For example,

(1) LJH: 现在农村里小孩子都重点培养，讲为孩子到城里买房子，为了孩子念书。

(1a) LJH: Nowadays in the countryside children are prioritized: purchasing houses in the cities for the children and earn money for their education.

The first clause in Example (1) is a passivization, which does not direct to the agent. Considering the interviewee's age, we can infer that the agent is not the US_1 group member, but the younger US_2 group member. This passive agent deletion excludes the actors who attach importance to their children's education. In the same way, the agent of "买房子" (purchasing houses) is also suppressed, or implicitly represented with no reference. This indicates that the disadvantageous position prevents the migrant worker from buying real estate in the city, and that he is not confident in their future concerning the children's education and their life in the city.

(2) HSY: 人总是要跟别人打交道，心态要放好些。不管做什么事，芝麻大的事情都想搞赢，总想横行霸道，怎么行？

(2a) HSY: People have to communicate with others, so they should keep a good state of mind. Whatever they do, no matter how trivial, they always want to win, and gain advantage over others. How can it be?

In Example (2), HSY, a cleaner, talked about how to get along with others. She suppressed the subject/agent of the verbal groups " 赢 " (win) and " 横行霸道 " (gain advantage). We are not sure who the actor is, maybe some of her colleagues who are aggressive, maybe people in general. This positions HSY as the defender of harmonious interpersonal relationship.

Backgrounding is different from suppression in which social actors appear in other places in the text, or the exact social actors can be inferred from the context. For example,

(3) LJH: 那时候刚改革开放，所以都很贫穷，不管是哪家。当时出去外去做买卖，一趟赚百把块钱就算不错了。

(3a) LJH: In the beginning of the reform and opening-up, all were very poor. At that time, it was pretty good to earn one hundred yuan out of one business transaction trip.

Migrant worker LJH talked about his experience of doing business in the cities. He omitted the subject/agent of " 贫穷 " (being poor) and " 做买卖 " (doing business). The agent of " 做买卖 " (doing business) is himself, but with no explicit reference. It is not difficult for the reader to deduce that his family was poor at that time so that he worked in remote areas to earn a living. Due to such negative and disadvantaged conditions, the narrator tends to exclude or background himself as the actor to save face.

(4) LXS: 比在老家稍微好一点吧，在老家，讲句实话，赚钱也不容易。有时间也收过垃圾，多少盈利点。

(4a) LXS: It is better compared with the hometown. To tell the truth, it is not easy to earn money in the hometown. At times collected some garbage and earned a bit.

LXS excludes himself as the agent of " 赚 钱 " (earn money) and " 收 垃 圾 " (collect garbage). The reason for the linguistic exclusion is that the two social actions mentioned are related with hard life and lower social status. For the positive face wants, LXS naturally deletes his agent role. In contrast, he includes himself in the positive representation in the following example:

(5) LXS: 我以前去过芜湖，待了几年，那时候当兵。

(5a) LXS: I have been to Wuhu and stayed there for several years. At that time, I was a soldier.

In the data, we do not find many uses of the first singular pronoun "I", which indicates that due to their vulnerable and powerless position, "I" is often backgrounded. However, in Example (5), the subject is " 我 " (I), undoubtedly showing that LXS is proud of his identity as a soldier and feels a sense of superiority.

It is clearly seen from the examples above that the vulnerable migrant workers tend to conceal the negative sides of their self, but reveal the positive sides. By such an underlying strategy, migrant workers want to construct their positive images and hope that they are equal to local urban people. It is also crucial for them to form in-group identification that supports them spiritually; thus they construct a strong sense of solidarity for in-group, upholding the values of honesty and hardwork. Their identification of group identity relieves them from being isolated from the local community.

6.2 Representation by categorization

Social actors can be represented in terms of categorization, i.e. functionalization and identification. Functionalization occurs when social actors are represented by an activity, an occupation or a role. Identification occurs when social actors are represented by their permanent quality, relationship or appearance (van Leeuwen 1996: 54). It can be further divided into classification, relational identification and physical identification. Table 2 lists the actors represented by occupation.

Table 2　Functionalization of social actors in the data

The vulnerable group (Total: 19)	The advantaged group (Total: 37)
瓦 工 / 瓦 匠 (tiler), 木 匠 (carpenter), 清 洁 工 (cleaner), 环卫工人 (sanitation workers), 裁缝 (tailer), 保姆 (housemaid), 楼管 (janitor), 司机 (driver), 工人 (worker), 小工 (coolie), 民工 (peasant worker), 农民 (farmer), 搬瓦的妇女 (women who move tiles), 力 工 (unskilled laborer), 技工 (mechanic), 劳力 (laborer)	城管 (urban inspectors/chengguan), 派 出 所 的 (local police station), 收留所的 (asylum), 劳务警察 (labor police), 劳动力保障单位 (Labor and Security Unit), 中央国务院 (Central State Council), 国家 (country), 干部 (cadre), 当官的 (official), 搞行政的 (administrator), 公务员 (civil servant), 老师 (teacher), 医生 (doctor), 律师 (lawyer), 会计 (accountant), 老总 / 老板 (boss), 老板娘 (proprietress), 大老板 (the big boss), 小老板 (the small boss), 雇主 (employer), 经理 (manager), 主管 (head), 车间主任 (workshop director), 领班的 (foreman), 头 (head), 包工头 (contractor), 组长 (team leader), 大工头 (big foreman), 小工头 (small foreman), 房东 (landlord), 念书的人 (the intellectual), 研究生 (postgraduate), 本科生 (undergraduate), 大专生 (junior college student), 中专生 (specialized school student), 高中生 (middle school student), 职校学生 (vocational school student)

Table 2 shows that the number of advantaged or elite group members represented almost doubles that of the vulnerable group. This indicates that firstly, social actors who have higher social power and social status are generally included in the representation, which is consistent with the above analysis on exclusion and inclusion of social actors; secondly, migrant workers individualize the advantaged group more often, but they themselves often appear in groups. It is understandable that the advantaged group who has decent jobs are more often represented by occupation. On the contrary, migrant workers who do indecent jobs such as garbage collecting are unwilling to represent themselves by occupations.

What's more, the functionalized advantaged group can be divided into four categories. The first is the national institutions or institutional authorities like "国家" (country), "派出所" (local police station), "劳务警察" (labor police) and "城管" (urban inspector), whose task is to protect migrant workers' interests or supervise them by regulations. The second category is the social actors who are generally believed to have the most decent occupations in China, like "干部" (cadre), "公务员" (civil servant), "律师" (lawyer), etc. This group is the most typical privileged group in migrant workers' eyes, whose advantaged identities form a sharp contrast with their own vulnerable identities. The third is the boss group. The bosses are also functionalized by different classes like "老板/老总" (boss), "包工头" (contractor), "头" (head), "组长" (team leader) and "车间主任" (workshop director). The last is the intellectual group like "研究生" (postgraduates) and "本科生" (undergraduates).

Besides functionalization, identification is also a significant way to categorize social actors. Migrant workers differentiate social actors according to five different factors, namely, age, gender, education, status and ability. Relational identification appears most frequently in the data. This is in accordance with the principle that identity representation is relational, and that the vulnerable are often represented in groups. The in-group identities are important for self-representation because people in an inferior status would like to gather the power of the group they belong to, and thus construct a strong sense of solidarity. They lack confidence to construct self so that their self-concept involves their group membership. In relational identification, most of the actors are categorized by kinship, which shows that migrant workers tend to strengthen the voices of their group by including their relatives who also work in the same field.

6.3 Representation by genericization and specification

Genericization and specification also play a crucial role in the representation. In general, the vulnerable are often referred to generically and the advantaged are often specified. The vulnerable group tends to rely on the group rapport by genericization to prove that their statements are convincing, especially when their self-identity is in crisis. However, they specify themselves as individuals when the positive social relationships are represented. If the negative appraisals are applied to THEM group, genericization occurs more frequently, which reflects their fear to offend the advantaged group.

Personal pronouns are frequently employed as a discursive strategy. As Chilton and Schaffner (1997: 30) suggest, pronouns such as *we/us*, *you*, *they/them*, and *others* can be used to construct group identity, either as insiders or as outsiders. The generic references like 人 (man), "人家" (others) and "别人" (others) are frequently used when the narrator cannot name a referent, a display of unwillingness instead of inability. Social status is one of the most significant factors which determine the choice of generic or specific reference of social actors. These findings can be well illustrated by the following examples.

(6) LQQ: 我家小孩也快毕业了，文凭高也不高，低也不低，比高中生好一点，就这种人找工作最不好找。你要找 1000 块一个月的，人家打工也 1000 块一个月。

(6a) LQQ: My child will graduate soon. It is hard for her to find a job because her diploma is not high, nor low. She is better than a senior middle student in job-hunting. It is hard for this kind of person to find an ideal job. You find a job with 1000 yuan a month, and those migrant workers also earn 1000 yuan one month.

In Example (6), LQQ talked about the embarrassing job-hunting of his child. "这种人" (this kind of person) is a generic reference to the migrant worker's child—an undergraduate, who earns a salary as low as that of migrant workers. "人家" (others) also generically refers to his own group, implicating the speaker "I" and in-group "we". This serves the purpose of protecting his self-esteem and avoiding offence to hide the negative side of self.

(7) LGS: 打工的都是系于别人底下的。人都有一种自卑感，讲出来难为情。其实没什么。

(7a) LGS: Migrant workers are positioned below others. People have a sense of inferiority. It is shameful to speak it out. In fact, it is nothing.

Example (7) shows the honest and straightforward self-recognition of LGS. "别人" (others) is a general term, which implicitly refers to the boss group. Though the generic reference "人" (man) at surface includes all people, it implicates a specific group of people, the migrant workers, including LGS himself. He feels inferior as a migrant worker, but he generalizes the subject as "人" (people)，which subconsciously denies his inferior position to others and protects himself from losing face. The negative sides of self are concealed by genericization, thus to achieve the positive self-representation.

(8) LJH: 我接触的人也多，企业公司老板都接触，低级的，农村的，农民工，小工也接触。公司老总见面说不到两句话，档次不一样，没必要，人家也不理你。人分三六九等。

(8a) LJH: I have had much contact with a lot of people, including bosses of enterprises or companies, some low-class people, such as people from the countryside, migrant workers and coolies. Bosses are unwilling to communicate because of the different social levels. It is unnecessary; they are unwilling to say anything with you. People are divided into different classes.

LJH talked about the boss's unwillingness to communicate with him, the US group. It seems a criticism on the dominant THEM group; however, the generic addressing form "人家" (they) implicitly shifts the agent, which lightens the criticism, excluding both the social actor and their activities. The boss was represented as the despised other. In reality people at different social hierarchies would rarely like to listen to each other. WE stick together and THEY are not mixing with US and refuse to let US in. "人" (people) is also a general and universal reference to both the advantaged group and the vulnerable group. Through social categorization and social comparison, the narrator assesses his own group in terms of deprivation of equal dialogue between groups. He implicitly admits that he lies at the lower level of society, which softens his vulnerable position through positive self-representation.

Within the range of specification, the representation of social actors can be realized by individualization. On the contrary, the social actors are realized as assimilation. Social actors of higher status are often individualized, whereas those of lower status are generally grouped (Tang 2010: 134). Assimilation can be divided into aggregation and collectivization. The former quantifies the participants by the presence of definite quantifiers or indefinite quantifiers like "极少数" (few) or indefinite pronouns or non-specific references like "有些/某些/这些/那些" (some, these, those)in the data. The latter is realized by plurality such as plural form of individuals, collective or plural pronouns, such as "我们" (we, us), "你们" (you), "他们" (they, them), "打工的/农民工" (migrant workers), "民工" (rural workers) and "外来务工人员" (workers from out of town), etc. The linguistic reference to in-group forms a joint or mutually shared understanding and empathy.

By analyzing the frequencies and forms of social actors in the context, we find that in the NMWs most of the aggregated social actors belong to THEM group. Migrant workers use aggregated addressing forms to represent the advantaged group, and collective addressing forms to represent US group members so as to express the voices of the whole group, not of individuals and reinforce a strong sense of in-group solidarity. This indicates that their discursive representations are affected by the power relations, implicitly ideologically loaded. THEM group is more often specified than US group. US group agents usually appear in groups, THEM group as individuals. Thus genericization is applied in the negative representation of the advantaged group, while specification is more often used in the positive representation of in-group and out-group. Aggregation is usually used to construct THEM group while collectivization is applied to construct US group. But if criticism goes to THEM group, genericization occurs instead of specification. Such linguistic pattern depends on how the interviewee perceives the role of social actors in social practice. This perception is strongly influenced by their cognition of the distance between different groups.

7. Conclusion

This study explores the self-representation of old-generation Chinese migrant workers. In the interview, the narrators do not categorize themselves as migrant workers, implying that this label is created by the powerful group. The stigmatized "migrant worker" is not a natural and intrinsic identity but the outcome of national policy, management and social structure. It should vanish from the public sphere because of its potential prejudice. Migrant workers position themselves as powerless, suppressed, and lower-status social actors. Vulnerable as they are, migrant workers try every means to maintain their positive self-image. In contrast, their representation of the advantaged group proves that they are still in a disadvantaged position, despised and excluded.

The discursive representation of self involves two main strategies: (1) referring to self and others in different forms, and (2) setting up a series of explicit or implicit contrasts between US and THEM to foreground differences. The vulnerable are characterized by being poor, fragile and marginalized, thus they have a strong sense of inferiority and deprivation. If measures are not taken to return them the rights of expression, and if public discourse still holds slanted view on them, their situation will deteriorate. The distrust between the groups is deepened and solidified. The accumulation of the moods of isolation, loneliness and depression may eventually lead to extreme acts like violence and suicides, thus social conflicts and clashes of the groups increase, because prejudices are not innate, but socially acquired, and such acquisition is the primary source of shared ethnic prejudices and ideologies.

References

Azrout, R, J. van Spanje and C. de Vreese. 2011. Talking Turkey: Anti-immigrant attitudes and their effect on support for Turkish membership of the EU. *European Union Politics,* 3, 3-19.

Baxter, J. and K. Wallace. 2009. Outside in-group and out-group identities? Constructing males solidarity and female exclusion in UK builders' talk. *Discourse & Society*, 4, 411-429.

Bucholtz, M. and K. Hall. 2005. Identity and interaction: A sociocultural linguistic approach. *Discourse Studies*, 4, 585-614.

Chilton, P. and C. Schaffner. 1997. Discourse and politics. In Teun A. van Dijk (ed.), *Discourse as Interaction*. 206-230. London: SAGE Publications.

de Fina, A. 2006. Group identity, narrative and self-representations. In A.de Fina, D. Schiffrin and M. Bamberg (eds.), *Discourse and Identity*. 351-375. Cambridge: Cambridge University Press.

de Fina, A., D. Schiffrin and M. Bamberg. 2006. *Discourse and Identity*. Cambridge: Cambridge University Press.

de Fina, A. and K. A. King. 2011. Language problem or language conflict? Narratives of immigrant women's experiences in the US. *Discourse Studies*, 2, 163-188.

Dobly, N. and C. Cornbleth. 2001. Introduction: social identities in transnational times. *Discourse: Studies in the Cultural Politics of Education*, 3, 293-296.

Duszak, A. (ed.) 2002. *Us and Others: Social Identities Across Languages, Discourses, and Cultures*. Amsterdam: John Benjamins Publishing Company.

Edwards, J. 2009. *Language and Identity: An Introduction*. London: Cambridge University Press.

Fairclough, N. 2003. *Analysing Discourse: Textual Analysis for Social Research*. London: Routledge.

Gabrielatos, C. and P. Baker. 2008. Fleeing, sneaking, flooding: A corpus analysis of discursive constructions of refugees and asylum seekers in the UK press, 1996-2005. *Journal of English Linguistics*, 1, 5-38.

Hayati, A. M. and M. Maniati. 2010. Beggars are sometimes the chooser. *Discourse & Society*, 1, 41-57.

Liamputtong, P. 2007. *Researching the Vulnerable: A Guide to Sensitive Research Methods*. London: SAGE.

Li, P. and W. Li. 2007. Economic status and social attitudes of migrant workers in China. *China & World Economy*, 4, 1-16.

Martin, J. R. and D. Rose. 2003. *Working with Discourse: Meaning Beyond the Clause*. London: Continnum.

Mieroop, D. V. 2011. Identity negotiations in narrative accounts about poverty. *Discourse & Society*, 5, 565-590.

Myers-Scotton, C. 1993. *Social Motivations for Code-switching: Evidence from Africa*. Oxford: Clarendon Press.

Oktar, L. 2001. The Ideological organization of representational processes in the presentation of us and them. *Discourse and Society*, 3, 313-337.

Reed, G. G. 2001. Fastening and unfastening identities: negotiating identity in Hawaii. *Discourse: Studies in the Cultural Politics of Education*, 3, 327-339.

Richards, K. 2006. *Language and Professional Identity: Aspects of Collaborative Interaction*. Basingstoke: Palgrave.

Rohrer, J. 1997. Identity and white privilege in Hawaii. *Social Process in Hawaii*, 38, 140-161.

Tajfel, H. 1978. *Differentiation Between Social Groups: Studies in the Social Psychology of Inter-group Relations*. London: Academic Press.

Tajfel, H. and Turner, J. C. 1979. An integrative theory of intergroup conflict. *The Social Psychology of*

Intergroup Relations, 3, 33-47.

Tang, B. 2010. The discourse representation of migrant workers in People's Daily (1987-2007). Unpublished doctoral dissertation. Shanghai International Studies University.

Tang Qingye. 2008. Multimodal positive discourse analysis of the TV news on people's livelihood. *Foreign Languages Research,* 4, 15-20.

Tang, Q. 2012. Positive discourse analysis on the identity representation of the vulnerable group. *Contemporary Foreign Languages Research,* 9, 10-14.

van Dijk, T. A. 2001. Multidisciplinary CDA: A plea for diversity. In R. Wodak & M. Meyer (eds.), *Methods of Critical Discourse Analysis.* 95-120. London: SAGE.

van Dijk, T. A. 1989. Mediating racism: The role of the media in the reproduction of racism. In R. Wodak (ed.), *Language, Power and Ideology.* 199-226. Amsterdam: John Benjamins.

van Leeuwen, T.A. 1995. Representation of social action, *Discourse & Society,* 4, 81-106.

van Leeuwen, T. A.1996. The representation of social actors. In C. R. Caldas-Coulthard and M. Coulthard (eds.), *Texts and Practices: Readings in Critical Discourse Analysis.* 32-70. London/New York: Routledge.

Discursive Construction of National Identity in Chinese and Canadian Press
—A Case Study of CNOOC's Takeover of Nexen

Jinjun Wang

Yunnan University, China

1. Introduction

Newspapers as a major form of mass media still remain powerful in the digital era. News reports are the main section of newspapers. As a kind of traditional discourse in modern society, they are often regarded as a social practice and can be constitutive and constituted by social structures, social relations and social identities. News reports concerning bilateral events between two nations can contribute to the construction and the representation of national identity to a certain degree. The paper aims to explore the discourse strategies for the construction of national identity in Chinese and Canadian newspapers by making a critical discourse analysis of news reports on the event of CNOOC's takeover of Canadian Nexen Oil Company. It is hoped that the analysis will discover some characteristics of national identity construction and the ways self and the others are represented respectively in the newspapers in China and Canada.

2. Background information about CNOOC and Nexen

Canada was among the first Western countries to establish diplomatic relation with the People's Republic of China in 1970 and since then Sino-Canadian relations have achieved great progress, although there have been noticeable disagreements between the two countries occasionally. Without doubt, the press witnesses the bilateral relations between the two countries and represents their respective national identities as well. On July 23rd 2012, China National Offshore Oil Company (CNOOC) launched China's largest overseas takeover bid by agreeing to buy Canadian oil producer Nexen Inc for US$15.1 billion and to undertake Nexen's debt of

US$33.6 billion. Newspapers in both China and Canada have given close attention to the economic event. The CNOOC's takeover of Nexen has aroused contentious debate within the Canadian government and the deal was postponed for approval twice. On December 7th 2012, after five months of uncertainty and arguing, the Canadian Conservative government finally approved the takeover, the largest one not only in Canada but also in China.

In recent years quite a number of state-owned Chinese companies have begun to take over some overseas companies due to their rising economic strength and the imperative demand for fast economic development. The takeover of CNOOC is one of them. CNOOC is one of the largest state-owned oil companies in China and it tended to take over American oil company Unocl Corporation in 2005 but failed. The CNOOC's tentative takeover of Nexen aroused the attention of the media at the very beginning as it is regarded as China's largest overseas takeover bid so far and CNOOC promised to retain all employees and to make Canada home base for its West Hemisphere operations.

Nexen Inc, located in Calgary, Alberta, is one of the largest independent oil and gas exploration and production companies in Canada and is listed on Toronto and New York stock exchanges. It operates oil sands and shale gas in Western Canada and has made conventional exploration and development primarily in the British North Sea, offshore West Africa and the Gulf of Mexico. It is reported that for both China and Canada, CNOOC's takeover of Nexen is the largest.

During the five months from July to December 2012, the takeover has gone through great pressure and obstacles, mainly from the Canadian side. On the one hand, the bid of $15.1 billion was very profitable because Canada needed the large sum of money to stimulate economy; on the other hand, the fear that foreigners would control Canadian energy and the threat to national security haunted the leaders. At the beginning the deal was approved by approximately 99 percent of the votes cast by Nexen common shareholders and approximately 87 percent of the votes cast by Nexen preferred shareholders. Later the opposite opinion became overwhelming; it was held by the opponents that the takeover would cause an energy threat to Canada and it could be treason to approve Nexen takeover, etc.

In contrast, the Chinese side has a dominantly positive opinion towards CNOOC's takeover due to the benefit and prospect that the takeover would bring about.

3. About the data

The collected data about CNOOC's takeover of Nexen come respectively from the Chinese newspaper *21st Century Business Herald*, which is one of Chinese financial newspapers with the largest circulation in China and from the Canadian newspaper *Financial Post*, the only national financial newspaper in Canada. The reason to choose financial or business newspapers is that though national newspapers like *People's Daily*[1] in China and *The Globe and Mail*[2] in Canada have reported the takeover, the amount of the news reports on the event was limited and the takeover's newsworthiness was not so highlighted when compared with other news.

The data cover the news reports during the whole process from the launching of the takeover bid on July 23rd 2012 to its approval on December 7th 2012. The data include 20 pieces of news reports (10 from each newspaper) collected respectively from the official websites of *21st Century Business Herald* and *Financial Post*. The collected bilingual (Chinese and English) data are set to be equal in quantity and similar in word count for the sake of comparison.

4. Theoretical background

Critical discourse analysis (CDA) has established itself internationally over the past thirty years as a new approach to discourse analysis, which aims at demystifying naturalized discourse and showing that grammatical and semantic forms have close connections with ideology and power. There are several schools in CDA, among which two are very influential in recent years, that is, the British School represented by Norman Fairclough which draws upon Foucault's theory of discourse and Halliday's systemic linguistic theory and social semiotics (in the paper it is called Fairclough's CDA), and the Vienna School or the discourse-historical approach (DHA) with Ruth Wodak as a representative.

Although Wodak's DHA and Fairclough's CDA have the same goal, which is to unmask how discourse is shaped by its relations with power and ideology and to reveal how discourse has effects upon social identities, social relations and systems of knowledge and belief, the two schools differ in their use of effective linguistic tools for critical analysis. Fairclough's CDA is mainly based on Halliday's systemic functional linguistics, despite taking other theories into consideration, such as pragmatics, speech act theory, schema theory, etc. Halliday (1985)'s functional grammar has been the main tool for critical discourse analysts, who have established the British school and made fruitful analyses of discourses, such as newspaper reports, political documents, etc. Halliday's three metafunctions have contributed a lot to written text analysis. When doing critical analysis, analysts often relate various linguistic forms to the three metafunctions. Some linguistic tools, namely passivization, nominalization, transitivity, modality, transformation, lexical choice, pronominalization, etc. are frequently adopted by critical discourse analysts to unmask the hidden ideology and power relation in texts. In addition, generalization, over-lexicalization, lexical cohesion and thematization are also used in CDA. In comparison, DHA is interdisciplinary and problem-oriented, and targets at the change of discursive practices over time and in various genres. Just like other schools in CDA, DHA concentrates on dealing with the three essential concepts, that is, critique, power and ideology in discourse analysis. DHA is specifically concerned with three dimensions of discourse, i.e. (1) the contents or topics of a specific discourse, (2) discursive strategies, and (3) linguistic means (Wodak and Meyer 2001).

Through careful comparison, it is not difficult to see the differences concerning analytical tools between Wodak's DHA and Fairclough's CDA. DHA pays more attention to interpreting how historical context is related to the understanding of the whole text, in what way argumentations are developed, from what perspectives discourses are produced, what is the genre that discourse belongs to, etc. In other words, DHA focuses more on the macro features of discourse. Despite that DHA also examines the micro-structure of discourse, such as lexis, including addressing, intensifying and mitigation of words, predication of sentences, Fairclough's CDA has more detailed and more powerful tools for critical analysis at the lexical-grammatical level as they are mainly derived from Halliday's functional grammar. Teo (2000: 24) argues that "SFG is rooted in structural grammar, focusing on selection, categorization, and ordering of meaning primarily at the clausal level rather than at the meaning of macro-structures of the larger, discoursal level" (original italics). It seems that Fairclough's CDA pays less attention to the macrostructure of discourse than DHA does although context is an essential element for CDA. DHA tends to do more macro analysis concerning historical context, genre analysis and argumentation, etc., which pave the way for the detailed micro linguistic analysis like lexis.

It can be said that Wodak's DHA and Fairclough's CDA have their own merits. Therefore, there is a need to complement the two approaches in CDA in accordance with the analytical orientation and the exact discourse to analyze. It is held that, in critical analysis, both the microstructure and macrostructure of discourse should be taken into consideration in order to make a sound and comprehensive critical analysis, especially when the discourse is concerned with social problems, like racism, sexism, migration, refugees, etc.

5. Defining identity and national identity

Identity is an everyday word for people's sense of who they are. It is also a complex concept in different disciplines and is referred to by different terms, such as "self" (Bersnier 1991), "ethos" (Fairclough 1992), "subject" or "subjectivity" (Foucault, 1980), "possibilities for self-hood" (Ivanič 1997), etc.

Bersnier (1991) regards "self" as an individual's feelings from an anthropological perspective. Fairclough (1992) uses "ethos" to refer to a person's identity in terms of world view and social practice when he discusses the relationship between discourse and social change. Foucault's tradition focuses on the impact of discourse and social practices on people's identities (Foucault 1980). Ivanič (1997) proposes the use of "possibilities for self-hood" to highlight the nature of identity which is socially constructed and constrained.

Not only are there different terms for identity in different disciplines, but there are different definitions of it. Generally speaking identity is "about who we are, and who and what we identify with. However, identity is also about who we want to be, and who we wish to be seen by others" (Douglas 2009: 11). Norton (2004) refers to identity as how a person understands his or her relationship to the world, how that relationship is constructed across time and space, and how the person understands possibilities for the future. Taylor (1989: 28-29) conceives of identity as "a fundamental moral orientation relative to which individuals can evaluate what is worth doing and what is not, what has meaning and importance for them and what is trivial and secondary". Taylor's definition of identity puts emphasis on the individuals' evaluation, judgment, or "a commitment to a faith, a nation, a community—provides a frame within which one can decide, from case to case, where one stands relative to what is good or valuable or what ought to be done" (Joseph 2004: 433). Therefore, identity is often classified into many kinds, such as social identity, group identity, individual identity, national identity, etc.

Nation is used sometimes in its etymological sense of people connected with one's birthplace according to Joseph (2004). "More often it is used in its extended sense of an expanse of territory, its inhabitants and the government that rules them from a single, unified center" (Joseph 2004: 92). Anderson (1991: 7) regards nation as "imagined communities" and "the nation is always conceived as a deep, horizontal comradeship". Cillia et al. (1999: 153) believe that "a nation is understood as mental constructs" and "a symbolic community constructed discursively" (Cillia et al. 1999: 155). Later, Cillia et al. (1999) further interpret national identity from four aspects: (1) national identity is specific forms of social identity represented by language; (2) national identity is a kind of habitus, that is, an internalized complex of shared ideas or concepts, similar emotional attitudes and behavioural dispositions; (3) the discursive construction of national identity is to find out the uniqueness and the differences; (4) national identity is dynamic instead of stable and immutable.

What is worth noticing is that national identity is a linguistic phenomenon. Language plays an important role in constructing, representing and shaping national identity. Anderson (1991) once claims that "language is the bedrock on which the fiction of the nation is built" (cited in Joseph 2004: 224). Joseph (2004) holds that identity is a type of representation and a type of communication as well. In fact, both nations of identity are realized by language. Billig (1995: 8) points out that the construction of national identity is discursive and "to have a national identity is to possess ways of talking about nationhood" as discursive practices contribute to the construction, reproduction and maintenance of national identity.

In addition, the existence of national identity depends on the existence of other nations.

Butler (1991) highlights the relationship between the self and the other when identity is discussed. There is a close relationship between the self and the other as "the self is from the start radically implicated in the 'other'" (Butler 1991: 26). She further elaborates,

> "The self becomes a self on the condition that it has suffered a separation, a loss which is suspended and provisionally resolved through a melancholic incorporation of some 'other'. That 'other' installed in the self thus establishes the permanent incapacity of that 'self' to achieve self-identity; it is as it were always already disrupted by that Other; the disruption of the Other at the heart of the self is the very condition of that self's possibility." (Butler 1991: 27)

Butler's words show that identity is concerned with the relationship between the self and the other and the otherness makes the identity or the other kinds of identity, like national identity possible. Likewise, Taylor (1991: 311) notices the otherness of identity and states that "much of our understanding of self, society and world is carried in practices that consist in dialogical action." It can be inferred from Taylor's words that the existence of "we" depends on that of the other, as Taylor (1991: 311) points out that "my self is socially constituted, through the attitudes of others, as the 'me'."

Concerning national identity, the existence of one nation is in comparison and contrast with the other nations. Therefore, there is a dialogic relationship between one nation and the other. When a nation is mentioned, it is always connected with other nations. The culture, the lifestyle, customs or thinking ways accrue with a nation and the existence of the national identity is in comparison with other nations.

Mass media like newspapers have proven to be excellent tools and sites for the dissemination and articulation of national identity. In recent decades, many studies have focused on the place of media in forming and sustaining national identities in different countries, such as Billig (1995), Wodak et al. (1999), Anderson (1991), and Chouliaraki and Fairclough (1999). It is found that all the previous studies are based on monolingual news reports and few are concerned with how national identity is constructed in newspapers in two different languages. Therefore, the present study tries to make a tentative research on how the self and the others are represented in newspapers in two different countries when the same news event is reported.

6. Comparative analysis of news reports on the CNOOC's takeover of Nexen

The study will adopt a comparative approach to reveal how news reports construct national identity in two newspapers from two nations within the framework of critical discourse analysis. Due to the limited space, the comparative analysis is undertaken in two steps and two perspectives. The headlines of the news reports will be analyzed first with a focus on their thematization, and then the nomination analysis of major stories of news reports will be undertaken.

6.1 Thematic analysis of news headlines in two newspapers

News reports aim to provide mass audience at different levels with news events in simple and easy-to-understand language. What attract the reader first is the news headlines, which in a very concise way generalize the whole of the news events and decide whether the reader reads on as the reader will grasp the accurate gist of a news event at a glance of the headline. Therefore, news headlines "have to be crafted in such a way as to employ the minimum number of words to package maximum information" (Teo 2000: 14) and hence the sharp, punchy, and dramatic quality of headlines. The lexical choice and sentential patterns in news headlines can often reflect news reporters' ideology, standpoints and attitudes.

Twenty headlines from news reports of the two newspapers are listed in the following two tables and Chinese headlines are translated into English by the author for readers' understanding.

According to Halliday (1985), theme is the element which serves as the point of departure of the message conveyed by the clause. The element put at the very beginning of a clause often becomes prominent or foregrounded as the writer wishes to contribute much to it. Hence the thematization of an element in a clause. The thematization of an element in news reports can reflect the ideology and viewpoint of the news writer as the thematized element often becomes the information focus and the highlight or topic of a news report. In the above tables, all the themes of the headlines are marked in bold. After the analysis of the thematization of the headlines in the above two tables, it is clear that in Table 1, 8 out of 10 headlines are concerned with the Chinese side like " 中海油 " (CNOOC), 中海油购尼克森 (CNOOC's takeover of Nexen), " 中国企业 " (Chinese enterprises), " 王宜林 " (the CNOOC's CEO), and only two headlines have " 加执政党议员 " (Canadian MP) as the themes. In comparison, in Table 2, it is much more obvious that almost all the headlines have themes concerning the Canadian side, such as "Canada opposition MP", "Harper", "Ottawa" and the only exception is a theme concerning the Chinese side, i.e. "China's Nexen offer". Table 3 shows such difference in a clearer way.

Through the content analysis of the headlines in the two tables, it is easy to discern the news reporters' ideology, standpoint and perspectives. The headlines in the two newspapers have their respective focus and concern, directly leading to the news stories in the news reports although they have covered the whole process of CNOOC's takeover of Nexen, that is, from the takeover launch to the obstacles faced and at last to the takeover approval. Specifically, from

Table 1 we can find that the news reports in the Chinese newspapers are more concerned with the success of the takeover as the deal is reasonable, profitable and can bring out prosperity to Chinese economy. The headlines also show the worries from the Chinese side when extensions occurred twice. After the approval of the takeover on December 7, three headlines are concerned with the future of CNOOC, including an analysis of the success of the takeover and its influence on the domestic situation of oil industry. Table 2 shows a complicated situation. One voice is to support CNOOC's takeover of Nexen as it is hard to turn down the offer provided by CNOOC; and the second voice is a complete opposition, a representation of "resource nationalism", as the opposition MP thinks that it is treason to approve Nexen takeover. The third voice is from Prime Minister Harper, who is in a dilemma as he has to consider the two quite different opinions from the leader's perspective. Therefore, Harper has to "weigh national security" on the one hand and to consider the profit that the takeover will generate on the other hand.

Table 1　News headlines in *21st Century Business Herald*

Date	Headlines/captions
7 月 23 日 (July 23)	中海油 151 亿美元收购加拿大 Nexen (CNOOC took over Canadian Nexen with the bid of US $15.1 billion)[3]
7 月 24 日 (July 24)	中海油购 Nexen 作价合理 页岩气具憧憬 (CNOOC took Nexen over with a reasonable bid and shale gas is prosperous)
9 月 27 日 (Sept 27)	中海油与加政界磋商后对获准收购 Nexen 有信心 (CNOOC is confident with the takeover of Nexen after negotiating with Canadian government)
10 月 3 日 (Oct 3)	加拿大议员：批准中海油收购 Nexen 是叛国行为 (Canadian PM says that approving CNOOC's takeover of Nexen is treason)
11 月 3 日 (Nov 3)	中国企业海外并购最大障碍——政治敌意 (Chinese enterprises are facing the biggest obstacle on the way of their overseas takeover: political hostility)
11 月 8 日 (Nov 8)	加执政党议员反对 中海油收购尼克森遇新忧 (Canadian MP opposed CNOOC's takeover of Nexen and the takeover is facing new problems)
11 月 8 日 (Nov 8)	王宜林：中海油收购尼克森有望 2012 年底完成 (Wang Yilin says CNOOC's takeover of Nexen is expected to be completed at the end of 2012)
12 月 8 日 (Dec 8)	中海油购尼克森获批 (CNOOC's takeover of Nexen is approved)
12 月 10 日 (Dec 10)	中海油收购尼克森落听 国内原油业或将三分天下 (CNOOC's takeover of Nexen succeeds and China oil industry may be divided into three main forces)

（待续）

（接上）

Date	Headlines/captions
12 月 14 日 (Dec 15)	**中海油**艰难海外找油 (CNOOC is on the hard way to find oil overseas)

(Themes in headlines are marked in bold)

Table 2   News headlines in *Financial Post*

Date	Headlines/captions
Aug 30	**China's Nexen offer** hard for Ottawa to refuse
Oct 2	**Canada opposition MP**: treason to approve Nexen takeover
Oct 12	**Harper** says must weigh national security in China ties
Oct 11	**Will Ottawa** take CNOOC at its word over Nexen deal?
Oct4	**NDP's rejection of Nexen deal** pushes Harper into tight corner
Oct23	**Canada "resource nationalism"** threatens CNOOC, Nexen deal, Fitch warns
Nov3	**Ottawa** extends review of controversial CNOOC-Nexen deal again
Dec 7	**Ottawa** approves **Nexen** and Progress takeover deals
	Nexen deal may not give CNOOC earnings boost
Dec 10	**Harper** defends takeover decision, says similar deals 'extremely unlikely' to be approved in future

(Themes in headlines are marked in bold)

Table 3   Number of themes in headlines of *21st Century Business Herald and Financial Post*

News headlines in *21st Century Business Herald*		News headlines in *Financial Post*	
Number of themes concerning China's side	Number of themes concerning Canada's side	Number of themes concerning China's side	Number of themes concerning Canada's side
8	2	1	9

It can be seen that the news headlines reflect the common concern of two nations, including not only the profit that a nation can obtain, but also national security and national development. Therefore, the headlines crystallize the national identity.

6.2 Nomination analysis of the news stories in the two newspapers

After the analysis of news headlines of the collected data, it is necessary to make an analysis of the news stories by using the linguistic tool of nomination.

Nomination is "the discursive construction of social actors, objects, phenomena/events and processes/actions" (Reisigl and Wodak 1997: 90) and it is a way to categorize membership and to construct national identity. Deictics like "I", "we" and "they" depend heavily upon the existence of the other. Nomination is a frequently used device in the discursive construction of national identity as it is a productive way of classification in order to distinguish "we" from "they". Billig (1995: 114-115) in *Banal Nationalism* points out that deixis in newspapers is a very forceful way to speak to and speak for a nation, and also to represent the nation as the deictic expressions can "evoke a national 'we' , which includes the 'we' of reader and writer, as well as the 'we' of the universal audience". Deixis, according to Matthews (2000: 89), is "the way in which the reference of certain elements in a sentence is determined in relation to a specific speaker and addressee and a specific time and place of utterance". Therefore, personal references, spatial references, demonstrative references, and temporal references are frequently seen as deixis. However, in newspapers many names or terms are flagged with nationhood or nationalism when the news events are concerned with two or more than two countries, and these names or terms often become contextually dependent references. Billig (1995: 105) explains that "There the national name can hang as sign, context and potentiality. These familiar words are like flags hanging in the cool air." He exemplifies the use of the deixis of homeland as it "invokes 'we' and places 'us' within 'our' homeland" (Billig 1995: 105). Therefore, in the paper, all the names concerning both Chinese and Canadian sides are considered as deictic expressions as they are flagged with nationhood or nationalism in the exact context of the takeover event.

In order to discriminate the nomination used in the news reports of the two newspapers, two tables are drawn to show the deixis used, and the deictic expressions in Chinese newspaper are translated into English by the author.

In Table 4, the deictic expressions about CNOOC include "中海油" (CNOOC), "中国企业" (Chinese enterprise), "中国经济界" (Chinese economic field) etc., while the deictic expressions about Nexen cover "加拿大人" (Canadians), "加拿大政府" (Canandian government), "加拿大企业" (Canadian enterprise), "加拿大能源公司" (Canadian energy company), etc.

Table 4　Deixis used in 21st Century Business Herald

Date	Deixis	
	CNOOC	Nexen
11 月 08 日 (Nov.8)	中海油 (CNOOC); 中国 (China);	尼克森 (Nexen); 加拿大主要的反对党 (The major opposition party in Canada); 加拿大人 (Canadians); 加拿大政府 (Canandian government); 加拿大企业 (Canadian enterprises)

（待续）

（接上）

Date	Deixis	
	CNOOC	Nexen
7月24日 (July 24)	中海油 (CNOOC)	加拿大能源公司 Nexen (The Canadian Energy Company Nexen)
7月23日 (July 23)	中国海洋石油有限公司 (China National Offshore Oil Corporation)	加拿大能源公司尼克森公司 (The Canadian energy company Nexen)
9月22日 (Sept 22)	中海油 (CNOOC)	尼克森公司股东特别大会 (The special meeting of shareholders of Nexen); 尼克森 (Nexen)
9月27日 (Sept 27)	中海油 (CNOOC); 中国 (China); 中海油高层 (The higher leaders of CNOOC); 中海油首席执行官 (The chief executive officer of CNOOC)	尼克森 (Nexen); 加拿大 (Canada); 加国省级领导组成的代表团 (the delegation of provincial officials in Canada); 加拿大官员 (Canadian officials)
12月10日 (Dec 10)	中海油 (CNOOC); 中国企业 (Chinese enterprises); 中国经济界 (Chinese economic field)	尼克森 (Nexen); 加拿大能源公司 (Canadian energy company); 加拿大 (Canada)

In Table 5, the deictic categories about CNOOC are concerned with "the Chinese company", "CNOOC", "the Chinese company", "Chinese state-owned oil and gas company", etc.,whereas the deictic expressions about Nexen include "Canada", "the Calgary-based oil and gas producer Nexen Inc", "Ottawa", "the Canadian government". It can be found that the deictic expressions are used to help cultivate the national belonging and shape the national identity. What's noticeable is that in the news reports of *Financial Post*, "we", "Ottawa", "Canadian Prime Minister Stephen Harper", and "The Canadian government" are frequently mentioned when reporting the CNOOC-Nexen deal. In *21st Century Business Herald,* neither "Beijing", nor "Chinese government" or Chinese national leaders are mentioned. The differences in the use of deixis show that the takeover is very controversial in Canada, which has led to the discussion of national security and resource threat. For the Chinese side, all the concern is on whether the takeover is successful or not and whether the takeover can bring profits. Therefore there is no worry about the threat to the nation and the only concern is whether it is profitable.

Table 5   Deixis used in *Financial Post*

Date	Deixis	
	CNOOC	Nexen
Oct 10	Chinese investment; CNOOC; the Chinese company;	the Canadian oil and gas sector Ottawa; Canadian

（待续）

（接上）

Date	Deixis	
	CNOOC	Nexen
Aug 30	China; CNOOC; a Chinese company;	a major Canadian petroleum producer; Nexen; the Harper government; the Canadian government
Oct 12	China; the Chinese state-owned oil company; a Chinese company	Canadian Prime Minister Stephen Harper; Ottawa; We; The Canadian government; Canada
Oct 11	CNOOC Ltd. Executives; China; the Chinese state-owned oil and gas company;	Nexen; the Calgary-based oil and gas producer; Ottawa;
Oct 23	China's CNOOC Ltd.	Canada; the Canadian government; Canada's resource nationalism
Dec 12	foreign governments; CNOOC;	the Conservative government; we; Canada; the Calgary-based oil and gas producer Nexen Inc.

7. Conclusion

Due to the space limit, the paper just compares the thematic expressions in news headlines and the use of nomination in the two newspapers. It is shown that the news reports are the site to represent, construct and maintain national identity as the thematization of an important element in headlines and the use of nomination in news stories are always the possible ways to realize and represent the national identity.

The present study is a preliminary and tentative research on the discursive construction of national identity in news reports of two different nations. In fact, more work can be done from the micro- and macro-structure perspectives, such as the analysis of perspectivization, lexical cohesion, transitivity and genre of the collected data. When a complicated and detailed analysis is undertaken on the collected data, it is possible to know more about the representation of self and the others in news reports in China and Canada.

Notes

1. *People's Daily* is regarded as the most authoritative and influential newspaper with a daily circulation of 3 million, which is ranked the second largest newspaper in China (http://www. people.com.cn/).

2. *The Globe and Mail* is one of the two national newspapers in Canada with national and worldwide fame, and is Canada's largest-circulation national newspaper and second-largest daily newspaper (http://www.theglobeand mail.com/).

3. The English translations for the Chinese data in Tables 1 and 4 are done by the author.

References

Anderson, B. 1991. *Imagined Communities: Reflections on the Origin and Spread of Nationalism*. London: Verso.

Bersnier, N. 1991. Literacy and the notion of person on Nukulaelae Atoll. *American Anthropologist*, 93, 570-587.

Billig, M. 1995. *Banal Nationalism*. London: SAGE.

Butler, J. 1991. Imitation and gender insubordination. In D. Fuss (ed.), *Inside/out: Lesbian Theories, Gay Theories*. 13-31. New York & London: Routledge.

Chouliaraki, L. and N. Fairclough. 1999. *Discourse in Late Modernity: Rethinking Critical Discourse Analysis*. Edinburgh: Edinburgh University Press.

Cillia, R., M. Reisigl and R. Wodak. 1999. The discursive construction of national identities. *Discourse & Society, 10* (2), 149-173.

Douglas, F. M. 2009. *Scottish Newspapers, Language and Identity.* Edinburgh: Edinburgh University Press.

Fairclough, N. 1992. *Discourse and Social Change*. Cambridge: Polity Press.

Foucault, M. 1980. *Power/knowledge: Selected Interviews & Other Writings 1972-1977.* C. Gordon (ed.). (C. Gordon L. Marshal J. Mepham and K. Sober, Trans.). New York: Pantheon Books.

Halliday, M. A. K. 1985. *An Introduction to Functional Grammar*. London: Edward Arnold.

Ivanič, R. 1997. *Writing and Identity: The Discoursal Construction of Identity in Academic Writing*. Amsterdam/Philadelphia: John Benjamins Publishing Company.

Joseph, J. E. 2004. *Language and Identity: National, Ethnic, Religious.* New York: Palgrave.

Matthews, P. H. 2000. *Oxford Concise Dictionary of Linguistics*. Shanghai: Shanghai Foreign Language Education Press / Oxford: Oxford University Press.

Norton, B. 2004. *Identity and Language Learning: Gender, Ethnicity and Educational Change.* Harlow: Longman.

Reisigl, M. and R. Wodak. 1997. The discourse-historical approach. In R. Wodak and M. Meyer (eds.), *Methods of Critical Discourse Analysis*. 87-119. London: Sage.

Taylor, C. 1989. Sources of the Self: The Making of the Modern Identity. Cambridge: Cambridge University Press.

Taylor, C. 1991. The dialogical self. In D. R. Hiley, J. F. Bohman and R. Shusterman (eds.), *The Interpretive Turn*. 304-314. Ithaca & London: Cornell University Press.

Teo, P. 2000. Racism in the news: A critical discourse analysis of news reporting in two Australian newspapers. *Discourse & Society*, 11(1), 7-49.

Wodak, R., M. Reisigl, and K. Liebhart. 1999. (A. Hirsch and R. Mitten, Trans.) *The Discursive Construction of National Identity*. Edinburgh: Edinburgh University Press.

Gender Construction in Pakistani Children's Literature: An Analysis of Taleem-O-Tarbiyat

Ambreen Shahnaz[a], Samina Amin Qadir[b] and Farah Riaz[c]

[a]COMSATS Wah Campus, [b]Fatima Jinnah Women University,
[c]COMSATS Wah Campus, Pakistan

1. Introduction

The relationship between language and gender is so intense that it cannot be ignored as it is language which determines what we are and we are helpless regarding this fact. The importance of considering language in the study of gender representation in children's literature is emphasized by Clark, who calls on researchers of children's texts to pay greater attention to "nuances of expression" and "a variety of voices" when reading gender in children's literature (2002: 292). No medium has been so extensively investigated than children's literature due to its importance as a powerful medium for transmitting cultural heritage. Children receive the blueprint of cultural values through various characters in books to which they follow to reaffirm themselves in the existing society as books mirror the values and culture transmitted to children by adults by functioning as a vehicle for transferring ideologies from generation to generation (Taylor 2003). In fact, by influencing the minds of children, one can shape the future directions. As a result, analysis of children's literature is required to update teachers, educators, parents and other concerned people regarding the negative aspects of books. The researcher hopes that this awareness will lead towards provision of more progressive reading material.

1.1 Research objectives

The present research aims at the study of gender construction in children's literature. Thus, the basic objective of the research will be to observe the frequency of males and females' visibility and examine the association and effect of various variables upon one another. The researcher will also analyze the assigned professions and interpret the ideology which has been built up according to socio-cultural point of view.

1.2 Research questions

RQ1: How are gender roles defined through linguistic and pictorial representation?

RQ2: How do male and female characters differ in term of professions assigned to them?

RQ3: What is the relationship of various variables with one another and how do they affect one another?

RQ4: Which ideology is built up through representation of male and female characters in children's literature?

2. Literature review

Gender role stereotyping is a widely investigated research area in children's literature (Hamilton et al. 2006; Turner-Bowker 1996). This study is important due to the belief that literature plays a pivotal role in shaping the personality of children which ultimately leads towards the construction of society (Diekman and Murnen 2004; Hamilton et al. 2006).

According to various studies related to gender issues and role specification in children's literature, representation of various characters has conventionally been stereotyped and gender-biased (Scott and Feldman-Summers 1979; Davies 1993, 2003; Evans and Davies 2000; Tsao 2008). The importance of the study of gender roles is based on the belief that children and young adults shape their view of themselves and society by reading books (Crabb and Bielawski 1993; Kortenhaus and Demarest 1993). Literature is one of the fundamental sources for dissipating gender stereotypes (Mendoza and Reese 2001). As noted by Desai (2001) and Gooden and Gooden (2001), children's literature has a crucial role in helping young children in this process of identifying and categorizing gender roles. Talbot (2010) also extends the view that books which are marketed as "for girls" tend to be pink, decorated with fairies for the young and fashion accessories for the older girls implying that their readers are only interested in their appearance and being attractive to the boys. Bradford (2007) concurs and stresses that while evaluating children's books, attention must be paid to messages about gender construction because they affect identity construction in young children. Particular attention must be paid to the identity of characters in the texts that depict oversimplified gender-role stereotypes which may contribute to establishing and reinforcing sexist attitudes (Christie 2000: 12). Moreover, Kramer (2001) affirms that the major problem of children's literature is the old and stereotypical representation of both the genders through biased language and images.

Keeping the importance and value of pictures in children's world, the present research has considered the pictorial aspect of the magazine too. A colored book with simple language and all those factors which involve a child is considered to be more appropriate and famous for kids. The text is not the only source of spreading messages as pictures also serve to depict more than just illustrations. They convey a specific ideology due to which they must be taken into consideration and interpreted. While addressing the same issue, Bechtel (1973: 180) argues that the function of well-decorated and well-organized page is "to make a page which will be more easily read by the child". Jackson and Gee (2005: 15) quote Chatton (2001) that pictures play a prominent role in conveying messages about males and females to immature minds. Hamilton et al. (2006) are in complete agreement with the previous researchers and assert that there can be more intricate ways of portraying stereotypical approach. Illustrations are significant, even much more powerful in conveying messages, specifically to children. Law and Chan (2004) observed illustrations at primary level depicting 32.19 percent females and 48.73 percent males and with a ratio of 68.67 and 77.94 percent major female and male characters respectively. The underrepresentation of females has also been asserted by Ferdows (1995) and Wood (2005). Brugeilles (2002) and Poarch and Monk-Turner (2001) also support the same argument that illustrated books for children are major source of gender construction. Children and parents are their main characters and their activities and characteristics are gender based. This demarcation is not limited to human beings only as even animals and real or imaginary characters are also defined through gender.

Pakistan is generally a patriarchal society which has traditional gender differences, expectations and gender roles in all walks of life. The importance of literature cannot be denied in Pakistan as it serves to reinforce the ideology of society due to its far-reaching influence. In this regard, Jha (2008) conveys a high rate of gender discrimination in favor of males in Pakistan. The gender discrimination is evident from the language of people and their literature. Extending the same point of view, Mushtaq and Rasul (2012) mentions that Urdu rhymes don't even depict the Pakistani society in a proper way. The researchers wind up the discussion by pointing out that nursery rhymes instead of revolutionizing or changing the society are not even representing the Pakistani society properly. They are, in fact, far behind the present society. Siddiquie's latest contribution is also very important in this regard as he is of the view that "The media is reinforcing stereotypes by legitimizing them and amplifying their impact" (2013: 125).

The way gender is portrayed in children's literature has far reaching effects upon children's behavior and their attitude towards gender related issues. Books are a major source of gender role stereotyping. Since infancy, the child is introduced to the social hierarchy of the stereotyped world through which a specific type of behavior, required from male and female gender, is inculcated. Gender development actually comprises a critical part of learning experiences of young children (Mathuvi et al. 2012). Kramer (2001) claims that children's literature provide characters and events which help children in identifying and considering their own beliefs, actions and emotions (Mendoza and Reese 2001). This corroborates with the findings from a study by Davies (2003) who analyze the influence of reading fairy tales to children. She asserts that children between the ages of 4 to 5 years relate males and females with superiority and dependence respectively.

All the above mentioned discussion makes the role of children's literature more imperative and critical in children's life. As a result, more in-depth research is required to point out the problematic areas by suggesting more positive reforms particularly from the gender construction point of view.

3. Research methodology

Data for the present study was taken from a children's magazine, i.e. *Taleem-o-Tarbiyat* which is one of the old and famous monthly magazines comprising a variety of short stories, biographies, poems and other items of entertainment. A total of twelve issues, including three issues of each year, were selected for the research. The three issues of each year have been taken from the start, mid and end of the year. Three stories from each issue have been selected. The stories have also been selected from the start, mid and end of the magazine. In this way, total thirty six stories have been taken for the present study. However, if any account related to any distinguished personality has been observed, it has been taken for the present study regardless of its position in the magazine. The total duration of time in which data has been taken is from January 2006 to 2012. In this regard, magazines of 2006 and 2007, and 2011 and 2012, have been selected.

There are various reasons for taking data for the research from children's literature. In order to analyze the process of gender construction quantitatively, immense data was required. Furthermore, the selection of children's literature is also more appropriate as it defines the course of action for future generation which results in the making of a society. Lastly, work on children's literature in Pakistan is less than the required need. So the present study will be a contribution to filling this gap.

The data for the present study has been collected from a number of categories. All these categories have been investigated under two major subcategories which are male and female. A theoretical framework, comprising the relationship among study variables with dimensions is presented below:

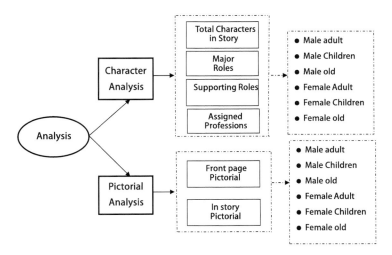

Figure 1　Theoretical model

Only those characters have been counted who have practically participated in any action. The important and central figures of the story have been considered the characters in major roles. Supporting characters are the second most important characters that helped and assisted the major characters. Similarly, assigned professions have been counted as per number of frequencies in which they have been mentioned in the stories.

4. Data analysis

The data has been analyzed through correlation, cross tabulation and ANOVA.

4.1 Correlation analysis

The correlation analysis helped in finding out the strength of relationship with each other. The details have been shown through Table 1 and follows up discussion.

Table 1　Correlation analysis

	Front page Pictorial (FPPM)	Front Page Pictorial (FPPF)	In Story Pictorial (M)	In Story Pictorial (ISPF)	Character in story adult (CSAM)	Character in story children (CSCM)	Character in story old (CSOM)	Character in story Adult (CSAF)	Character in story children (CSCF)
Front page Pictorial (FPPM)	1								
Front Page Pictorial (FPPF)	0.184	1							
In Story Pictorial (ISPM)	0.174	0.567	1						
In Story Pictorial (ISPF)	0.378	0.214	0.276	1					
Character in story adult (CSAM)	0.221	-0.066	0.332	0.163	1				
Character in story children (CSCM)	-0.437	-0.287	0.177	-0.244	0.351	1			
Character in story old (CSOM)	-0.287	-0.205	-0.379	-0.438	-0.374	0.183	1		
Character in story Adult (CSAF)	-0.272	0	0.303	0.247	0.094	0.287	-0.181	1	
Character in story children (CSCF)	0.306	-0.397	-0.21	-0.428	0.119	.741**	.657*	-0.075	1
Character in story old (CSOF)	0.393	.735**	.640*	0.008	-0.171	0.165	-0.032	-0.057	-0.045
Assigned Profession (APM)	-0.022	0.161	.637*	0.251	0.375	0.131	-0.346	0.118	0.019
Assigned Profession (APF)	0.129	-0.24	-0.145	-0.132	-0.439	-0.048	-0.186	0.299	-0.064
Major Role (MRM)	0.399	0.23	0.213	0.455	0.236	-0.561	-0.257	-0.019	-0.331
Major Role (MRF)	0.142	0.088	0.182	0.063	-0.25	-0.164	-0.127	0.325	-0.073
Supporting Role (SRM)	0.184	-0.402	0.008	0.286	0.228	0.166	-0.278	0	-0.027
Supporting Role (SRF)	-0.047	0.175	-0.172	-0.093	-0.546	-0.219	-0.313	0.289	-0.327

Table 1 shows the results of Pearson correlation in detail. It is evident from the table that FPPM is negatively associated with APM whereas positively associated with APF but the relationship is weak. Contrary to this, FPPF are positively associated with APM whereas negatively associated with APPF. The relationship between FPPM and APF and FPPF and APM show affirmative relationship. Furthermore, FPPF and APF are again negatively associated but the association between FPPM and MRM, and that between FPPM and MRF are found to be positive. The correlation between FPPF and MRM, and that between and that between FPPF and MRF are again positive. Similarly, FPPM and SRM indicate positive connection whereas FPPM with SRM and FPPF with SRM show negative association.

The association between APM and ISPM points out positive relationship and the correlation between ISPM and APF shows a negative association. The connection between ISPF and APM points out a positive association while the correlation between ISPF and APF is positive. The association between ISPM and MRM, ISPM and MRF is positive. The correlation between ISPF and MRM is positive while the correlation between ISPF and MRF is positive. The relationship between ISPM and SRM supporting role males indicates a positive association while the correlation between ISPM and SRF is negative. The correlation between ISPF and SRM points out a positive relationship and the association between ISPF and SRF is negative, indicating negative association. All the mentioned correlations are hinting a weak relationship.

The relationship between CSAM and APM, between CSAF and APF, and between CSAF and APM, each indicates a positive association while the correlation between CSAM and APF points out a negative relationship. The correlation between CSCM and APM signifies a positive link while the correlation between CSCM and APF, CSOM and APF and CSOM and APM is negative. The correlation between CSAM and MRM, between CSAF and MRF signifies a positive link while the connection between CSAF and MRM, between CSAM and MRF, between CSCM and MRM, between CSOM and MRM, and between CSOM and MRF indicates a negative association.

4.2 Cross tabulation analysis

Cross tabulation analysis is particularly helpful for the present study as it shows how increase in one variable influence increase, decrease or curvilinear changes in other variables. The following tables give a complete detail of association among the variables.

Table 2   Front page pictorial * assigned profession cross tabulation

Front Page Pictorial (FPP)	Assigned Profession (AP)		Total
	Male (APM)	Female (APF)	
Male (FPPM)	161	53	214
Female (FPPF)	15	4	19

Front Page Pictorial (FPP)	Assigned Profession (AP)		Total
	Male (APM)	Female (APF)	
Total	176	57	233

Table 2 shows that the assigned professions for males are higher in number if the front page males' pictorials are greater. The front page males' and the males' assigned professions shows a straight affirmative link. However, front page pictorials have negative relationship with females' assigned professions. It means that increased front page males' pictorials have negative influence upon females' assigned professions. The situation is reverse with females where even if the front page females' pictorials are higher, the assigned professions are still reserved for males. It indicates that despite possessing front page pictorial, females are not allotted professions; rather, the occupations are reserved to males.

Table 3   Front page pictorial * major role cross tabulation

Front Page Pictorial (FPP)	Major Role (MR)		Total
	Male (MRM)	Female (MRF)	
Male (FPPM)	153	61	214
Female (FPPF)	15	4	19
Total	168	65	233

Table 3 indicates that if major roles have been assigned to males, the front page pictorials are also surrounded with males. However, the case is reverse with females as no matter females are depicted in front page pictorials, the major roles are still held in reserve for males, which shows a sense of discrepancy and imbalance.

Table 4 shows that if more supporting roles are assigned to males, there is possibility that front page pictorials will also be crowded with males. However, the situation is contradictory with females as no matter the front page pictorials are possessed by females, the majority supporting roles have been allocated to males which expose the asymmetry in representation of females.

Table 4   Front Page Pictorial * Supporting Role Cross Tabulation

Front Page Pictorial (FPP)	Supporting Role (SR)		Total
	Male (SRM)	Female (SRF)	
Male (FPPM)	153	61	214
Female (FPPF)	13	6	19
Total	166	67	233

Table 5 shows that the more males in the in-story pictorial, the more assigned professions are kept for them. Females' in-story pictorials and assigned professions also have positive relationship as females possess equal exposure in both in-story pictorials and assigned professions. It shows that there is a sense of proportion between assigned professions and in-story pictorials for both males and females.

Table 5   In Story Pictorial * Assigned Profession Cross Tabulation

| In Story Pictorial (ISP) | Assigned Profession (AP) | | Total |
	Male (APM)	Female (APF)	
Male (ISPM)	173	52	225
Female (ISPF)	3	5	8
Total	176	57	233

Table 6 indicates that if more major roles are assigned to males, they are more likely to dominate in in-story pictorials. The same rule is applicable to females as well because the increase in major roles for females leads towards more chances of their domination in in-story pictorials. It shows a symmetrical representation of both sexes.

Table 6   In Story Pictorial * Major Role Cross Tabulation

| In Story Pictorial (ISP) | Major Role (MR) | | Total |
	Male (MRM)	Female (MRF)	
Male (ISPM)	165	60	225
Female (ISPF)	3	5	8
Total	168	65	233

Table 7 is also in agreement with the previous findings as there is a strong sense of proportion between males' supporting roles and males' in-story pictorials. However, the opposite is true to females as the greater number of in-story pictorials will lead towards equal possibility for both the genders to be in supporting roles. It is against the balance as contrary to males, females have not been provided the complete opportunity to dominate in supporting roles despite being present in in-story pictorials.

Table 7   In Story Pictorial * Supporting Role Cross Tabulation

| Front Page Pictorial (FPP) | Supporting Role (SR) | | Total |
	Male (SRM)	Female (SRF)	
Male (ISPM)	162	63	225
Female (ISPF)	4	4	8
Total	166	67	233

Table 8 makes it evident that the more males in the in-story characters, the more professions are kept for them. However, in-story female characters (adult females, children females, old females) and assigned professions have negative relationship with assigned professions. It means that despite being present in in-story characters, females are deprived of professions as they are reserved for male characters in enormous majority.

Table 8   Character in Story * Assigned Profession Cross Tabulation

Character in Story (CS)	Assigned Profession (AP)		Total
	Male (APM)	Female (APF)	
Adult Male (CSAM)	34	9	43
Children Male (CSCM)	18	11	29
Old Male (CSOM)	35	8	43
Adult Female (CSAF)	33	10	43
Children Female (CSCF)	28	10	38
Old Female (CSOF)	28	9	37
Total	176	57	233

Table 9 shows that if there are more male characters in story, there are probably more chances of their appearance in major roles. However, female characters and assigned professions have negative relationship with each other. It means that even if the characters in story are females, the major roles have still not been provided to them generously; rather, they are limited to male characters in a huge proportion.

Table 9   Character in Story * Major Role Cross Tabulation

Character in Story (CS)	Major Role (MR)		Total
	Male (MRM)	Female (MRF)	
Adult Male (CSAM)	32	11	43
Children Male (CSCM)	20	9	29
Old Male (CSOM)	28	15	43
Adult Female (CSAF)	36	7	43
Children Female (CSCF)	26	12	38
Old Female (CSOF)	26	11	37
Total	168	65	233

Table 10 shows that the more male characters in story lead towards more appearance of male characters in supporting roles. However, adult females, children females, old females and supporting roles have undesirable link with each other. It shows a strong unevenness and inequality as the power of supporting roles is highly in favor of males even if the in-story characters are females.

4.3 Analysis of variance

Table 11 indicates that the magazines published in the start and end of decades reflect values differently. Analyses revealed significant differences in the extent to which various categories differ from one another. The results show that both males and females' front page pictorials are higher at the end of the decade. Both males and females have more presence in in-story pictorial at the end of the decade. No difference has been found in in-story character male adults; however, in-story female adult characters have an increase in female adults' presence at the end of the decade. No dissimilarity has been found in male children's presence in the start and end of the decade but more female children characters are found at the end of the decade. Both male and female old characters' presence is stronger at the end of the decade.

Table 10   Character in Story * Supporting Role Cross Tabulation

Character in Story (CS)	Supporting Role (SR)		Total
	Male (SRM)	Female (SRF)	
Adult Male (CSAM)	31	12	43
Children Male (CSCM)	21	8	29
Old Male (CSOM)	34	9	43
Adult Female (CSAF)	29	14	43
Children Female (CSCF)	27	11	38
Old Female (CSOF)	24	13	37
Total	166	67	233

Males have been assigned more professions at the end of the decade while females are assigned more professions at the start of the decade. Males have been assigned more major roles at the end of the decade while females are shown in major roles at the start of the decade. Both male and female characters have been shown more in supporting roles at the start of the decade.

4.4 Discussion and analysis

The basic aim of this study was to expose the pattern of gender construction in children's magazine. According to the results of the present study, male characters have been overrepresented in term of frequencies and privileged in term of professions.

Male characters are often portrayed in a diverse array of roles possessing majority of major and supporting roles with various characteristics. The female images are mostly invisible in the illustrations as well as in the content. In this way, the researcher agrees with Khurshid et al.

(2010: 183), who are also of the view that "the proportion of male human character is greater than females" in the literature. Males are playing the lead roles and enjoying the prestigious position while females are shown much less even in supporting roles. The results indicate that of the relatively few times female characters appeared in these texts, they were largely confined to the home settings in stories and accompanying illustrations. Their presence in some stories is just nominal. The present study is in agreement with the previous researches which observe the same old pattern of depiction of women in the background (Scott and Feldman-Summers 1979; Davies 1993, 2003; Evans and Davies 2000; Tsao 2008).

Table 11   Analysis of Variance (ANOVA)

ANOVA		
Variables	**F-statistics**	**p-value**
Front page Pictorial Male	21.24*	.005
Front Page Pictorial Female	13.798*	.000
In Story Pictorial Male	12.075*	.010
In Story Pictorial Female	13.084*	.042
Character in story male adult	8.539	.060
Character in story male children	0.000	.500
Character in story male old	6.200*	.043
Character in story Female Adult	18.118*	.000
Character in story Female children	11.110*	.007
Character in story Female old	6.019*	.037
Assigned Profession Male	.192	.670
Assigned Profession Female	2.426*	.010
Major Role Male	11.077*	.007
Major Role Female	5.000*	.000
Supporting Role Male	11.450*	.026
Supporting Role Female	5.227*	.044

*significant at 5% level

Varieties of professions have been assigned to males. These professions belong to every walk of life, for example, soldier, businessman, teacher, spiritual guide, social worker, employee, watchman, contractor, dacoit, student, abductor, factory owner, pirates, captain, sailors, pilot, doctor, landlord and teacher, etc. This diversity of professions indicates the power and legitimacy of choice of occupations in the society. On the other hand, females have been ignored in occupations. This occupational sex segregation is an instance of the stereotyping towards females. Women have been observed as being nurturing, caring and possessing experience and skills in childrearing and domestic chores. Their appearance is mostly as a mother who is doing household chores and taking care of her family with complete devotion. A caring mother who is flattering her kids to eat food; a worried mother who is restless in providing comfort and care to her family. The short biographies of some historical personalities have also been conveyed by the name of *"Sunehry Log"* in this magazine; however, not a single female personality has been included in this portion. All the male celebrities have been taken from diverse fields of life but women despite being eminent in that field have not been considered eligible to be depicted in this important section of the magazine. This again does not confirm to the attitude of Pakistani society as according to Gallup Poll Pakistan (2013), 63% Pakistanis believe that women can lead a country, which shows that the stereotypical attitude of Pakistani society is changed now towards more a progressive direction.

This non-recognition of contribution and employed degradation is perpetuating a negative and stereotyped ideology which can lead towards low self-respect of girls (Khurshidet al. 2010). The magazine fails in following the modern trend of the Pakistani society where females are competing and sometimes excelling in various aspects of life. As a result, we can conclude that instead of revolutionizing and changing the society, the magazine is even lagging far behind the modern trend of society.

5. Conclusions and recommendations

The researcher employed co-relational, cross- tabulation and ANOVA to find out the association and effect of one variable upon other. This analysis helped in understanding the stereotypical representation to suggest who has more power in terms of visibility and how this power is accomplished and realized.

It is apparent from the stories and illustrations in the start and end of the decade that the authors are following the same old and traditional patriarchal ideology by providing more attention to males and depicting them more powerful. Males are possessors of a variety of positions as compared to females who are mostly depicted as mothers and wives busy in household tasks (Abdul Hamid et al. 2008). This numerical unevenness in favor of males is transformed into hierarchical dominance when we observe the assigned occupations where the demarcation and division is strictly based on gender. The dangerous aspect of this type of representation is that it provides a limited perception and negative ideology of world to the coming generation and it is accepted as naturalized or in other words "the way things are" if left unquestioned (Talbot 2003: 14). It is also noticed that this magazine do not even represent

Pakistani society well. This magazine is lagging even far behind the society itself.

Based upon the present research, the researcher hopes that the findings will contribute to make Pakistani writers and publishers vigilant about children's books so that they may address the gender stereotyping in their writing to help counteracting the sexist attitude of the society. The government as well as the relevant NGOs should provide proper boundaries and guidelines regarding ethical standards, codes of conduct and responsibility of literature. A systematic policy should be introduced to get rid of asymmetry for a better and progressive Pakistan. The results work as a guide as what is supposed to be done to bring a balance that may permit children to observe an "equitable representation" of males and females (Nair and Talif 2010). The common people as well as the media practitioner should make it sure to portray both male and female characters in the same background with similar characteristics and roles to be played in the society and both of them should have equal right to feel the same range of feelings and reactions in different contexts.

References

Abdul Hamid, B. D. H., M. S. M. Yasin, K. A. Bakar, Y.C. Keong and A. Jalaluddin. 2008. Linguistic sexism and gender role stereotyping in Malaysian English language text books. *GEMA Online Journal of Language Studes, 8* (2), 45-78.

Bechtel, L. S. 1973. The art of illustrating books for the young readers. In V. Haviland (ed.). *Children and Literature Views and Reviews.* USA: Scott. Foresman and Company.

Bradford, C. 2007. Reading children's literature: Theories and strategies. In T. Rosli and M. J. Jariah (ed.), *Understanding Children's Literature.* 1-21. Petaling Jaya: Sasbadi.

Brugeilles, C., I. Cromer and S. Cromer. 2002. Male and female characters in illustrated children's books or how children's literature contributes to the construction of gender. *Population English Ed., 57* (2), 237-267.

Christie, C. 2000. *Gender and Language: Towards a Feminist Pragmatics.* Edinburgh: Edinburgh University Press.

Clark, R. 2002. Why all the counting? Feminist social science research on children's literature. *Children's Literature in Education, 33* (4), 285-295.

Crabb, P. and Bielawski, D. 1994. The social representation of material culture and gender in children's books. *Sex Roles, 30* (1/2), 69-79.

Davies, B. 1993. *Shards of Glass: Children Reading and Writing beyond Gendered Identities.* New Jersey: Hampton Press, Inc.

Davies, B. 2003. *Frogs and Snails and Feminist Tales: Preschool Children and Gender.* New Jersey: Hampton Press, Inc.

Desai, C.M. 2006. National identity in a multicultural society: Malaysian children's literature in English. *Children's Literature in Education, 37* (2), 163-184.

Diekman, A. B. and Murnen, S. K. 2004. Learning to be little women and little men: The inequitable gender equality of nonsexist children's literature. *Sex Roles, 50* (5/6), 373-85.

Evans, L. and Davies, K. 2000. No sissy boys here: A content analysis of the representation of masculinity in elementary school reading textbooks. *Sex Roles, 42* (3/4), 255-270.

Ferdows, A. K. 1995. Gender roles in Iranian public school text books. In E. W. Farnew (eds.). *Children in the Muslim Middle East*. Austin: University of Texas Press.

Gallup Poll Pakistan. 2013. Data retrieved from http://www.gallup.com.pk/pollsshow.php?id=2013-12-04 on June 14, 2013.

Gooden, A. M. and M. A. Gooden. 2001. Gender representation in notable children's picture books: 1995-1999. *Sex Roles, 45* (1/2), 89-101.

Hamilton, M., D. Anderson, M. Broaddus, and K. Young. 2006. Gender stereotyping and under representation of female characters in 200 popular children's picture books: A twenty first century updates. *Sex Roles, 55* (11-12), 757-765.

Jackson, S. and S. Gee. 2005. She might not have the right tools and he does: Children's sense-making of gender, work and abilities in early school readers. *Gender and Education, 19* (1), 61-77.

Jha, J. 2008. Gender equality in education: The role of schools. Retrieved from www.nottingham.ac.uk/shared/shared_uccer/unescopdfs/Gender_Equality_in_Education.ppt on January 10, 2013.

Khurshid, K., I. G. Gillani and M. A. Hashmi. 2010. A study of the representation of female image in the textbooks of English and Urdu at secondary school level. *Pakistan Journal of Social Sciences (PJSS), 30* (2), 425-437.

Kortenhaus, C. M. and J. Demarest. 1993. Gender role stereotyping in children's literature: An update. *Sex Roles, 28* (3-4), 219-232.

Kramer, M. A. 2001. *Sex-role stereotyping in children's literature.* Unpublished master's thesis, Pennsylvania State University, University Park, PA.

Law, K. W. K. and A. H. N. Chan. 2004. Gender role stereotyping in Hong Kong's primary school Chinese language subject text books. *AJWS, 10* (1), 49-69.

Mathuvi, P. N., A. M. Ireri, D. M. Mukuni, A. M. Njagi and N. I. Karugu. 2012. An analysis of gender displays in selected children picture books in Kenya. *International Journal of Arts, 2* (5), 31-38.

Mendoza, J. and D. Reese. 2001. Examining multicultural picture books for the early childhood classroom: Possibilities and pitfalls. *Early Childhood Research & Practice, 3* (2), 1-38.

Mushtaq, K. and Rasul, S. 2012. Identity construction in nursery rhymes: A gender based study. *Language in India, 12* (2), 1-34.

Nair, R. and R. Talif. 2010. Lexical choices and the construction of gender in Malaysian children's literature. *Kajian Malaysia, 28* (2), 137-159.

Poarch, R. and E. Monk-Turner. 2001. Gender roles in children's literature: A review of non-award-winning "easy-to-read" books. *Journal of Research in Childhood Education* 16 (1), 70-6.

Scott, K. P. and S. Feldman-Summers. 1979. Children's reactions to textbook stories in which females are portrayed in traditionally male roles. *Journal of Educational Psychology, 71* (3), 396-402.

Siddiquie, S. 2013. *Language, Gender and Power: The Politics of Representation and Hegemony in South Asia.* Karachi: Oxford University Press.

Talbot, M. 2003. Gender stereotypes: Reproduction and challenge. In J. Holmes and M. Meyerhoff (eds.),

The Handbook of Language and Gender. 468-486. Hoboken: Blackwell Publishing.

Talbot, M. 2010. *Language and Gender* (2nd edition). Polity Press UK.

Taylor, E. B. 1974. *Primitive Culture: Researches into the Development of Mythology, Philosophy, Religion, Art and Custom*. New York: Gordon Press.

Tsao, Y. L. 2008. Gender issues in young children's literature. *Reading Improvement, 45* (3), 108-114.

Turner-Bowker, D. M. 1996. Gender stereotyped descriptors in children's picture books: Does "curious Jane" exist in literature? *Sex Roles, 35* (7/8), 461-488.

Wood, J. T. 2005. *Gendered Lives Communication, Gender & Culture* (6th edition). Belmont: Wordsworth Publishing Company.

Image-text Discourse: An Intermodal Perspective on the Construction of Institutional Identity

Jing Xu

Guizhou Minzu University, China

1. Introduction

Previous studies on institutional identity have primarily focused on the mono-modality of language, and the main issues of such studies include macrostructures, turn-takings and asymmetrical discursive rights, tending to explicate the orderly social activities. However, in terms of the perceivable realizations of institutional identity, there has been a lack of systematic studies at the lexico-grammatical stratum, and lexical choices in particular have been rarely explored (Benwell and Stokoe 2006). Recently, there are a few researches on identity from an intermodal perspective on the basis of Systemic Functional Semiotics (Bednarek and Martin 2010). As this intermodal study of institutional is still at its infant stage, there leaves much room for improvement.

The current study will take a different path to institutional identity construction (IIC), that is, an intermodal approach in accordance with the three hierarchical dimensions of Systemic Functional Linguistics (SFL), namely realization, instantiation and individuation. A combination of quantitative and qualitative methods is adopted. An image-text realization model of IIC at the lexico-grammatical level is established in accordance with the metafunction theory. It is expected that the institutional identity of each genre will be construed through its unique discursive pattern.

2. Data collection

The data collected in the study are the genres of print advertisements (PA) and linguistic research articles (LRA) that show the identities of advertising and academic institutions respectively. The multimodal print advertisements are collected from the British news weekly *Broadcast* dated from January of 2010 to March of 2011. The academic articles of linguistics are collected from two books of SFL, *New Discourse on Language* (Bednarek and Martin 2010) and *New Directions in the Analysis of Multimodal Discourse* (Royce and Bowcher 2007), and from four academic journals of linguistics, *The Modern Language Journal* (2008), *ELT Journal* (2010), *Applied Linguistics* (2010) and *Journal of English Linguistics* (2010; 2011). One hundred multimodal texts of each genre will be analyzed and counted in detail in accordance with their specific realizations.

3. The image-text realization of IIC

The following three points account for the theoretical basis of the study. The first is the idea of construing experience through grammar, that's to say, it is the grammar itself that construes our world of events and objects (Hjelmslev 1943; Firth 1957). In the view of Hjelmslev (1943), reality is unknowable and only things that are known are our construal of them—that is, the meanings. Meanings do not "exist" before the wordings that realize them. They are formed out of the impact between our consciousness and its environment. The second is the view of semiotic resources, which does not treat language as the only source for construing the reality (Halliday, 1978). Other semiotic resources such as displayed art (O'Toole 1994), actions (Martinec 1978), visual images (Kress and van Leeuwen 1996), and sound (van Leeuwen 1999) are also employed to construe human experience. The third is meta-redundancy— a symbolic construal between signifier and signified proposed by Saussure (Thibault 1997: 154) that was developed by Halliday (1978: 225) to refer to the mutual realizing relationships among the three layers of language. Following Martin's stratification of context (Martin 1992, 1997), this study holds that the institutional identities of specific genres at the sub-cultural stratum along the individuation cline (Martin 2010) can be realized by specific semantic and lexicogrammatic resources.

The study of IIC is explored from the perspective of the three meta-functions. Meta-functionally speaking, the interpersonal meaning is concerned with the relationship between the addresser and the addressee, and hence is closely related to IIC. However, the inseparability and complementarity among the three meta-functions makes it less likely to exclude the other two meta-functions' contributions to IIC. With regard to the relation between the representational meaning and institutional identity, Martin and Rose (2008: 13-14) confirm:

Field is concerned with the discursive pattern that realizes the activity that is going on. Technically speaking, a field consists of sequences of activities that are oriented to some global institutional purpose, whether this is a local domestic institution such as family or community, or a broader societal institution such as bureaucracy, industry or academia.

It is found that the analysis of the ideational meaning cannot do without that of the textual meaning. Drawing on Martin's concept of "coupling" (Martin 2010: 20), in this study names the combination of ideational and textual meanings is called the coupling of the ideational meaning and the textual meaning. Therefore, the image-text realization means chosen in this model are based on the following two points: the coupling of ideational and textual meanings, and the interpersonal meaning. An institution, as a social construction, produces binary and asymmetrical roles, and possesses the characteristics of dynamic and multiplicity (Benwell and Stokoe 2006). Based on the principles stated above, the image-text realization model of IIC is set up, as shown in Table 1.

Ideationally and textually, the paper argues that the institutional texts of different genres will present various visual representational processes and discursive patterns. It assumes that the frequencies of represented and interactive participants (Kress and van Leeuwen 2006: 48), combined with their transitivity analyses (Halliday 1994: 143) can better explore ideationally the logico-semantic relation (Halliday 1994) of the image-text relation unique to each genre. Based on the unique nature of each mode, the paper holds that images and texts are in complementary relation. Besides, the sense relations among the visual representative participants of each genre in combination with the analysis of textual organizations also will reflect the unique descriptive pattern of each institutional text.

Table 1   Image-text realization model of IIC

Meta-functions	Images	Texts	Image-text relations
Ideational coupled with Textual	Representational processes Textual organizations	Transitivity; Participants' tracking Descriptive patterns	Logico-semantic relations Sense relations
Interpersonal	Coding orientations Modality	Attitude; Use of "we" and "you"; Modality	Congruence vs. dissonance in terms of subjectivity and objectivity

Interpersonally, the focus lies in the analysis of the congruency obtained by images and texts in embodying the authors' subjectivity and objectivity. The paper holds that for different readers different types of institutional texts will have their own visual coding orientations and modality (Kress and van Leeuwen 2006: 165). With regard to the verbal description of the images, the attitudinal meaning at both clausal and lexical levels (Martin 2000: 156-160) can display in detail how the addressers appreciate as well as judge their products or achievements. The use of the first personal and the second personal plurals "we" (Wodak 1999: 44) and "you", as the markers of group identity alignment, will reveal the degree of the addressers' negotiation with the audience. In addition, the verbal modality (Halliday 1994; Palmer 2001) of each genre is expounded to show whether the keynote of the genre is subjective or objective.

According to Table 1, this paper will elaborate the discursive features closely related to the institutional identity construction of the two genres in the following two aspects. With respect to the coupling of the ideational and textual meanings, the representational meaning of images is explored first, which is followed by the transitivity analysis of verbal texts. Participant tracing is analyzed to explore the image-text relations, showing how the verbal texts describe the visual images. Interpersonally, the images' coding orientations are explored first, the attitudinal meanings are analyzed both at the clausal and lexical levels, and then the use of the interactive participants and modality is then discussed.

4. Instantiation of institutional identity

In the view of Halliday and Matthiessen (1999: 323), as a scale of generalization, instantiation relates the system to the instance, aggregating the meaning potential of a culture across instances of use. Martin (2010) and Matthiessen (2007) further develop the theory of instantiation by introducing the concepts of "coupling" and "commitment", which are crucial concepts in multimodal discourse analysis where synergies between modalities of communication are a major concern. Coupling is defined as the way in which meanings combine—across strata, meta-functions, ranks, and simultaneous systems (and across modalities), as pairs, triplets, quadruplets or any number of coordinated choices from system networks (Martin 2010: 20). Coupling analysis in this paper focuses on the way in which meanings combine across modalities and meta-functions. Commitment refers to the amount of meaning potential activated in a particular process of instantiation—the relative semantic weight of a text in other words (Martin 2008: 497), and the semantic weight of each mode in this paper will be explored through the analysis of the image-text relations. System and instance are not in a static but dialectic relation, in the middle of which there exist "domains" with different degrees of generality. Specific genre is one of the layers between the IIC system and the actual discourses.

4.1 The coupling of ideational and textual meanings

4.1.1 The visual representational meaning

According to Kress and van Leeuwen (2006: 59), representational structures fall into two kinds: conceptual structures and narrative structures. While conceptual structures represent participants in terms of their class, structure or meaning, in other words, in terms of their generalized and more or less stable and timeless essence, narrative structures serve to present unfolding actions and events, processes of change, and transitory spatial arrangements. Representational analysis of the data shows that the most frequently-used images of PA are conceptual representations, accounting for 92% of the total, among which symbolic suggestive images make up the highest percent (48%). Figure 1 is an example of suggestive images.

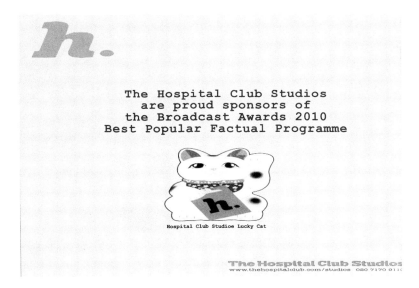

Figure 1   A symbolic suggestive process in PA (*Broadcast*, February, 2010)

As seen in Figure 1, there is only one participant (the Carrier) in this image, placed frontally in the centre of the page, against a de-emphasized background in light blue. There is no other participant but the letter "h" in the card held in the cat's right paw, representing the symbolical meaning attached to the Carrier, i.e. the hospitality of The Hospitable Club Studios. Here, the visual intuitive perception and the verbal symbolic value are combined together to attract the audience's attention and influence the consumers' behavior.

Inclusive analytical images account for 28% of all the conceptual representations. Inclusive analytical images contain no vector and display the commodities more or less frontally, against a de-emphasized background. The images only show some of the possessive attributes of the commodities, leaving many of the commodities unaccounted for. In PA, under normal conditions, the striking possessive attributes concerning the commodities, consumers or services are visualized to replace the whole commodity. Figure 2 is an example of inclusive analytical images.

Figure 2   An inclusive analytical image in PA (*Broadcast*, January, 2010)

It is shown in Figure 2 that the partial material image (Possessive Attribute) of the *Avid Media Composer 4* (Carrier) is placed frontally on the upper side of the page, representing the whole commodity and its function, as shown in the primary announcement "the world's most advanced film and video editing system". Here, the indefinite meaning of the commodity's excellent quality attached to the image is articulated by the verbal text.

Apart from the static presentations, the commodities can be visualized in narrative ways, which is shown in Figure 3. In the view of Kress and van Leeuwen (2006: 78), in a unidirectional transactional reaction, there is only one participant (Actor or Goal) at the two ends of an arrow-shaped vector. The vectors in Figure 3, in various shapes and pointing to different directions, are highlighted with dark colors, against a de-emphasized grey background, pointing out the locations of *bespoke studios* (Goal), that is, "anywhere in the UK" stated in the primary announcement (the words in red according to Cheong's (2004) classification). The emphasis lies in the Goal, as stated in the Enhancer (the words in grey) that "Let us build you a temporary or permanent studio on your own doorstep", and the Actor (*roll to record*), i.e. the advertiser, is shown on the bottom right.

Figure 3   A unidirectional transactional action in PA (*Broadcast*, March, 2010)

Similar to PA, conceptual images are still favored by AA, accounting for 91.6% of the total LRA images, but their forms are much more complex, as is shown in Table 2.

Table 2   Visual representational meanings of LRA

Representational meanings	Processes	Realizations	Occurrences	Frequencies
Conceptual	Classification;	Tree diagram	89	11.1%
	Inclusive analytical;	Drawing	72	9%
	Exhaustive analytical;	Table	286	35.8%
		drawing	102	12.7%
	Dimensional and	Bar chart	112	14%
	quantitative topographical;	pie chart		
	Spatio-temporal	Line graph	72	9%
Narrative	Bidirectional;		28	3.5%
	Unidirectional;	Drawing and	21	2.6%
	Nontransactional reaction;	photo	12	1.5%
	Mental		6	0.8%

The statistics show that the conceptual images in LRA are mainly composed of analytical and classification images. Among the analytical images, exhaustive analytical images make up the largest proportion (48.5%), followed by dimensional and quantitative topographical images (14%) and spatio-temporal images (9%). Specifically, exhaustive analytical images consist of tables and drawings, in which tables, as the most text-like visual displays (Lemke 1998), can condense or quantify the authors' achievements, and make up the highest percentage of 35.8% in LRA.

Apart from the text-like visual display, the exhaustive analytical processes can also be realized by drawings or diagrams.

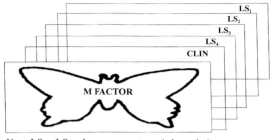

Note. $LS_1 - LS_4$ = language systems 1 through 4;
CLIN = crosslinguistic interaction.

Figure 4   An exhaustive analytical process in LRA
(*The Modern Language Journal*, 2008: 276)

Figure 4 from *The Modern Language Journal* (2008: 276) is an exhaustive analytical process, which exhaustively represent the possessive attributes of the Carrier with all of its space taken up by possessive attributes. As can be seen in this figure, there is an assembly (Carrier) in which the Possessive Attributes, including the rectangles labeled *M Factor, CLIN, L4, L3, L2 and L1*, are joined together to display the author's findings or achievement (Carrier). In order to convince the audience, the author exhaustively diagrams the factors (Possessive Attributes) related to his concept (Carrier).

4.1.2 The verbal ideational meaning

Due to the limited space, nominal groups, accounting for 18.9% of the total verbal descriptions of the images in PA, are a vital means for information transmission. The advertisement of *FTV* is a prime example, and the screenshot of the verbal text is shown in Figure 5.

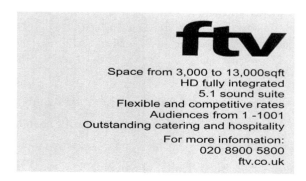

Figure 5   The verbal text of a PA in the realization of nominal groups
(*Broadcast*, February, 2010)

The transitivity structure of the processes implied by the nominal groups in Figure 4 is analyzed as follows:

(1) Space (is) from 3,000 to 13,000sqf (circumstantial attributive).

(2) Sound suit (is) 5.1 (intensive identifying).

(3) The rates are flexible and competitive (intensive attributive).

(4) (The phone number is) 020 8900 5800(intensive identifying).

In LRA, the nominal groups only account for 5.3% of the total verbal descriptions of the images, and the processes are mainly intensive identifying in their omitted forms or embedded forms, which are indicated in the prepositional phrases "as [Token]/ [Value]" like (5) or in the brackets like (6) or behind the verbs like (7).

(5) Accordingly each clause places *this information in first position* [Value] (**as** *Theme* [Token])…

(6) …the model in Figure 1.6, which displays the meta-functional proportion, outlined above-with *field* [Token] (*a co-pattering of ideational meanings* [Value]…)

(7) Meta-redundancy in this context refers to the way in which the model **interprets** *lexico-grammar* [Token] **as** *an emergently complex pattern of phonological patterns* [Value]…

Apart from "be" and "become", lots of "equative" verbs are used in LRA to realize intensive identifying clauses, including "signal", "include", "illustrate", "equate to", "comprise", "require", "illustrate", "involve", "provide", "be represented as", "make up", "target at", "begin with", "serve to", "combine into", "show", "depict", "detail", "make reference to", "appear to", etc. In PA, the percentages of material processes (45.8%) and relational processes (45.5%) are almost the same, showing the advertisers' equal emphasis on the introduction of the commercial goods or services and the identifying of what they are and what they can do for the consumers. In LRA, the material processes (31.6%) are less than relational processes (55.8%), among which intensive identifying processes (39.9%) are most favored by authors as a vital means for the introduction of the elements in the images, including their definitions, characteristics, functions, relations and the authors' attitudes toward them. Take *Thairath* (on March 15, 2007) for example:

(8) In total, there are 30 visual units on the page, and *these* [Token] **combine** *into 14 textual units* [Value] *each of which* [Token] **consists of** *one or more visual units* [Value]. *Textual units on the page* [Token] **are** *texts* [Value] (e.g. advertisement, masthead, news story), *which* [Token] **consists of** *one or more visual units* [Value].

In this verbal interpretation, there are five clauses, among which one is possessive attributive clause and the other four are intensive identifying clauses, introducing the elements in the image and the relation among them.

Participants tracking shows that the image-text relation of enhancement in PA is reflected by the highest percentage of the participants not contained in the images, including representative participants of companies or enterprises realized by explicit proper nouns as in (9) or similar substitutes (35.7%) as in (10), specific elements concerning the commodities (15.5%) which qualify the images with circumstantial features of time and place like contact information in (4), and interactive participants in the realizations of non-addressee "we" as in (11) and "you" referring to the potential consumers (48.8%) as in (12).

(9) ...**twofour54intaj** *offers* you and your team 6 fully equipped HD production studios, 22 post-production suites, a playout centre with teleport and the Arab World's first commercially available media asset management and digital archiving service...

(10) ... **a production partner** who'*s* at the cutting edge

(11) **We** *are* twofour54...

(12) ..., **you** *need* a production partner...

In LRA, the image-text relation of elaboration is shown by the highest percentage of the represented participants of images (87.5%) with super-ordinates (19%) and co-hyponyms (53.9%). Superordinates here refer to the represented participants generalizing the core ideas of the images, which mainly denote the abstract relations, perspectives, aims or conclusions of the study. Co-hyponyms refer to the members of the same class. Two examples are listed to show what the superordinates are.

(13) As it says, "**The point of this discussion** [Aim] of the privileging of paradigmatic relations is to illustrate the way in which meta-functional complementarity adds dimensionality to realization hierarchy in SFL-the meta-functions in other words provide an additional perspective on meanings that are organized as layers of abstraction."

(14) **A crude representation of the interplay of realization and metafuntion** [Conclusion] is outlined in Fig. 1.4 above.

As regards the textual organization of images, the "center marginal" type (34%) is frequently used in PA with the visual images in the center and the verbal texts in the marginal, followed by the "up down" type (26%) with the visual images in the upper part and the verbal text in the lower part, and by the "foreground background" type (18%) with the verbal text in the foreground and the visual images in the background. In reference to the verbal descriptive manner, the verbal descriptive pattern of PA is Generic→ (Specific), which is reflected by the highest percentage of the generic description (53.6%) in the realizations of the proper nouns or the substitutes (including "we") and lower percentage of the specific elements concerning the commodities (15.5%). In LRA, the verbal descriptive pattern is "Generic↔Specific→ (Generic)" shown by the frequently-used represented participants in the images (Co-hyponyms), which are generalized by certain represented terms or concepts (Superordinates). As seen in this pattern, the first two stages "Generic↔ Specific" are bidirectional and the last one "(Generic)" is optional. An example is cited from Martin's (2010: 24) "individuation and affiliation cline" to illustrate how the pattern "Superordinate Co-hyponyms Superordinate" works.

(15) Before turning to a brief discussion of genesis in relation to realization, instantiation and individuation, let's pause again to remind ourselves that **all strata** [Superordinate] individuate. In linguistics in general, **low level individuation** (i.e. phonological and morphological variation) [Co-hyponym] has tended to be referred to as dialectal; **semantic variation** [Co-hyponym], as explored in SFL, has generally been termed codal. Dialectal and codal variation can be generalized in relation to individuation in the model being developed here since all strata of realization are relevant. **This complementarity of realization and individuation** [Superordinate] is reinforced in Figure..."

4.2 Interpersonal meaning

4.2.1 Visual coding orientations and modality

62% of the PA images feature natural coding orientations, 28% of the images feature abstract coding orientations, while 12% are a coupling of natural and technological coding orientations. Usually, the images in print advertisements are coded within the bounds of naturalistic depiction that all members of the culture share. This "just being themselves" orientation provides the consumers an intuitional presentation of the commercial products or services. Obviously, parts of the real commercial products presented in inclusive analytical processes are of this kind, and so are the story-telling images presented in the narrative processes. Typical examples include the partial presentation of *Avid Media Composer 4*, the partial outlooking of *3 Mills Studios* and the representative consumer of a real or famous person in *Broadcast*. These photographic images are real and objective correspondences of realities. Being faithful to the appearances, these photographic images are endowed with the highest modality, somewhat less than full color saturation along the color continuum.

Apart from the naturalistic images, PA in *Broadcast* is unique in its degree of employing abstract and technological images. Take Figure 6 for example. Obviously, the *Broadcast Digital Awards 2010* is symbolized as colorful radio waves against a black background, whose commercial information is specified in the verbal text.

In LRA, the coding orientations are mainly abstract and technological, which show a course of abstraction declination and can be explored as a cline in relation to their degree of self-sufficiency or abstractness. In accordance with Lemke's classification (1998: 88-96), and with the views of Kress and van Leeuven's (2006: 164) and Myers's (1990) on the modality value of color, the images can be listed in the decreasing order of the degree of abstractness of the coding orientations they realize as follows: tables, tree diagrams, bar charts, pie charts, line graphs, drawings or diagrams in conceptual images, and drawings and photos in narrative images. The higher degree of abstractness of LRA is reflected by the high percentage of tables, followed by the percentage of bar charts and pie charts, tree diagrams and line graphs successively, which represents the authors' academic achievements obtained from a combination of the qualitative and quantitative methods.

Figure 6　A symbolic suggestive process in PA (*Broadcast*, March, 2010)

However, narrative images still account for 8.4%. Besides, the geometric shapes of exhaustive analytical processes in the conceptual images still have some natural or organic elements represented by circles or curved arrows. With regard to the interpersonal meaning of these geometric shapes, Kress and van Leeuwen (2006) conclude that circles, curved lines, and more naturalistic shapes alike are loaded with organic and natural interpersonal meaning, while squares, rectangles and straight lines alike are embodied with mechanical and technological interpersonal meaning. In order to explore features unique to LRA, the visual resources of the conceptual drawings or diagrams in the journals and books of linguistics are classified and counted, as is shown in Table 3.

Table 3   Visual resources of conceptual drawings in LRA

Abstractness	Geometrical Shapes	Occurrences
Abstract	Circles	28
	Circles with irregular shapes	34
	Rectangles with irregular shapes	4
	Irregular shapes	8
	Vectors	36
	Rectangles	32
Concrete	Naturalistic images	26

Their frequencies show that circles take the highest percentage, followed successively by irregular shapes, vectors, rectangles and naturalistic images. The "natural" and "organic" features of conceptual processes are illustrated in Figure 7.

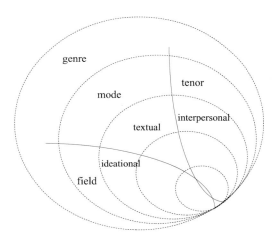

Figure 7   Image in the realization of circles (Martin 2010: 16)

In SFL, this diagram visualizes the relationships between human language and social context in a compact way. Context is stratifified into genre and register (a patterning of field, tenor and mode variables), while the other three circles indicate the three strata of language (phonology, lexicogrammar and semantics). The co-tangential circles describe the metareduant relation between the strata of language and context, that is, a lower stratum is reduant (mutually predictable) with an upper layer, and the integration of the two strata is again reduant with an even upper-strata. The demarcation of the circles by the two curves into three areas depicts the trinocular perspectives (mutafunctional diversity) of SFL to the language and context.

4.2.2 The verbal interpersonal meaning

In terms of the attitudinal meaning, in PA, the advertisers tend to appreciate the quality, impact and value of the commercial products or services, particularly their commercial significance in a positive way, which is marked by the highest percentage of positive valuation. In the mean time, the commercial products and services are judged with respect to their normality and capacity, particularly their leading or pioneering status in media industry. At times the advertisers' and consumers' imagined positive attitudes towards the commercial products and services are used to arouse similar feeling of the audience and drive consumers' behavior. In addition, the keynote of PA is more subjective, which is reflected by the addressee-exclusive "we", the directives of consumers' actions and less use of modality expressing uncertainty.

In LRA, there is no affect and the subcategories of appreciation and judgement are more various than those in PA. Generally the authors will not overtly show their emotions in consideration of the need of objectivity in academic articles. However, their appreciation and judgement about their ideas or achievements are inevitable. On one hand, their academic achievements are treated as products to be appreciated in terms of their quality, reaction, composition and valuation, among which the appreciation of quality and composition are more frequently used, reflecting the authors' explication of their original ideas or achievements. On the other hand, in order to show their rationality and to obtain the recognition of the audience, the authors will make judgements about their academic ideas or achievements in terms of normality, capacity, tenacity, propriety and veracity, among which normality and capacity appear more frequently, reflecting the authors' explanation of the popularity and functions of their achievements in their respective fields. As for modality, the modals used in LRA and their frequencies are overviewed in Table 4.

Table 4　Frequencies of modality in LRA

Modals		Modality categories	Occurrences	Frequencies
Central modal verbs	will	epistemic deductive	32	12.2 4.2 39.2 4.6 15.2 12.2
	would	epistemic deductive	11	
	can	evidential sensory	103	
		epistemic speculative	12	
	may	epistemic speculative	40	
Modal adverbs	probably perhaps	epistemic probability	32	
Verbs with Model meanings	seem; suggest argue	epistemic probability	33	12.4

Total occurrences of these modals divided by 100 show that there are 2.63 modals in a linguistic research article, much higher than 0.22 in a print advertisement. Specifically, the evidential sensory modal "can" appears frequently, reflecting the authors' invitation of the same or similar perceptions or thoughts of the audience, as is exemplified in (16) and (17).

(16) …we **can** *think of* individuation along two trajectories, basically asking whether we are classifying identities or negotiating them. …we **can** *conceive of* a culture dividing into smaller and smaller communities as *we* move form the community as a whole…What we are concerned with here is power…Revising direction, we **can** *conceive of* persona aligning…Along this trajectory we are concerned with…

(17) …through this representation, we **can** *get a sense of* the metafunctions mapping relatively well onto one another to achieve a certain level of coherence…

5. Affiliation of institutional identity

In SFL, individuation specializes meaning potential according to users rather than uses of language (Martin 2010: 22). Bernstein (1996: 158) regards individuation as a cline, at one end of which individuation has to do with the reservoir of meanings in a culture, and at the other with the repertoire a given individual can mobilize. In Bernstein's (ibid.) code theory, realization rules enable speakers to produce culturally specific texts and practices. Based on Bernstein's individuation cline, Martin (2010: 24) develops his own cline of individuation and affiliation for construing identity, and concludes that the main concern of affiliation is negotiating identities. Along the affiliation trajectory, personas align themselves into sub-cultures, configuring master identities and constituting a culture. Guided by this cline, the current study focuses on the construing of the group identity of each institution. Along the affiliation cline, authors of institutional texts are conceived of aligning themselves into their own institutions at the sub-cultural stratum through the shared visual and verbal discursive features at the lexico-grammatical stratum. Accordingly, the proof of the institutional identity of each genre lies in its unique image-text discursive pattern.

In my data, each genre has its specific discursive pattern and the institutional identities of the two genres are restricted to the broadcasting advertising and academic institutional identities, showing the delicacy of the model of IIC. A comparison of the two genres will be made to illustrate how these institutional identities are construed through their discursive patterns. The comparison is two-fold: the coupling of ideational and textual meanings, and the interpersonal meaning.

In terms of the coupling of the ideational and textual meanings, the discursive pattern of

PA is reflected in the image-text relation of enhancement and the verbal descriptive pattern of "Generic→(Specific)", and the discursive pattern of LRA is reflected in the image-text relation of elaboration and the verbal descriptive pattern of "Generic↔ Specific→(Generic)".

As far as the images' representational meaning is concerned, PA is unique in its highest percentage of symbolic suggestive images followed by inclusive analytical images, mainly representing the commercial services or goods in media industries; LRA is distinctive for its highest percentage of conceptual images, among which the most frequent is exhaustive analytical processes, followed successively by dimensional and quantitative topographical processes, classification processes, inclusive analytical processes and spatio-temporal processes, representing the authors' academic achievements obtained from a combination of the qualitative and quantitative methods.

As regards the verbal texts, in PA, the material and intensive identifying processes take up higher percentages and are used to introduce the commercial goods or services, identifying what they are and explaining what they can do for the consumers. In addition, the higher percentages of the participants qualifying the images with circumstantial features of time and place indicate the image-text relation of enhancement. In LRA, the highest percentage of relational identifying processes strengthens the scientific and objective features of LRA, reflecting the academic authors' intention to objectively explicate what their results or achievements are.

The pattern of the interpersonal meaning of PA is reflected by the congruence between the advertisers' subjectivity of visual images and that of verbal texts; the pattern of the interpersonal meaning of LRA is reflected by the congruence between the academic authors' objective attitude and mutual consultation of visual images and those of verbal texts.

As far as the visual coding orientations are concerned, the specialty of PA lies in its adoption of abstract and technological coding orientations apart from the naturalistic one, which reflects the scientific and technological features of the commodities in media industry. The coding orientations of LRA are mainly abstract and technological, in accordance with the scientific and objective features of academic articles. Color is mainly black and white with highest modality in terms of color saturation. Besides, a fewer percentage of naturalistic coding orientation and the organic and human geometrical shapes used in the drawings reveal the social and human features of LRA in linguistics.

With regard to the verbal interpersonal meaning, the two genres are different in their use of interactive participants and modality. PA has a highest percentage of interactive participants (including the addressee-exclusive "we" and the direct involvement of "you") and a lower percentage of modality, to show the advertisers' implicit subjectivity when explicitly negotiating with the consumers. Strikingly, the percentage of the interactive participants in LRA is more than double that of PA. Their participants include the addressee-inclusive "we", the direct involvement of "you" in imperative mood and the authors related to the images, reflecting the authors' negotiation with the audience with respect to their academic ideas. The objectivity of the LRA is enhanced by the frequent use of addressee-inclusive "we" followed by the mental verbs to arouse the same perceptions and thoughts of the audience concerning their academic achievements.

In addition to the use of interactive participants and modality, the attitudinal meanings of the two genres also differ in some way. Though the images of the two genres are all treated as products that are appreciated as well as judged, the advertisers in PA tend to appreciate the quality, impact, and particularly the value of the commodities in a positive way and judge their normality and capability, so as to announce their leading and innovative status in the media industry; the authors of LRA show their concern over the appreciation of the quality, balance and complexity of their results and the judgement of their social esteem such as normality, capacity and tenacity as well as their social sanction like veracity and propriety.

To sum up, the specific institutional identity of each genre is constructed through its distinctive intermodal discursive pattern. In terms of the fixed, pre-discursive and complementary pair roles (Benwell and Stokoe 2006: 87) in each genre, the broadcasting advertising institutional identity of PA in *Broadcast* integrates the roles of the authoritative advertisers and the specific consumers; the social scientific academic institutional identity of LRA integrates the roles of objective academic authors and professional audience.

6. Conclusion

This study has adopted an intermodal perspective to institutional identity construction on the basis of the semantic dimensions of realization, instantiation and individuation in SFL. It aims at establishing a viable image-text realization model to construe institutional identity. The specific process of institutional identity construction has been explored through the analysis of ideational-textual meaning coupling and interpersonal meanings in two genres (print advertisements and linguistic research articles) realized by both image and verbal resources.

It is found that the institutional identity of PA in *Broadcast* is broadcasting advertisement, which integrates roles of both authoritative advertisers and target consumers. Ideationally and textually, its discursive pattern is reflected in the image-text relation of enhancement and the Generic→(Specific) verbal descriptive pattern. Particularly, the images of PA in *Broadcast* is unique in its highest percentage of symbolic suggestive processes in abstract and technological coding orientations, which is unlike food advertisement with images of inclusive analytical processes usually coded in naturalistic coding orientations.

The institutional identity of LRA is socially and scientifically academic, integrating roles of both objective academic authors and professional audience. Ideationally and textually, its discursive pattern is reflected in the image-text relation of elaboration and the "Generic↔Specific→(Generic) verbal descriptive pattern". The scientific identity of LRA is reflected in its highest percentage of conceptual images visualized in tables, bar charts and line graphs to represent authors' quantitative work, and its social nature in the frequent use of the geometrical shapes loaded with organic and natural interpersonal meaning as circles, curved lines, and the like in diagrams.

The embedded institutional features of the images have justified the addition of semiotic modes other than language as effective resources to facilitate the construction of institutional identity. It is suggested that future studies of image-text construction of institutional identity be carried out on the basis of in larger corpora to further improve the model.

Notes

1. Discourse in the study refers to text realized both linguistically and visually, while text in "image-text" relation only refers to the associated verbal interpretation of the images.

References

Bednarek, M. and J. R. Martin (eds.). 2010. *New Discourse on Language: Functional Perspectives on Multimodality, Identity and Affiliation*. London: Continuum.

Benwell, B and E. Stokoe. 2006. *Discourse and Identity*. Edinburgh: Edinburgh University Press.

Bernstein, B. 1996. *Pedagogy, Symbolic Control and Identity: Theory, Research, Critique*. London: Taylor and Francis.

Cheong, Y. Y. 2004. The construal of ideational meaning in print advertisements. In K. L. O'Halloran (ed.), *Multimodal Discourse Analysis: Systemic-Functional Perspectives*. 163-195. London: Continuum.

Firth, J. R. Modes of meaning. 1957. In J. R. Firth (ed.), *Papers in Linguistics*. 190-215. London: Oxford University Press.

Halliday, M. A. K. and C. Matthiessen. 1999. *Construing Experience through Meaning: A Language-based Approach to Cognition*. London: Continnum.

Halliday, M. A. K. 1961. Categories of the theory of grammar. *Word*, 17 (3), 241-292.

Halliday, M. A. K. 1978. *Language as Social Semiotic: The Social Interpretation of Language and Meaning*. London: Edward Arnold Limited.

Halliday, M. A. K. 1994. *An Introduction to Functional Grammar*. London: Edward Arnold Limited.

Hjelmslev, L. 1943. *Prolegomena to a Theory of Language*. Madison: University of Wisconsin Press.

Kress, G. and T. van Leeuwen. 2006. *Reading Images* (2nd edition). London: Routledge.

Lemke, J. L. 1998. Multiplying meaning: Visual and verbal semiotics in scientific text. In J.R. Martin and R.

Veel (eds.), *Reading Science*. 87-113. London: Routledge.

Martin, J. R. 1992. *English Text: System and Structure*. Amsterdam: John Benjamins Publishing Company.

Martin, J. R. 2000. Beyond exchange: Appraisal systems in English. In S. Hunston and G. Thompson. *Evaluation in Text: Authorial Stance and the Construction of Discourse*. 142-175. Oxford: Oxford University Press.

Martin, J. R. 2008. Tenderness: Realization and instantiation in a Botswanan town. In Z. H. Wang (ed.), *The SFL Theory, Volumn 1: The Collected Works of J. R. Martin*. 484-513. Shanghai: Shanghai Jiao Tong University Press.

Martin, J. R. 2010. Semantic Variation—Modelling realization, instantiation and individuation in social semiosis. In M. Bednarek and J. R. Martin (eds.), *New Discourse on Language: Functional Perspectives on Multimodality, Identity and Affiliation*. 1-34. London: Continuum.

Martin, J. R. and D. Rose. 2008. *Genre Relations: Mapping Culture*. London: Equinox.

Martinec, R. 1998. Cohesion in action. *Semiotica*, 120 (1-2): 161-80.

Matthiessen, C. M. I. M. 2007. The multimodal page: A systematic functional exploration. In T. D. Royce and W. L. Bowcher, *New Directions in the Analysis of Multimodal Discourse*. 1-62. New Jersey: Lawrence Erlbaum Associates.

Myers, G. 1990. *Writing Biology*. Madison: University of Wisconsin Press.

O'Toole, M. 1994. *The Language of Displayed Art*. Leicester: Leicester University Press.

Palmer, F. R. 2001. *Mood and Modality*. Cambridge: Cambridge University Press.

Royce, T. D. and W. L. Bowcher. 2007. *New Directions in the Analysis of Multimodal Discourse*. New Jersey: Lawrence Erlbaum Associates.

van Leeuwen, T. 1999. *Speech, Music, Sound*. London: Macmillan.

Wodak, R., R. de Cillia., M. Reisigl. and K. Liebhart. 1999. *The Discursive Construction of National Identity*. (Translated by A. Hirsch and R. Mitten). Edinburgh: Edinburgh University Press Ltd.

Part Four

Translation and Computational Linguistic Studies

Nominalization and Pinyin in Chinese-to-English Translation

Tangjin Xiao

Guizhou Minzu University, China

1. Introduction

Nominalization is a grammatical metaphor in Systemic Functional Grammar. It embodies the functions of static information packaging, probably first occurring in texts of science and technology and then extending to other fields. In translation from Chinese to English, Pinyin (Romanization using the Chinese letter pronunciation marking) is more often than not adopted, particularly when events, objects and persons uniquely related to China are concerned. In this paper we will first explore the notion of nominalization from such perspectives as Systemic Functional Grammar, cognitive linguistics and cultural linguistics. Afterwards, we will illustrate that as a translation device Pinyin can be regarded as nominalization, highlighting discourse ideology. Nevertheless, there are disadvantages in using Pinyin. Hence, it is necessary to use Pinyin with caution in the Chinese-to-English translation.

2. Nominalization

In Systemic Functional Grammar nominalization is related to grammatical metaphor, which differs from lexical metaphor. "*A flood of people*" is simply a lexical metaphor, equivalent to "*many people*". In a similar vein, the word "*fox*" in "*he is a fox*" is a lexical metaphor, meaning "*cunning*". In the eyes of Systemic Functional Grammar, metaphor is interwoven with syntax or morphology and nominalization is a powerful means of grammatical metaphor. For instance, "*the car industry was nationalized in this city in 1956*" can be converted to a nominalization—"*the nationalization of car industry in this city in 1956*". In terms of origin, Chaucer first used nominalization in 1391 during the Renaissance. Halliday and Matthiessan (2008: 284) hold that nominalization is an information packaging. Hu (2004: 186) distinguishes the "rough" from "refined" expressions, corresponding to non-nominalization and nominalization termed as Doric and Attic respectively by Halliday.

Cognitive linguists explore nominalization from the perspectives of experience philosophy. Hayvaert (2003: 42-50) expounds the cognitive features of nominalization from the angle of usage-based model. First, nominalization reflects the schemata and schematic expansion of low-level and high-level cognitive components. Take *"all the interesting people"* for example. *"People"* is a high-level cognitive component, whereas *"all"*, *"the"* and *"interesting"* are low-level cognitive components, their composition being a result of schemata and schematic expansion. Second, nominalization occurs as language use interacts with linguistic system, displaying such features as entrenchment and specificity. In the diachronic light it has been prolific. Third, nominalization demonstrates rank shift, reclassification, and especially functional reclassification.

Nida (2004: 75-77), a famous translatologist and cross-cultural expert, analyzes the nominal group *"the reinforcing impacts of natural resource depletion and human destitution"* in *"the reinforcing impacts of natural resource depletion and human destitution are exemplified by trends in the world's farmlands"*. He argues that the difficulty of understanding this clause lies in structural complexity, while in translating the specified nominal group attention must be paid to semantic features and relations as well as the stylistic demand of the target language. Nida's cross-cultural view reminds us that nominalization is related to translation strategies.

3. Pinyin and nominalization

In translation from Chinese to English, particularly when unique Chinese events, objects and persons are involved, Pinyin is commonly adopted. In fact, Pinyin pertains to a matter of translatability vs. untranslatability. Feng (1996: 11-13) proposes the dichotomy of translatability and untranslatability. First, untranslatability is inextricably a byproduct of context. Different people have different understandings of a certain expression in the target language. Hence, untranslatability may come into being. The Chinese medical term *"qi"* is a good example. Literally, it means *"air"*. Nevertheless, in Chinese medicine it means something very much different. *"Qi"* is considered to be the most fundamental and minute material constituting human body and maintaining life activities as well as physiological functions. It seems that no better expression than Pinyin can reveal the meanings of this Chinese medical term. Second, cultural ideology is relevant to untranslatability. In *The Analects* *"ren"* (literally meaning *"virtue"*) is not simply a virtue, but the sum of all virtues. Sun and Tian (2008: 30-32) translate *"ren"* as *"perfect virtue"*. This is in fact a semantic translation or a demonstration of domestication, which can hardly reveal the profound Chinese culture advocated in Confucianism. We argue that in this case semantic translation is not as effective as Pinyin or "Pinyin + English explanation"—a strategy of foreignization or semi-foreignization. As a translation strategy, foreignization can better display an awareness of Chinese culture and contribute to the avoidance of missed translation. According to Xinhuanet.com on Aug. 16, 2013, "*dama*" (literally meaning "*aunts*") become a powerful force of gold purchase as reported by *The Wall Street Daily*, pushing the prices of gold higher than before. The word "*dama*" illustrates the influence of Chinese culture on the world. Meanwhile, it tells us that Pinyin has strong vitality.

As mentioned above, nominalization is featured with information packaging and schemata in terms of Systemic Functional Grammar and cognitive linguistics, and related to stylistic demand in terms of cultural linguistics. Our examination on Pinyin shows that most Pinyin expressions in Chinese-to-English translation are nouns or nominal groups, and consist with the definition and traits of nominalization. Hence, Pinyin can be assumed as a device of nominalization in the English version texts of Chinese information. Pinyin is a phonetic loan or a means of transliteration, and expresses unique Chinese events, objects and persons. For instance, "*yin*" (a Chinese philosophical notion), "*yang*" (a Chinese philosophical notion), "*jiaozi*" (a Chinese food), "*qigong*" (a Chinese fitness exercise) and "*fengshui*" (a Chinese divination) are loaded with strong Chinese cultural traits. If they are put in English rather than Chinese Pinyin they can hardly mean what they are intended to mean. The mascot of 2008 Beijing Olympic Games is another case in question. It was originally expressed as "*Friendlie*", but later changed to the Pinyin version "*Fuwa*". In Chinese, "*Fuwa*" means good luck, loveliness, and friendship. Thus, the English version "*Friendly*" does not suffice to convey the Chinese connotations. In contrast, the Pinyin expression serves the point. What should be noticed here is that Pinyin can express something good as well as something bad which is uniquely Chinese. "*Chengguan*" (administrators in charge of urban order*)*, "*fangnu*" (people who have to work most of their life for an apartment), "*dingzihu*" (urban residents who refuse to move from their original houses to be demolished), "*xiaokang*" (a well-off life as advocated by the Communist Party of China) are cases in this sense. Liu (2010: 38-41) and Zhu (2010: 53-56) have done research on some of these expressions unique in China.

Pinyin expressions in the Chinese-to-English translation may appear in two ways. First, there are literal direct Pinyin expressions, for example, "*tai chi*" (a Chinese fitness program), "*tangyuan*" (a Chinese snack or delicay), "*majiang*" (a Chinese game), and "*moutai*" (a famous Chinese liquor). It is noted here that some Pinyin expressions are not derived from the contemporary Modern Chinese Pinyin system but the Wade system, for instance "*tai chi*" and "*moutai*". Second, there are "Pinyin + English" expressions, for example, "*Gong Bao diced chicken*", "*Dong Po stewed pork*", and "*Ma Po tofu*". In this case, the Chinese Pinyin highlights Chinese origins while the English explanations add information to the designated events, objects and persons which may be confusing to those who are unfamiliar with Chinese culture. It is safe to argue that Pinyin is an important device to demonstrate the Chinese culture and ideology. As a means of foreignization, Pinyin contributes to Chinese discursive power on the world stage.

4. Pinyin and discourse ideology

Through our discussions, we can find that Pinyin contributes to discourse ideology in translated texts. Ru (2008: 50-54) suggests that translation can serve the "others" (i.e. the target language readers) as well as a cultural pursuit. Pinyin expressions are conducive to the cultural pursuit of the translator's own culture, hence indicating its specialties and even superiority in cross-cultural communication. The translator's role is evident here. Slingerland (2003) recommends that we translate Chinese culture-loaded words using the formula of "original Chinese character + English + Pinyin", for instance, "孝：filial piety (xiao)". Wang (2006) assumes that "cultural turn" has occurred in translation since the 1990s. Ge (1980) proposes the term "China English" for unique Chinese events, objects and persons. "*Baihua wen*" is the simplified Chinese expressions in contrast to ancient complex Chinese expressions. Like "*bagu wen*" (old official stereotyped Chinese essay), such Pinyin expressions record history and Chinese features. Chen (2013: 95-100) thinks that we should have a "cultural self-awareness" in translation and publicity, which is a way to establish a positive image for China on the global stage.

Take Chinese cultural publicity for instance. The following is about *hutong*, a narrow alleyway in Beijing (from www.bjta.gov.cn):

Beijing's hutongs are a glimpse - fast disappearing - of what the city used to look like before the skyscrapers started munching the skyline. A hutong is a narrow alleyway formed by joining together courtyard residences. When you hear people speak of 'the hutongs', they will often be referring to the neighborhoods formed by these alleys.

In this example, "*hutong*", revealing classic Beijing features and Chinese culture, cannot be replaced by the word "*alleyway*". Nevertheless, the English explanation helps foreigners roughly understand what this Chinese cultural phenomenon means. However, as the translation says, "*hutong*" also means "*the neighborhoods formed by these alleys*". Hence, the Pinyin expression "*hutong*" communicates something unique and valuable about Chinese culture to foreigners.

Sometimes, in a text about Chinese culture there may be a number of Pinyin terms. The adoption of multiple Pinyin expressions is conducive to the construction of a set of Chinese images. Consider the following example (from www.bjta.gov.cn):

As an ancient performing art in China, quyi is a general term that covers several different types of performances in which speech, singing or both are used. As an independent art, it was formed in the middle of the Tang Dynasty and flourished in the Song Dynasty. Now more than 300 forms of quyi are popular among all ethnic groups throughout the country. The most influential and widespread forms are jingyun dagu, meihua dagu, shulaibao, danxian, xiangsheng, pingshu, kuaiban, Tianjin shidiao, xihe dagu, Dongbei dagu, er'-renzhuan, Suzhou pinghua, Yangzhou pinghua, pingtan, Fengyang huagu, Shandong ginshu, Shandong kuaishu, Henan Zhuizi, Sichuan qingyin, Hubei daoqing, yuequ, Shanbei shuoshu and Mongolian haolaibao. Performances consist usually of only one, two or three people, with simple props and no stage scenery. Major singing forms, such as danxian, jingyun dagu and meihua dagu, normally tell short stories and the songs are short. Some combine singing with speech, such as Suzhou pingtan and Xihe dagu, and these are often long pieces. Some are half sung and half spoken, such as kuaiban and Shandong Kuaishu. Talking forms include pingshu and pinghua, which are used to tell long stories which continue over several months, in addition to xiangsheng, which involves short pieces that can be finished in a few minutes or even in a few lines. The performers sit as they sing in some forms, such as tanci, qinshu and pingshu, but walk up and down when singing in the er'renzhuan mode of Northeast China and the Fengyang huagu mode of Anhui Province. In other forms the performers stand, including dagu, uaiban, zhuizi, and qingyin. Singing is accompanied by musical instruments, clappers or drums. Instruments include sanxian, sihu and yangqin.

This text is about Chinese opera and drama art. It is unique, and no equivalent English expressions can be found for the Chinese artistic terms. As a result, Pinyin turns out to be the best way of advocating excellent Chinese art on the international stage. "Quyi" consists of many modes and schools; the further explanations of the latter contribute to the development of comprehensive, positive, influential images of the former. It can be argued that Pinyin expressions, used appropriately in a set, do not prevent foreign readers from understanding Chinese culture positively.

Xiao and Fan (2012: 145-148) advocate that discourse ideology be classified into deference, solidarity and hierarchy. In fact, we can even more specifically classify discourse ideology into crediting, neutralizing and devaluating. The Chinese Pinyin expression "*the Duanwu Festival*" rather than "*the dragon-boat Festival*" is an example to credit Chinese culture. Wang (2004: 36) argues for "psychological recognition", which means the translator's recognition of his or her own culture and values. Webster (2011) defends for the Pinyin expressions of *"Heung Gong Ya*n" using the local dialect rather than *"Hong Kong people"*. In Webster's view, *"Hong Kong people"* is a name given by westerners, alluding to something inferior or second-class citizenry while *"Heung Gong Yan"*, based on Cantonese, can better show the local people's discursive power and positive cultural identity.

5. Reflections on Pinyin in translation

As a means of nominalization, Pinyin can have a positive impact on the publicity of Chinese culture. Nevertheless, some principles should be abided by in using Pinyin for translation from Chinese to English.

First, the principle of gains and losses should be noticed. As Halliday (1994: 353) mentions, nominalization can be seen as a condensation of clause information and hence some information may be lost in using it. For instance, *"alcohol impairment"* can be explained as *"alcohol impairs"* or *"alcohol is impaired"*. In the former case "alcohol" is an agent while in the latter case it is a patient. The semantic difference is obvious here. The Pinyin expression *"fangnu"* emphasizes distinctive Chinese features, but may be confusing to foreign readers. However, those curious foreign readers may spend much time searching for relevant information in order to understand the expression. In this way, information gap is bridged. Zeng (2009: 59-60) mentions that the Chinese expression *"buzheteng"* should be translated as *"no faith wavering, no effort relaxation, and no self-defeating campaign"*. In fact, *"buzheteng"* is an expression imbued with Chinese cultural features. If we simply use the Chinese Pinyin *"buzheteng"* in the translated texts, it may evoke a response in foreign readers as *"encore"* (a French expression meaning *"one more"*) in English readers. The target language readers can find information complementary to *"buzheteng"* in translated texts. The English language is not purely British or American in these days. The publicly-accepted term "world Englishes" indicates that English expressions are pluralized in modern times, justifying the usage of Pinyin in translation from Chinese to English.

The following example is from www.cntv.cn. In this example, both Pinyin and domesticated English versions are used, which can be seen as a complementation in rendering clear information:

This is a bill of exchange of the Daoguang Period of the Qing Dynasty which is now collected in China Piaohao Museum). The bill of exchange is rectangular. There are characters of "Hui Quan" on the right while "Xin Xing" on the left. It was the unified form of bill of exchange at that time.

Here, "*a bill of exchange*" means the same as "*Piaohao*". Such a translation strategy or technique highlights Chinese culture while offering clear information to foreign readers or viewers.

Second, the adequacy of cultural information should be stressed. In texts Pinyin should show its information transparency and adequacy. Zheng (2010: 86-87) proposes four elements in text translation: wholeness, focus, logical rationality, and cohesion and coherence. If these four elements are adopted, the cultural information conveyed by Pinyin can be revealed.

Take the following Chinese tourism publicity for example (from www.bjta.gov.cn):

Kunninggong (Palace of Earthly Tranquility), built in 1420, is one of three palaces in the living zone of the Forbidden City. Both in 1514 and 1596, Kunninggong was destroyed by fire disasters, and in 1605 it was rebuilt. In 1798, it was also restored. Qianqinggong traditionally is representative of yang and Kunninggong is yin. These two palaces are built together to show the harmony and oneness of heaven and earth.

In this part, "*Kunninggong*" is a Chinese palace. In translating this name, both Pinyin and English annotation ("*Palace of Earthly Tranquility*") are used. The Pinyin expression reminds readers that this is a text about Chinese culture while the English annotation indicates the meaning of the Chinese name sounding blessing. The purpose of advocating Chinese culture is strong by means of this translation strategy. Also, in the above excerpt, "*yin*" and "*yang*", which are two important Chinese philosophical notions, are mentioned, followed by clear English explanations of their meanings. The intention of using Pinyin to show unique Chinese ideas is fully conveyed in this way.

"*Guizhou Minzu University*" rather than "*Guizhou University for Nationalities*" may be confusing to foreign readers at the first sight, but if they read an introduction to the university, they may find ample information about minority people and cultures, interethnic studies and minorities-oriented work. Then, they should be able to understand the term. Seen in this way, Pinyin can activate readers' interest in consulting relevant information, which is a means of recontextualization. Part of the introduction to Guizhou Minzu University is:

Guizhou Minzu University was founded on May 17, 1951 under the jurisdiction of the People's Government of Guizhou Province. As one of the first minorities-oriented universities in China, it is a key provincial higher education institute sponsored jointly by the People's Government of Guizhou Province and the State Commission for Nationalities, awarded the rank of A in the 2007 National Evaluation of Undergraduate Education. The university is located in Huaxi District of Guiyang City, a scenic spot with green mountains and bright waters renowned as "Pearl of Yunnan-Guizhou Plateau".

Two more examples can be shown to illustrate the use of "*minzu*" for minorities-oriented university in China: *Minzu University of China*, and *Yunnan Minzu University*.

There are also cases where "*nationalities*" rather than "*minzu*" is used, but the text concerned highlights minority features, for instance:

Southwest University for Nationalities; South-central University for Nationalities; Guangxi University for Nationalities; Northwest University for Nationalities; Dalian Nationalities University. Part of the introduction to South-central University for Nationalities is: Located in Wuhan, the political, economic, financial, cultural, educational and transportation center of central China，South-Central University for Nationalities (SCUN) is a comprehensive and key university directly under the administration of the State Ethnic Affairs Commission. Founded in 1951 as South-Central College for Nationalities, it was renamed as South-Central University for Nationalities in March, 2002. Since its foundation, SCUN has implemented the educational policy and ethnic policies of the state. It is committed to cultivation of talents for ethnic communities while following general principles of higher education, thus achieving a rapid and comprehensive development in past decades.

In this introduction, *the State Ethnic Affairs Commission* and *ethnic communities* show that this university places much emphasis on the education of minority people.

Pinyin expressions are understood through a sound context of information. With sufficient information in texts, the messages that Pinyin indicates are properly revealed. The above two instances—one with Pinyin and the other without Pinyin indicate that Pinyin is a context-bound device in Chinese-to-English translation. As Xin and Lai (2010: 32-39) argue, recontextualization is an extension of intertextuality. The strategy of Pinyin rooted in message communication corresponds to the principle of cultural information adequacy.

Third, contextual applicability is worth noticing. At present there are a considerable number of Pinyin expressions in English, such as "*guanxi*" (nepotism) and "*baozi*" (Chinese food). This situation is much related to the impact of media and publicity. In the adoption of Pinyin in such a context, however, there are some variations worth noticing.

Sometimes, straightforward Pinyin expressions are adopted without further English explanations. This might be related to the extensive influence of Chinese culture. Consider the following two examples (from www.chinadaily.com.cn):

> Five hundred people practice tai chi at the "Kung Fu Tai Chi Day" fair held at Plaza de Cesar Chaves Park in downtown San Jose on May 18, 2014;
>
> US first lady Michelle Obama practices tai chi with students at Chengdu No 7 High School during her visit in Chengdu, Sichuan province, March 25, 2014.

Here, "*tai chi*" is a Chinese fitness program well known abroad; like "*kung fu*", it has entered the English vocabulary, and in using it no further explanation is needed. Notice here that the Pinyin expression is in the fashion of the Wade system—somewhat modified from Putonghua—standard Chinese pronunciation.

However, contrasts always appear in the translation of Chinese culture to English. "*The Book of Change*" is not called "*Yijing*", and "*The Analects*" can hardly be as equal as "*Lunyu*". Both terms, translated in the strategy of domestication, have been widely accepted, and they are not advised to be reformulated in Pinyin. "*Bank of Communications*" cannot be changed to "*Jiaotong Bank*", as the former has been widely accepted and Pinyin does not work here. In contrast, "*Shanghai Jiaotong University*" is not called "*Shanghai University of Communications*" though in both expressions the same Chinese word "*jiaotong*" is involved. There are indeed some cases where both Pinyin and English expressions are accepted or used together in translating a text from Chinese to English, for example (from www.chinadaily.com.cn):

> In the final scene of the movie, Fearless, Jet Li, who plays Huo Yuanjia, one of China's historical heroes and wushu (martial arts) master, wins a Shanghai tournament by beating four international champions, his feat raising the spirits of his countrymen.

This example shows that "*martial arts*" may be more familiar to foreigners while "*wushu*"— a Pinyin expression is gaining understanding and recognition internationally.

6. Conclusion

In this paper nominalization is explored, and Pinyin expressions in the Chinese-to-English translation are found to demonstrate the features of nominalization. Pinyin has its advantages, i.e. highlighting cultural distinctiveness, and its disadvantages, i.e. information adequacy to be revealed through texts. Considered overall, Pinyin is conducive to introducing Chinese culture to foreign readers and highlighting Chinese discursive power. It can be said that the explorations on Pinyin complement the translation studies from such perspectives as domestication, foreignization, translator's subjectivity and eco-translation. The present research indicates that linguistics and translatology can interact with each other and yield beneficial results.

References

Chen, X. W. 2013. Cultural self-awareness and audience's awareness in translation for international publicity. *Chinese Translators Journal*, 2, 95-100.

Feng, Y. L. 1996. *A Brief History of Chinese Philosophy*. Beijing: Beijing University Press.

Ge, C. G. 1980. On translation from Chinese to English. *Translation Correspondence*, 2.

Halliday, M. A. K. 1994. *An Introduction to Functional Grammar*. London: Edward Arnold Limited.

Halliday, M. A. K. and C. Matthiessan. 2008. *Construing Experience Through Meaning: A Language-based Approach to Cognition*. Beijing: The World Publishing House.

Heyvaert, L. 2003. *A Cognitive-Functional Approach to Nominalization in English*. Berlin/New York: Mouton de Gruyter.

Hu, Z. L. 2004. *Cognition and Metaphor*. Beijing: Beijing University Press.

Liu, X. Q. 2010. Transliteration and dissolution of translatability limitation. *Chinese Science & Technology Translators Journal*, 2, 38-41.

Nida, E. A. 2004. *Language, Culture, and Translating*. Shanghai: Shanghai Foreign Language Education Press, 75-77.

Ru, F. 2008. Study on the translation strategies of the Analects. *Chinese Translators Journal*, 5, 50-54.

Slingerland, E. 2003. *Confucius Analects*. India: napolis Hackett Publishing Company, Inc.

Sun, W. L. and D. B. Tian. 2008. Review of Feng Youlan's translation ideas. *Chinese Translators Journal*, 2, 30-32.

Wang, H. Y. 2004. On the background variables in literary translation criticism. *Chinese Translators Journal*, 2, 36.

Wang, N. 2006. *Preface for "Perspectives: Translatology Studies"*. Beijing: Qinghua University Press.

Webster, J. 2011. Reflections on Hong Kong's culture of translation. In Guizhou Minzu University (ed.) *Collection of China-ASEAN Education Communication Week Proceedings* (unpublished).

Xiao, T. J. and Y. L. Fan. 2012. Discourse ideology and C-E translation of national culture. *Journal of Hunan University of Science and Technology*, 6, 145-148.

Xin, B. and Y. Lai. 2010. Analysis of intertextuality: theories and methods. *Modern Rhetoric*, 3, 32-39.

Zeng, L. S. 2009. The contextual implications and English translation for "buzheteng". *Chinese Science & Technology Translators Journal*, 3, 59-60.

Zheng, L. Q. 2010. Four elements in text translation. *Chinese Translators Journal*, 1, 86-87.

Zhu, A. B. 2010. Cultural interpretation of "fangnu" in English translation. *Chinese Science & Technology Translators Journal*, 3, 53-56.

A Transitivity Analysis of Manipulation in Howard Goldblatt's Translation of Red Sorghum

Chengyu Liu[a] and Xu Zhang[b]

[a]Southwest University, China; [b]Southwest University, China

1. Introduction

With the rapid development of China in the past few decades, Chinese contemporary literature has won more worldwide publicity than ever before. In 2012, the Nobel Prize in Literature was awarded to Mo Yan "who with hallucinatory realism merges folk tales, history and the contemporary" (http://www.nobelprize.org/nobel_prizes/literature/laureates/2012/). Apart from this remarkable literary style, it is generally acknowledged that the successful translation of many of his works into various foreign languages also contributes to Mo Yan a distinct fame at home and abroad (Hu 2010; Xie 2012). Among his various works, *Hong Gaoliang Jiazu* is one of the most prominent. Its English version *Red Sorghum,* translated by the renowned American translator Howard Goldblatt, has won such extensive recognition in the Western world that Mo Yan remarked that "My novel could have been translated by someone else and published in the United States, but the English version would never have been so beautifully translated, if not for him." (Mo 2000: 473). The preeminent translation, however, does not necessarily mean the absolute fidelity to the source text (Xie 2012; Xu 2013). Even Goldblatt himself admits that translation is a kind of treason and rewriting is inevitable in the translation process (Goldblatt 2002), which suggests that rewriting activities have really occurred in his translation.

The present paper aims to scrutinize Glodblatt's manipulation in the translation of *Red Sorghum* by revisiting the Rewriting Theory from the perspective of systemic functional linguistics to explore how rewriting strategies are linguistically realized in translation, focusing particularly on the transitivity system. It seeks to illuminate how the translator's lexicogrammatical choices would possibly help reconstruct the characters and plots in the translated version, thus achieving the various manipulation goals of translation.

2. Theoretical background

2.1 Rewriting theory

Translatology is a newly developed inter-disciplinary research area dating from the second half of the 20th century. Traditionally, translational studies focused on linguistic comparison and text analysis. In the 1980s, however, translatology experienced "a Cultural Turn", i.e. a shift from a more formalist approach to one that places more emphasis to exterior factors. Accordingly, a number of new approaches emerged, such as the Poly-system Theory, the Manipulation Theory, the Feminist Translation Theory and the Post-colonial Translation Theory, among which, Lefevere's Rewriting Theory is one of the most representative theories. It holds that translation is a rewriting of an original text and that all rewritings, whatever the intention, reflect some ideology and as such manipulate literature to function in a given society in a given way (Lefevere 1992: viii).

According to Lefevere (1992), there exist two controlling mechanisms in a literary system. While the first mechanism largely functions within the literary system by employing professionals and poetics as its operative force, the other mechanism functions outside the literary system, with patronage and ideology as its key factors. Hence the following three constraining factors are proposed in the Rewriting Theory: (i) ideology, which refers to "the conceptual grid that consists of opinions and attitudes deemed acceptable in a certain society at a certain time, and through which readers and translators approach texts." (Hermans 2004: 126-127) (ii) poetics, which is the dominant concept of what literature should be, or is allowed to be, in a given society, and is a code which makes literary communication possible (ibid: 127). (iii) patronage, which, as an organic component of literary system, can be understood as "the powers (persons, institutions) that can further or hinder the reading, writing, and rewriting of literature" (ibid: 15) to make sure that the literary system does not fall too far out of step with other systems in the society.

As a whole, the Rewriting Theory focuses more on translation strategies than on linguistic choices in the manipulation. As a remedy, this paper adopts the perspective of Systemic Function-al Linguistics (SFL) so as to scrutinize the lexicogrammatical realizations (particularly realiza-tions through the TRANSITIVITY system) involved in various kinds of rewriting in translation.

2.2 Transitivity system

In SFL, language is defined as a social semiotic. Accordingly, language is interpreted "within a sociocultural context, in which culture itself is interpreted in semiotic terms—as an information system" (Halliday 1978: 2). On the other hand, language is a complex semiotic system which has various levels (or strata), with semantics and lexicogrammar as the content strata and phonology and phonetics as the expression strata. (Hallday 2014: 24-27) As for the basic functions of language in relation to the ecological and social environment, SFL holds that language has three metafunctions: ideational (i.e. making sense of our experience), interpersonal (i.e. enacting interpersonal relations) and textual (i.e. enabling the first two modes of meaning in the construction of a text) (Halliday 1985).

With focus on the experiential metafunction, language can be employed to construe human experiences. In SFL, transitivity is defined as one of the major lexicogrammatical realizations of the experiential function. It is "a system for describing the whole clause rather than just the verbal group" (Thompson 1996: 78). According to Halliday (1985: 106), transitivity "specifies the different types of process expressed in the clause and potentially consists of three components: process, participants in the process and circumstances associated with the process." The concepts of process, participant and circumstance, in the Hallidayan perspective, are semantic categories which explain in the most general way how the real world is represented as linguistic structures. The transitivity system in English falls into six process types: (i) material process (i.e. process of "doing"): this expresses the notion that some entity "does" something – which may be done "to" some other entity; (ii) mental process (i.e. process of "thinking"): this deals with the internal world of the mind; (iii) relational process (i.e. process of "being"): this displays the relationship among entities. It can be subdivided into three types: intensive, circumstantial and possessive; (iv) behavioral process (i.e. process of "behaving"): this describes the psychological and physiological behaviors, like breathing, dreaming, laughing, etc.; (v) verbal process (i.e. process of saying): this covers any kind of symbolic exchange of meaning; and (vi) existential process (i.e. process of existing): this presents that something exists or happens.

To sum up, SFL emphasizes the study of language in relation to its ecological and social environment. In translating, the translator does not merely do the word-by-word rephrasing between the source text and the target text. Instead, he should try to employ his meaning potential to understand the source text and then choose appropriate lexicogrammatical resources to produce the target text. In this process, he has to rewrite the text in accordance with the ideology deemed acceptable in a given society, the dominant poetic concept in the society, and the will of the patronage, i.e. the powers (individual persons and/or institutions) which can further or hinder the reading, writing, and rewriting of literature.

In the field of translation studies, House (1997) and Reiss (2000) seek to construct a framework of translation criticism in the metafunctional approach. Halliday (2010) also realizes the applicability of SFL in translation studies, and reveals that translators achieve functional equivalences through lexicogrammatical choices. At home, Hu et al. (1989: 188-189) proposes that a successful translation must realize equivalence in the three metafunctional aspects. Huang (2002a, 2002b, 2002c) analyzes the English translation of some classical Chinese poems from the perspective of the three metafunctions.

The previous literature indicates that the Rewriting Theory and SFL have both made remarkable achievements in translation studies. Whereas the Rewriting Theory mainly deals with problems on the macro level, such as culture, ideology, poetics, etc. SFL attempts to illuminate translation from the micro angles by examining the dynamic choices involved in interpreting and then analyzing metafunctional equivalences between the source text and the target text. However, as Snell-Hornby (2001: 25) observes, "neither the perspective of literary studies nor the methods of linguistics have provided any substantial help in furthering translation studies as a whole".

In the present paper, a systemic-functional approach is proposed for the study of Goldblatt's translation of *Red Sorghum* by incorporating SFL into the Rewriting Theory. This is postulated as a "middle way" to root downwardly in linguistic factors and meanwhile look upwardly at cultural elements, seeking to reveal how various rewriting strategies are realized via the translator's conscious or unconscious choices in the transitivity system.

3. Transitivity analyses of manipulation in Red Sorghum

The English version *Red Sorghum* proves to be a successful but not necessarily faithful translation. Based on the assumption that various manipulation activities occur in Goldblatt's translation, the current section intends to detect how Goldblatt realizes his rewriting goals via choices in the transitivity system.

3.1 Transitivity rewriting dictated by ideology

According to Lefevere (1992), ideology exerts a great impact on rewriting in translation, which is in turn reflected on the translator's lexicogrammatical choices, including choices in the transitivity system. In Goldblatt's translation of *Red Sorghum*, the transitivity rewriting dictated by ideology can be dictated by religion, politics and ethical values.

3.1.1 Transitivity rewriting dictated by religion

It is generally acknowledged that the Chinese people are either atheists or adhere to a traditional religious belief which can be roughly characterized as a blending of Confucianism and Taoism on the one hand and Buddhism on the other. In contrast, religious beliefs, especially Christianity, exert considerable influences on the Western society. When translating, Goldblatt has to take the target readers' religious preference into account. Hence, in his translation, information that eulogized the Mighty God was appended while information that might go against Christianity was altered or even omitted, so as to be in conformity with the Western readers' religious beliefs, as shown in the following examples:

(1) a. 余司令说：" <u>你好大的命</u>！ "（《红高粱家族》，莫言 2007：8）

b. "<u>The heaven has smiled on you</u>," Commander Yu said. (*Red Sorghum*, Goldblatt 1993: 12)

Table 1　Transitivity rewriting in Example (1)

你	好大的命！
Carrier	Process/Attribute

The heaven	has smiled	on you.
Behaver	Process	Circumstance

As is displayed in Table 1, the original underlined Chinese clause in (1a) entails the Buddhist belief of destiny to praise someone who could have good luck to avoid disaster. It could be regarded as an attributive relational process with the Process " 是 " (is) conflated with the Attribute, revealing that the writer attributes one's good fortune to destiny, thus conveying the traditional Chinese value of Fatalism and Karma.

However, in its English version (1b), the underlined clause is rewritten into a behavioral process of the God. The introduction of "heaven" brings the religious color. When getting into trouble, the Westerners, unlike the Chinese who are used to resorting to destiny, always turn to the God for help. In such sense, Goldblatt's rewriting proves to be reasonable, because when God behaves a kind smile, the human could survive then.

From the transitivity analysis, we can see that these two clauses belong to different processes. The original one is a relational process that attributes good fortune to destiny, while the translated version rewrites it into a behavioral process to imply that God behaves kindly to save people. This manipulation clearly illustrates Goldblatt's adaptation of religious information to cater to the Western readers' religious preference.

In the following example, the same image may convey quite different or even opposite religious senses and consequently the translator has to rewrite the transitivity system to cater to the intended readership.

(2) a. 奶奶在唢呐声中停住哭，像聆听天籁一般，<u>听着这似乎从天国传来的音乐</u>。（《红高粱家族》，莫言 2007: 39）

b. Grandma's stopped crying at the sound of the woodwind, <u>as though commanded from on high</u>. (*Red Sorghum*, Goldblatt 1993: 45)

Table 2　Transitivity rewriting in Example (2)

[奶奶]	听着	从天国传来的音乐
Behaver	Process	Matter

(the sound of the woodwind)	commanded	from on high
Sayer	Process	Circumstance

The background of the cited clause is that the grandmother just learns from the bearers that the man she is going to marry is a leper. The original underlined clause (2a), as analyzed above, is a behavioral process, describing grandmother as listening to the sound of woodwind. Since she does not like the man she is going to marry, the sound of woodwind makes her feel like the weeping from the heaven. This image, however, would be in conflict with the Christian belief, in which the music from the heaven should always be pleasant, soft and melodious. The description of the weeping sounds from heaven is far from being pleasant, and would cause a weird sense among Western readers.

To avoid arousing such undesirable feelings, Goldblatt rewrites this sentence into a verbal process, in which the original "(unpleasant) sound of the woodwind" is altered into a "command from God", the original "天国" (heaven) is obscured into "on high" to further weaken the offensive senses to God since the target readers hold that the heaven is always the representative of peace, harmony and happiness and cannot bear any unpleasant description for it.

From the transitivity analysis of the above two examples, it can be figured out that in order to avoid conflicts with the target readers' religious beliefs, the translator has to rewrite the relevant lexicogrammatical expressions as a means of ideological manipulation.

3.1.2 Transitivity rewriting dictated by politics

The story told by Mo Yan in *Hong Gaoliang Jiazu* took place during the Anti-Japanese War between 1937 and 1945, which involved Japanese invaders and puppet troops on the one hand and the Communist Party of China, the Kuomintang Party and other political forces on the other. A faithful translation of this complicated political situation would be laborious and somewhat sensitive. To cope with that such historical information, Goldblatt chooses to omit or replace the original expressions with some expressions with less political weight to achieve a relatively less politically related tone, as can be seen in the following example:

(3) a. 父亲对我说过，任副官八成是个共产党，除了共产党里，很难找到这样的纯种好汉。(《红高粱家族》，莫言 2007：52)

b. Father told me that Adjutant Ren was a rarity, a true hero. (*Red Sorghum*, Goldblatt 1993: 59)

As is shown in Table 3, two processes are involved in the original Chinese version: one is attributive relational process which characterizes Adjutant Ren as a Communist Party member; the other is a material process which states that such a real hero could only be found in the Communist Party. The two processes contribute to presenting the fact that Adjutant Ren is a rarity since he is a member of the Communist Party, which is so superb that real fighters will be attracted to join. The pro-communist attitude could be easily seen from such a description. However, in the target culture, such praises may arouse political disputes. Therefore, Goldblatt rewrites the original two processes into only one attributive relational process, in which the attribute "a Communist Party member" is replaced by "a rarity, a true hero". As a result, Adjutant Ren is depicted as a hero rather than a Communist Party member. By cutting down the processes and shifting the attributes, Goldblatt successfully gets rid of the subtle political information.

Table 3　Transitivity rewriting in Example (3)

任副官	（八成）是	个共产党，
Carrier	Process	Attribute
除了共产党里，	[你]（很难）找到	这样的纯种好汉。
Circumstance	Process	Goal

Adjutant Ren	was	a rarity, a true hero.
Carrier	Process	Attribute

Besides process shifts, participant shifts within the same process clause could also serve as a strategy for rewriting. For example:

(4) a. 我们村里一个九十二岁的老太太对我说："……女中魁首戴凤莲，花容月貌巧机关，调来铁耙摆连环，挡住鬼子不能前……"（《红高粱家族》，莫言 2007：8）

b. An old woman of ninety-two sang to me "…the beautiful champion of women, Dai Fenglian, ordered rakes for a barrier, the Jap attack broken …" (*Red Sorghum*, Goldblatt 1993: 13)

Example (4a) is said by a woman who has survived from the Japanese massacre. From her narration, we can see how hateful she is to the Japanese soldiers and how admirable she is to the heroine Dai Fenglian. In the original clause, an active material process is employed to relate the heroic event: the Actor "Dai Fenglian" is so witty and courageous that she defeats the Goal "the Japanese invaders". The hatred of Japanese invaders and the praise for the Chinese heroine are emotively phrased in the process. Goldblatt holds an objective view on such an event. Although the material process is retained, he eliminates the Actor "Dai Fenglian" and puts the Goal "the Jap attack" to be the subject to form a middle voice, seeking to achieve a relatively objective statement about the event: the Japanese attack is broken. The political concern may be one of the convincing reasons for such rewriting.

Table 4　Transitivity Rewriting in Example (4)

[戴凤莲]	挡住	鬼子
Actor	Process	Goal

The Jap attack	broken
Goal	Process

From the transitivity analysis of the above two examples, we can conclude that in order to avoid political disputes, the translator may rewrite the relevant lexicogrammatical expressions as a means of political manipulation.

3.1.3 Transitivity rewriting dictated by ethical values

Due to their distinct traditions, cultures and customs, Chinese and Westerners hold different ethical values. Goldblatt, as a sinologist, is fully aware of such differences and manipulate those distinctions deliberately, as can be seen in following example:

(5) a. 爷爷说："你打开天窗说亮话，<u>要我干什么？</u>"（《红高粱家族》，莫言 2007：157）

b. "Let's open the skylight and let the sun shine in," granddad said. "<u>Just what do you have in mind</u>?" (*Red Sorghum*, Goldblatt 1993: 208)

Table 5　Transitivity rewriting in Example (5)

（你）	要	我	干	什么?
Actor	Process	Goal		
		Actor	Process	Goal

What	(do) you	have	in mind?
Attribute: Possessed	Carrier: Possessor	Process	Circumstance

What	(do) you	think?
Phenomenon	Sensor	Process

The original clause complex is extracted from a conversion in which Jiang, a government military officer, tries to persuade granddad, a leader of an illegal military force, to merge his force into Jiang's. According to the traditional Chinese ethical value, Jiang is superior to granddad, for Jiang is a government military officer while granddad is a bandit. The officer is granted the right to command a bandit. Mo Yan adopts a material process in the original version, in which Jiang is the Actor, while granddad is the Goal, displaying an image that the officer is oppressing the bandit. Nevertheless, Westerners believe in the doctrine that "Human beings are created equal" and consequently, the original clause complex cannot be literally translated lest it may impose the Chinese ethical value on Western readership.

To get rid of the sense of oppression, Goldblatt rewrites this clause complex into a relational process "what do you have in mind". It is actually an ideational metaphor of the congruent mental process "what do you think". The original material process, which conveys a sense of the addressee's imposition on the addresser, is rewritten by the translator into a relational process, which is a metaphor of a mental process, thus evaporating the flavor of oppression in the original expression.

3.2 Transitivity rewriting dictated by poetics

In literary translation, translators will inevitably encounter the incompatibility between the poetics of a source text and that of the target text. In most cases, translators are likely to cater to the dominant poetics in the target culture by employing of the following rewriting strategies in the transitivity system.

3.2.1 Simplification

Due to distinct aesthetic expectations towards literature, the translator sometimes has to simplify or delete some expressions or description deliberately to cater to the preference of the target readers. Such simplification can also be identified in Goldblatt's translation of *Red Sorghum*. Generally speaking, Chinese writers tend to attach more importance to detailed descriptions than Westerners. Consequently, Goldblatt has to simply some descriptions in the English version to avoid redundancy, as is illustrated in the following example.

(6) a. 他确实是饿了，<u>顾不上细品滋味，吞了狗眼，吸了狗脑，嚼了狗舌，啃了狗腮，把一碗酒喝得罄尽</u>。（《红高粱家族》，莫言 2007：90）

b. He was ravenously hungry, so <u>he dug in, eating quickly until the head and the wine were gone</u>. (*Red Sorghum*, Goldblatt 1993: 102)

Table 6   Transitivity rewriting in Example (6)

[他]	顾不上细品 吞了 吸了 嚼了 啃了	滋味， 狗眼， 狗脑， 狗舌， 狗腮，
Actor	Process	Goal
把一碗酒	喝得	罄尽。
Goal	Process	Circumstance

he	dug in,	eating	quickly	until the head and the wine were gone.
Actor	Process	Circumstance		
		Process	Circumstance	Circumstance

In the source text, the author employs six consecutive material processes to portray every detail of grandpa's eating actions vividly. Moreover, the six process verbs " 品 " (taste)," 吞 " (swallow), " 吸 " (suck up), " 嚼 " (chew), " 啃 " (nibble) and " 喝 " (drink) are all hyponyms of the action " 吃 " (eat), contributing to a parallel structure that impresses readers how hungry grandpa is. Besides, each process verb is collocated with a distinct Goal denoting a certain part of the dog's body to indicate different eating manners. These six material processes serve to form a subtle description of eating actions.

But in the target text, Goldblatt compresses the six vivid material processes into only one material process, and neglects the Goal, the dog's body. A superordinate word "eat" replaces all the details of the eating action. From a Chinese translator's view, it is a pity to lose all the exquisite description. But for Goldblatt, a Western translator who cares more about the aesthetic flavor of Western readers, he probably thinks that those detailed descriptions are redundant and thus simplifies them into one efficient process. Besides, the behavior of eating a dog is too cruel for Westerners, as a dog is a symbol of loyalty in Western culture. Therefore, the Goal "dog" is eliminated in the translated version.

From the above analysis, it can be seen that aesthetic tendencies differ between Chinese and Westerners. It seems that Chinese people would like to appreciate parallel structures and delicate descriptions interwoven in literary works while Westerners pay more attention to the clear interpretation of the plot. This accounts for the simplification in the rewriting.

3.2.2 Narrative rewriting

According to Lodge (1994), fictional language changes between two basic forms of narration, i.e. showing and telling. By employing pure showing, the narrator quotes the character's talking and doing directly, while pure telling is just the narrator's own comments. Showing is usually regarded as a narrative discourse while telling is deemed as non-narrative. For Chinese and Western authors and literary critics, the balance between narration and non-narration differs. Mo Yan, a typical Chinese contemporary writer, would like to tell his understanding and evaluation in the novel. Contrarily, showing is a skill quite important to contemporary American fiction-writers. Confronting the distinct narrative preference, Goldblatt has transitivity to make his own choice, as is shown below.

(7) a. 奶奶死后面如美玉，微启的唇缝里皎洁的牙齿上，托着雪白的鸽子用翠绿的嘴巴啄下来的珍珠般的高粱米粒。<u>奶奶被子弹洞穿过的乳房挺拔傲岸，蔑视着人间的道德和堂皇的说教，表现着人的力量和人的自由、生的伟大爱的光荣，奶奶永垂不朽！</u>（《红高粱家族》，莫言 2007：119）

b. Even in death her face was as lovely as jade, her parted lips revealing a line of clean teeth inlaid with pearls of sorghum seeds, placed there by the emerald beaks of white doves. (*Red Sorghum*, Goldblatt 1993: 135)

From the contrast of the above two versions, we can see that the underlined part in the original expressions have been deleted in the English translation. The underlined part involves five consecutive processes, showing Mo's comments on Grandma's courageous behaviors. But Goldblatt chooses to omit those processes, leaving an objective and concise description, as the Western readers do not appreciate such intrusive comment tones. The narrative rewriting by Goldblatt also implies that it is necessary for a translator to consider the narrative language and patterns if he attempts to subvert the dominant poetics and narrative patterns through translation, especially when the translated text does not comply with the "horizon of expectation" of most readers.

3.3 Inappropriate rewriting

Although Goldblatt is a senior sinologist, he still cannot understand all the Chinese euphemisms and metaphors generated by Chinese culture and ideology. This probably accounts for some inappropriate rewritings that occur in his translation.

(8) a. 罗汉大爷说："<u>行了，老啦！</u>"（《红高粱家族》，莫言 2007：255）

b. "Okay", Uncle Arhat said, "<u>she is old now</u>." (*Red Sorghum*, Goldblatt 1993: 191)

As the Chinese are conservative when talking about death, euphemism is always introduced on such occasions. As is shown in Table 7, the original Chinese clause is a material process, euphemizing the death of someone in an indirect tone. The process verb "老" (literally meaning "getting old") here is a euphemism indicating death (i.e. pass away). Nevertheless, Goldblatt wrongly perceives the verb "老" literally as an attribute meaning "getting/being old", thus misinterpreting this clause as an attributive relational process, and then mistranslating it as "She is old now".

Table 7　Transitivity Analysis of Example (8)

[她]	老啦!
Actor	Process

she	is	old	now.
Carrier	Process	Attribute	Circumstance

The following is an example to demonstrate Goldblatt's misunderstanding of Chinese cultural metaphors.

(9) a. 奶奶不理孙五，向倚在墙边的一个长脸姑娘走去。长脸姑娘对着奶奶吃吃地笑。奶奶走到她眼前时，她忽然蹲下身，<u>双手紧紧地捂着裤腰</u>，尖声哭起来。她的两只深潭般的眼睛里，跳出疯傻的火星。（《红高粱家族》，莫言 2007：46）

b. Ignoring Sun Five, Grandma walked up to a long-faced girl leaning against the wall, who smiled weakly, then fell to her knees, <u>wrapped her arms tightly around Grandma's waist,</u> and began to cry hysterically. (*Red Sorghum*, Goldblatt 1993: 52)

Table 8　Transitivity analysis of Example (9)

[她]	双手紧紧地	捂着	裤腰
Actor	Circumstance	Process	Goal

(She)	wrapped	her arms	tightly around Grandma's waist
Actor	Process	Goal	Circumstance

This episode is extracted from the situation that Sun Five has raped a girl, and Grandma tries to comfort her. In the traditional Chinese ethic value, people hold quite conservative views on sex, holding that virginity is crucial to maids. The loss of virginity has driven that girl to insanity. In the original version, Mo Yan adopts a material process in the underlined sentence: "捂"

(wrap) is the process verb, while "裤腰" (trouser belt) is the Goal. In the Chinese language, the subconscious action of wrapping the trouser belt can be used as a metaphor to indicate the girl's mental shadow of the rape. However, Goldblatt fails to perceive the metaphorical connection between rape and the action of "wrapping her trouser belt". Consequently, he rewrites the "weird" action as "wrapped her arms tightly around Grandma's waist". The process remains to be a material one, but the Goal has been changed into "Grandma's waist", displaying that the weak girl is turning to Grandma for help. Unfortunately, the mental sufferings of the raped girl described in the source text have been completely ignored in the target text.

4. Conclusion

Translation is a process of language choices in a certain ecological and sociocultural environment. In order to make the translated text well received by the target readers, the translator must take into account the prevailing ideology and poetic preferences of the target readership as well as the patronage. Consequently rewriting is inevitable in translation in that the translator has to manipulate the lexicogrammatical expressions so as to cater to the reading habits and expectations of the target speech community. In this sense, translation is intrinsically a process of linguistic accommodation towards the target readership as well as a betrayal from the source text.

As the above analysis indicates, Howard Goldblatt's translation of Mo Yan's works, particularly of *Red Sorghum*, is a successful example for Chinese literary works to be well received by the English-speaking readers. A comparison between Mo Yan's original work and Goldblatt's translated text indicates that ideological and poetic rewriting prevails as a means of cross-cultural communication. The various manipulation strategies are linguistically realized by a series of conscious or unconscious choices among the available lexicogrammatical expressions and discourse patterns.

To ensure effective cross-cultural communication via translation, an ideal translator should be one who not only has a comprehensive knowledge of the source language and culture to ensure a profound understanding of the source text in relation to its ecological and sociocultural environment, but is also equipped with profound knowledge of the reading habits and subtle expectations of the target readership so that he or she can employ appropriate rewriting strategies to achieve the various manipulation goals.

By incorporating the Hallidayan systemic functional linguistics with Lefevere's Rewriting Theory, we can scrutinize the various rewriting strategies as well as their lexicogrammatical realizations in the translated texts. In the present paper we merely focus on the manipulation in the transitivity system. Further research should be conducted on rewriting in other linguistic systems, such as manipulation on interpersonal and textual resources, to illuminate how effective rewriting can be linguistically realized in translation to facilitate cross-cultural communication in this increasingly globalized world.

References

Goldblatt, H. 1993. Trans. *Red sorghum* (by Mo Yan). New York: Penguin.

Goldblatt, H. 2002. The writing life. *The Washington Post*, April 28, BW10.

Halliday, M. A. K. 1978. *Language as Social Semiotic: The Social Interpretation of Language and Meaning*. London: Edward Arnold Limited.

Halliday, M. A. K. 1985. *An Introduction to Functional Grammar*. London: Edward Arnold Limited.

Halliday, M. A. K. 2010. Pinpointing the choice: Meaning and the search for equivalence in translated texts. In A. Mahboob and N. K. Knight (eds.), *Appliable linguistics*. 13-24. London: Continuum.

Halliday, M. A. K. 2014. *Halliday's Introduction to Functional Grammar*. Revised by C. M. I. M. Matthiessen. New York: Routleldge.

Hermans, T. 2004. *Translation in Systems: Descriptive and System-oriented Approaches Explained*. Shanghai: Shanghai Foreign Language Education Press.

House, J. 1997. *Translation Quality Assessment: A Model Revisited*. Tubingen: Gunter Narr Verlag.

Hu, A. 2010. Translator model, translating strategy, and the "going out" project to promote Chinese literature abroad: With American sinologist Howard Goldblatt as an exemplar. *Chinese Translators Journal*, 6, 10-16.

Hu, Z., Y. Zhu, and D. Zhang. 1989. A Survey of Systemic Functional Grammar. Changsha: Hunan Education Press.

Huang, G. 2002a. A metafunctional-experiential analysis of Du Mu's poem "Qingming" and its translated versions. *Foreign Languages and Their Teaching*, 5, 1-6, 11.

Huang, G. 2002b. An interpersonal analysis of Du Mu's "Qingming" and its translated versions. *Foreign Language Education*, 3, 34-38.

Huang, G. 2002c. A logical analysis of Du Mu's "Qingming" and its translated versions. *Foreign Languages and Translation*, 2, 1-6.

Lefevere, A. 1992. *Translating Literature: Practice and Theory in a Comparative Literature Context*. Beijing: Foreign Language Teaching and Research Press.

Lefevere, A. 2004. *Translation/history/culture: A Sourcebook*. Shanghai: Shanghai Foreign Language Education Press.

Lodge, D. 1994. *The Art of Fiction: Illustrated from Classic and Modern Texts*. London: Penguin Books.

Mo, Y. 2000. My three American books. *World Literature Today*, 74, 473.

Mo, Y. 2007. *Red Sorghum*. Beijing: People's Literature Publishing House.

Reiss, K. 2000. *Translation Criticism, The Potentials and Limitations*. Manchester: St. Jerome Publishing Company.

Snell-Hornby, M. 2001. *Translation Studies*. Shanghai: Shanghai Foreign Language Education Press.

Thompson, G. 1996. *Introducing Functional Grammar*. London: Edward Arnold Limited.

Xie, T. 2012. The enlightenment of successful translation of Mo Yan's works into foreign languages. *Wenhui*

Book Review, December 17, 3.

Xu, F. 2013. Mo Yan's winning the Nobel Prize in Literature and the translation of his works. *China Reading Weekly*, June 19, 14.

Chinese Grammar Engineering: A Case Study of Mandarin Grammar Online

Chunlei Yang[a] and Dan Flickinger[b]

[a]Shanghai International Studies University, China;
[b]Stanford University, USA

1. Introduction

Deep linguistic processing, or constraint-based processing, has grown steadily in the past 15 years. Much successful experience has been accumulated in terms of linguistic theoretical support, cross-language coverage, implementation techniques, commercial applications, etc. (Oepen et al. 2002; Bender 2008; Bender et al. 2010) However, the deep linguistic processing of Chinese is still in its beginning stage. A precise computational grammar is the key to deep linguistic processing. It is a complex system including lexicon definition, phrase and grammar rules, semantic representation, information structure, etc. Lu (2000) points out that the processing of Chinese "badly needs more research in lexical, syntactic and semantic studies and should focus on how to process clauses."

He also emphasizes the practicality of adopting HPSG as a theoretical framework for the analysis of Chinese. Mandarin Grammar Online (ManGO) is a computational grammar whose characteristics meet Lu's goals for future Chinese processing in the sense that 1) ManGO is based on sound ontological studies and therefore lays a solid theoretical foundation for further development and application; 2) based on Head-driven Phrase Structure Grammar (HPSG) (Pollard and Sag 1987, 1994; Sag et al. 2003; Boas and Sag 2012), ManGO (Yang and Flickinger 2014) is highly lexicalized and treats syntax and semantics as equally important components; 3) ManGO now is capable of handling clauses and has potential for discourse analysis (e.g. information structure). Besides ManGO, Zhang et al. (2012) are also developing a Mandarin computational grammar named Mandarin Chinese Grammar (MCG). Like ManGO, it is still a medium-sized grammar under active development (Fan et al. 2013).

2. HPSG-based grammar engineering for deep linguistic processing

Feng (2005:1) believes that although linguistic processing is an interdisciplinary field involving contributions from computer science, mathematics, psychology, logic, statistics, etc., its basis should be in linguistics. In the past 15 years or so, many prominent Chinese linguists have reiterated the significance of employing HPSG to analyze and describe Chinese, not only because this framework has a strong descriptive capacity of a wide range of language phenomena, but also because its description is more natural (Fang and Wu 2003:40). In addition, Lu (2006) points out that because rich grammar features are absent in Chinese but Chinese lexical features are very important and effective, HPSG is extremely suitable for Chinese analyses. For example, in Mandarin, grammar concepts like agreement and case are absent, inflectional forms are comparatively rare, and tense and aspects are mainly realized with a very small number of lexical forms such as *le*, *zhe* and *guo*. Finally, according to a report by the European Expert Advisory Group, HPSG is the linguistic theory most widely used in computational linguistics (Uszkoreit et al. 1996).

2.1 The DELPH-IN collaboration

The Deep Linguistic Processing with HPSG Initiative (DELPH-IN)[1] was cofounded around the beginning of the new millennium by the Language Technology Lab of German Research Center for Artificial Intelligence (DFKI) and the Linguistic Grammar Online (LinGO) Laboratory at the Center for the Study of Language and Information (CSLI) of Stanford University. Currently there are 18 renowned member institutions across the world, including the Computer Laboratory of Cambridge University, the Language Technology Group of Melbourne University, the Linguistic Intelligence Research Group of NTT Communication Science Laboratories, the Division of Linguistics and Multilingual Studies of Nanyang Technological University and the Computational Linguistics Laboratory of University of Washington. They have all adopted HPSG and Minimal Recursion Semantics (MRS) as their models of formal linguistic analysis.

MRS is a representation for computational semantics, introduced in (Copestake et al. 2005). It is suitable for parsing and generation and can be implemented in typed feature structure formalisms such as HPSG. It has been integrated with many HPSG grammars, for research and teaching, and for applications.

One of the three main research areas of DELPH-IN is multilingual grammar engineering. Eight resource grammars and nine medium-sized grammars have been developed so far[2].

2.2 Grammar foundation: grammar matrix

The Grammar Matrix (Bender 2002) is a framework for the rapid prototyping and scalable development of broad-coverage, precision, implemented grammars for diverse languages[3] and has been under active development for more than a decade. It includes types defining the basic language-independent feature geometry and technical devices, types associated with MRS, general classes of rules, and types for basic constructions. ManGO is one of several DELPH-IN grammars based on the Grammar Matrix.

2.3 Semantic representation: minimal recursion semantics

MRS is a representation for computational semantics, introduced in Copestake et al. (2005). It is suitable for parsing and generation and can be implemented in typed feature structure formalisms such as HPSG. It has been integrated with many HPSG grammars, for research and teaching, and for applications. In its design, it provides for underspecification of quantifiers and scopal operators, enabling the encoding of the constraints on meaning that a word or construction imposes, without imposing the need for spurious syntactic ambiguity where the syntax does not fully specify such constraints.

3. The development of ManGO

The development of ManGO consists of three stages, namely, linguistic ontological analyses, encoding the ontological findings in a computable formalism (e.g., Type Description Language, TDL) and implementation with software including the Linguistic Knowledge Building (LKB) system (Copestake 2002) as a development platform and [incr tsdb ()] (Oepen 2000) as a competence and performance profiling tool to assist in grammar development.

In stage 2, some specific steps were taken to build up ManGO, including grammar customization, creation of a Chinese MRS test suite, lexicon building, definition of grammar rules and MRS representation. These will be discussed in turn.

3.1 Grammar customization

Based on Grammar Matrix, ManGO starts with an online customization system[4]. It is a web-based service which prompts typological descriptions of languages and produces customized grammar fragments which are ready for sustained development into broad-coverage grammars (Bender et al. 2010). By completing questionnaires about the target language grammar, e.g., word order, number, person, gender, case, sentential negation, tense, aspect and mood, etc., this system will produce a basic but functioning grammar as the starting point for a more precise and larger-scale grammar produced by manually adding new definitions by the developers for expanded coverage.

3.2 Creation of a Chinese MRS Test Suite

The MRS test suite is a short but representative set of 107 sentences, originally in English, designed to illustrate some of the MRS phenomena. At present there are translated and suitably adapted test suites for 12 languages.

The basic information of this Chinese MRS test suite includes parts of speech (POS), grammar phenomena, example sentences, etc. There are some differences between the English and Chinese versions. For example, English tense and aspect are indicated by particular verb forms and additional auxiliary verbs, whereas Chinese tense and aspect are indicated by functional words like *le*, *zhe* and *guo*. In some cases, there is more than one interpretation of tense and aspect when it is indicated by *le* in a sentence. Also, some phenomena such as agreement, gerunds, particles, etc. in the English test suite are not present in its Chinese counterpart.

3.3 Lexicon building

A lexical entry in ManGO usually consists of three parts, namely, lexical type, orthographical form and semantic representation. Take zhui1gan3 (" 追 赶 "; chase) for example. Each part is written on a separate line as follows:

追赶 _v := v_trans-verb-lex &
    [STEM < " 追赶 " >,
    SYNSEM.LKEYS.KEYREL.PRED "_zhui1gan3_v_rel"].

In ManGO, syntactic concepts are written with lower-case letters, for example, *v_trans* for transitive verb, *arg* for argument, *lex* for lexical entry, *crs* for sentence-creating lexical entry, *s* for sentence, etc. On the first line, the lexical item is defined as a transitive verb. On the second line, STEM is the orthographical form. On the third line, SYNSEM is the concatenation of syntax and semantic constraints; LKEYS refers to the pointers into the semantics of lexical items; KEYREL is the pointer to the main relation in RELS; PRED is the predicate name of the relation. The period between the features indicates the path from outer to inner levels in the feature structure defining the attributes and values of the lexical item.

In Chinese lexicon building, words with more than one part of speech are very common. Take the lexical form *le* ("了") as an example. It is generally agreed that this form splits into le_1 and le_2 (Lv 2000:351-358; Wu 2002; Chen 2007). The former indicates the perfective when it appears after a verb and the latter helps to create a sentence when it appears at the end of a sentence. Two lexical entries should therefore be added. Consequently, for a simple "NP + VP" structure like (1), there are two parsing results illustrated in Figures 1 and 2.

1)

(猫　　　　叫　　　　　了

　Mao1　　　jiao4　　　le

　Cat　　　　meow　　　le

"The cat has meowed. / The cat meows."

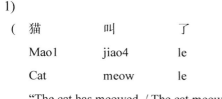

Figure 1　Parsed tree and feature structure for *le₁*

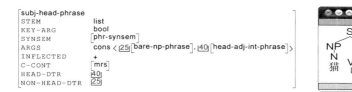

Figure 2　Parsed tree and feature structure for *le₂*

We also investigate and define the characteristic features of some POS subtypes, such as quantifier, reflexive, locative, predicative adjective, determiner, compound, dative, preposition, etc. in the lexicon of ManGO.

3.4 Definition of type hierarchy and rules

With lexical items provided, we then need to define the type hierarchy and rules so that lexical items can be combined to produce larger well-formed constructions. For example, the type definition of transitive verb is as follows. First, we stipulate that transitive verbs involve two arguments (the two elements of the list value of the ARG-ST feature in the lexical type definition below) whose heads are both nouns. This transitive verb type also identifies the semantic index of the first element of the argument structure (normally the subject) with the appropriate role (ARG1) of the two-place predication introduced by the verb.

v_trans-verb-lex := transitive-verb-lex.

transitive-verb-lex := main-verb-lex & transitive-lex-item &

　　[SYNSEM [LOCAL.CAT.VAL.COMPS < #comp >,

　　　　LKEYS.KEYREL.ARG1 #index],

ARG-ST < [LOCAL [CAT.HEAD **noun**,

CONT.HOOK.INDEX #index]],

#comp &

[LOCAL.CAT [VAL [SPR < >,

COMPS < >],

HEAD **noun**]] >].

Then in the following type we establish the link between the semantic index of the second argument and the appropriate role (ARG2) in the two-place predication supplied by the transitive verb which instantiates this type.

transitive-lex-item := basic-two-arg-no-hcons &

[ARG-ST < [ ],

[LOCAL.CONT.HOOK.INDEX ref-ind & #ind2] >,

SYNSEM.LKEYS.KEYREL.ARG2 #ind2].

As for phrase rules, take the "numeral +classifier" construction and bare NP as an example. In Chinese, the "numeral +classifier" construction can serve as a full NP such as yi1zhi1 ("一只"; one + classifier) in (2):

2)

(猫　　　追赶　　　一　　　只

Mao1　　zhui1gan3　yi1　　zhi1

Cat　　chase　　one　　CL

"The cat chases one."

To enable the grammar to parse (2), we need a number of phrase rules illustrated in Figure 3.

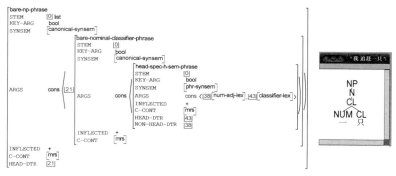

Figure 3　Parsed tree and feature structure for *yizhi*

In the feature structure of Figure 3, item [38] is yi1 (" 一 "; one) and item [43] is zhi1 (" 只 "; CL). The definition of two phrase rules are employed to form the ultimate bare NP. First, the following rule allows a classifier to be the head of a "numeral + CL" structure. In the HEAD value, the type is the underspecified supertype of several parts of speech, where *j* is for adjective, *r* for adverb, *p* for preposition and *d* for determiner.

head-spec-h-sem-phrase := basic-head-spec-phrase & head-final
  [SYNSEM.LOCAL.CAT.VAL.COMPS #spcomps,
    HEAD-DTR.SYNSEM.LOCAL [CAT.HEAD +**jrpd**,
          CONT.HOOK #hook],
  NON-HEAD-DTR.SYNSEM.LOCAL.CAT.VAL.COMPS #spcomps,
  C-CONT.HOOK #hook].

The next rule allows a classifier phrase to be a bare NP. Note that the type +*jd* has three subtypes in ManGO, namely, *det* (determiner), *adj* (adjective) and *classifier*.

bare-nominal-classifier-phrase := basic_bare-nominal-phrase &
  [ARGS < [SYNSEM.LOCAL.CAT.HEAD +**jd** &
      [MOD < [LOCAL.CONT.HOOK [LTOP #ltop,
          INDEX #index]] >]] >,
  C-CONT.HOOK [LTOP #ltop,
    INDEX #index]].

3.4.3 Basic syntactic rules

To form clauses, we need some basic syntactic rules such as the "subject + HEAD" rule and "HEAD + complement" rule illustrated in Figures 4 and 5, respectively:

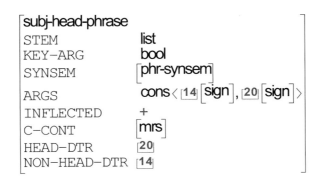

Figure 4　Feature structure for "subject + HEAD" rule

In Figure 4, item [14] is the non-head daughter subject, positioned before item [20], which is the head daughter (the single element of ARGS) for lexical rules.

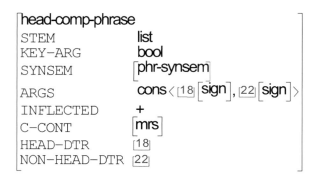

$$
\begin{bmatrix}
\text{head-comp-phrase} \\
\text{STEM} \quad\quad\quad\quad \text{list} \\
\text{KEY-ARG} \quad\quad \text{bool} \\
\text{SYNSEM} \quad\quad \begin{bmatrix}\text{phr-synsem}\end{bmatrix} \\
\text{ARGS} \quad\quad\quad \text{cons} \langle [18]\begin{bmatrix}\text{sign}\end{bmatrix}, [22]\begin{bmatrix}\text{sign}\end{bmatrix} \rangle \\
\text{INFLECTED} \quad + \\
\text{C-CONT} \quad\quad \begin{bmatrix}\text{mrs}\end{bmatrix} \\
\text{HEAD-DTR} \quad [18] \\
\text{NON-HEAD-DTR} \quad [22]
\end{bmatrix}
$$

Figure 5   Feature structure for "HEAD + complement" rule

Likewise, Figure 5 defines the "HEAD + complement" rule as the head daughter [18] comes before the non-head daughter [22] as its complement.

These two rules should suffice for basic SVO structures, as in (3) and Figure 6 and SVC structures, as in (4) and Figure 7.

3)

(张三   追赶   李四

  Zhang1-San1   Zhui1gan3   Li3si4

  Zhang-San   chase   Li-Si

"Zhang San chases Li Si."

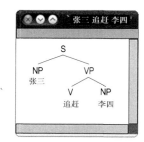

Figure 6   Parsed tree for an SVO structure

4)

(张三   认为   李四   在   叫。

  Zhang1-San   ren4wei2   Li3-Si4   zai4   jiao4

  Zhang-San   think   Li-Si   progressive   shout

"ZhangSan thinks Li-Si is shouting."

Figure 7   Parsed tree for an SVC structure

The semantic representations (the MRSs) for each of these sentences are composed by having each syntactic rule simply append the lists of relations of its daughters, starting at the bottom with the lexically supplied relations, normally one per lexical item. Syntactic rules may also add semantic content directly, but the basic rules discussed here only gather up the semantic contents of their daughter words and phrases, leaving the precise constraints on semantic composition to be ensured by the rich lexical types, as illustrated above for transitive verbs.

To parse some characteristic Chinese structures, we need to add more rules based on the customized grammar. For example, the customized grammar fails to parse (5):

(5)

追赶	猫	很	无聊。
Zhui1gan3	mao1	hen3	wu2liao2
Chase	cat	very	boring

"Chasing the cat is boring."

Judging from its parsing flowchart (Figure 8), we can see no syntactic rules are available that allow the VP *zhui1gan3* (" 追赶 "; chase) as a subject.

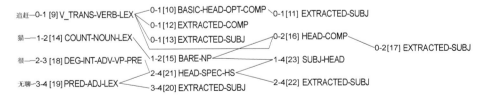

Figure 8   Parsing flowchart of *Zhui1gan3 mao1 hen3 wu2liao2*

Actually, a VP as the subject of a clause is very common in Chinese. In inflectional languages like English, non-predicative forms like gerunds help identify a subject with a verb stem such as (6) and Figure 9.

(6) Chasing the cat is boring.

Figure 9   Parsed tree and feature structure for Chasing the cat is boring

The absence of such inflectional forms as gerunds in Chinese leads to the parsing failure of (5), at least with the basic rule inventory produced directly by the Grammar Matrix as directed by the language-specific information supplied at the outset. To tackle language-specific phenomena such as this, we need some additional device to allow a VP as a subject. In ManGO, we make use of the list type *olist* to achieve this purpose. The type *olist* is a list of optional arguments, and we define the SUBJ value for normal verbs in Mandarin to be an *olist,* so that a VP can be treated as a saturated constituent, and hence as a suitable phrase to serve as the subject of a clause. With this treatment of verb phrases and the resulting interaction with the standard subj-HEAD phrase, ManGO successfully parses (5) as illustrated in Figure 10.

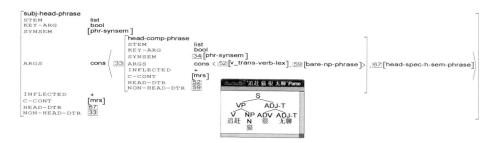

Figure 10   Parsed tree and feature structure for Zhui1gan3 mao1 hen3 wu2liao2

ManGO covers a fairly wide range of language phenomena in Chinese, including tense, aspect & mood, genitives, prepositional modifiers, resultative constructions, coordination, pivotal constructions (Yang 2013), embedded clauses, questions, imperatives, passive voice, nominalization, the *ba*-construction, etc. The results of batch parsing and inspection in the resulting [incr tsdb()] profile show that ManGO fully covers the Chinese MRS test suite (Yang & Flickinger 2014); However, the parsing efficiency still needs improvement. Take coordination structure as an example. In matrix.tdl file, the definition of coordination is as follows.

This shows that the heads of the coordinated daughters are both verbs. Based on this definition, ManGO produces 6 readings of (7).

s-coord-phrase := event-coord-phrase &

[SYNSEM.LOCAL.CAT.VAL.SUBJ < >,

SYNSEM.LOCAL.CAT.HEAD verb,

LCOORD-DTR.SYNSEM.LOCAL.CAT.HEAD verb,

RCOORD-DTR.SYNSEM.LOCAL.CAT.HEAD verb].

(7) 狗   到   了   而且   叫   了
     gou3   dao4   le   er2qie3   jiao4   le
     dog   arrive le   and   bark   le

"The dog arrived and barked."

Some of the readings such as the one in Figure 11 are natural; some others such as the one in Figure 12 are not.

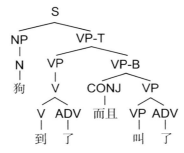

Figure 11   A natural parsing of *gou3 dao4 le er2qie3 jiao4 le*

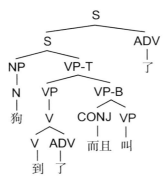

Figure 12   An unacceptable parsing of *gou3 dao4 le er2qie3 jiao4 le*

To improve the parsing efficiency, i.e, to enable the grammar to produce the acceptable readings only, more linguistic constraints are needed for more exact definitions. For example, to avoid the reading in Figure 12, the exact scope of *le* in a coordination structure needs to be defined. What's more, we expect some other readings like the one in Figure 13.

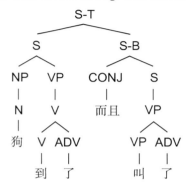

Figure 13　An expected parsing of *gou3 dao4 le er2qie3 jiao4 le*

Considering the fact that Chinese is a pro-drop language, the right coordinated daughter is possibly a clause with an omitted subject "the dog". However, if we add a definition to allow a clause to be a coordinated daughter, the number of readings of (7) increases dramatically to 21. Some of the readings are not acceptable and again this shows that the definition of coordination needs to be refined. Finally, punctuations could also affect the parsing of coordination structure.

4. Conclusion

ManGO is one of the first medium-size computational grammars of Chinese, expressed in a rich and detailed theoretical framework, HPSG. It serves as a bridge and effective carrier of the interdisciplinary studies across formal grammatical theory and computational linguistics. Constructed using the Grammar Matrix, it produces a compositional semantic analysis for each parse, expressed in Minimal Recursion Semantics, and has the additional desirable property of being a fully reversible grammar, meaning that it can be used to generate well-formed sentences of Mandarin from input MRSs, in addition to its more conventional use in parsing.

Our next steps will include further linguistic analysis and implementation to expand its coverage of interesting and frequently occurring phenomena, and also to improve its processing efficiency. These efforts at greater coverage will include building an expanded test suite with a richer inventory of phenomena, and enlarging the lexicon, while work on efficiency will focus on reducing the number of unwanted parsing results by fine-grained tuning of the rules, and by examination of unwanted output sentences when using the grammar for generation.

Acknowledgement

This research is supported by Innovative Research Team and General Program Foundation of Shanghai International Studies University "The Multidimensional Studies of Quantification in Language" No. 2013XJGH023.

Notes

1. http://www.delph-in.net
2. http://wiki.delph-in.net/moin/GrammarCatalogue
3. http://www.delph-in.net/matrix/
4. http://www.delph-in.net/matrix/customize/matrix.cgi

References

Bender, Emily M. 2008. Grammar engineering for linguistic hypothesis testing. In N. Gaylord, A. Palmer, and E. Ponvert (eds.). *Proceedings of the Texas Linguistics Society X Conference: Computational Linguistics for Less-Studied Languages*. 16-36. Stanford: CSLI Publications.

Bender, E. M., D. Flickinger, and S. Oepen. 2002. The Grammar matrix: An open-source Starter-Kit for the rapid development of cross-linguistically consistent broad-coverage precision grammars. In Carroll, John, Nelleke Oostdijk, and Richard Sutcliffe (eds.). *Proceedings of the Workshop on Grammar Engineering and Evaluation at the 19th International Conference on Computational Linguistics*. 8-14. Taipei, Taiwan.

Bender, E. M., S. Drellishak, A. Fokkens, L. Poulson, and S. Saleem. 2010. Grammar customization. *Research on Language & Computation* 8, 23-72.

Boas, H. C. and I. A. Sag. 2012. *Sign-Based Construction Grammar*. Stanford: CSLI Publications.

Chen, X. 2007. The discerning of the grammatical meaning of Le1 from That of Le2. *Language Teaching and Linguistic Studies*, 5, 54-60.

Copestake, A, D. Flickinger, C. Pollard, and I. A. Sag. 2005. Minimal recursion semantics: An introduction. *Journal of Research on Language and Computation*, 4, 281-332.

Fan, Z., H. Wang, and J. Zhang. 2013. Review of head-driven phrase structure grammar. *New Technology of Library and Information Service*, 4, 40-47.

Fang, L. and P. Wu. 2003. A review of head-driven phrase structure grammar. *Language Teaching and Linguistic Studies*, 5, 31-43.

Feng, Z. 2005. Academic position of natural language processing. *Journal of PLA University of Foreign Languages*, 3, 1-8.

Lu, J. 2000. Aspects of language use in China. *Applied Linguistics*, 2, 4-8.

Lu, J. 2006. On interface between syntax and semantics. *Journal of Foreign Languages*, 3, 30-35.

Lv, Shuxiang. 2000. *Xiandai Hanyu Babai Ci* (Eight Hundred Major Words in Contemporary Chinese).

Beijing: The Commercial Press.

Oepen, S., D. Flickinger, J. Tsujii, and H. Uszkoreit. 2002. *Collaborative Language Engineering: A Case Study in Efficient Grammar-based processing.* Stanford, CA: CSLI Publications.

Pollard, C. J. and I. A. Sag. 1987. *Information-based Syntax and Semantics, Volume 1: Fundamentals.* Stanford: CSLI Publications.

Pollard, C. J. and I. A. Sag. 1994. *Head-Driven Phrase Structure Grammar.* Chicago: The University of Chicago Press.

Sag, I. A., T. Wasow and E. M. Bender. 2003. *Syntactic Theory: A Formal Introduction.* Stanford: CSLI Publications.

Uszkoreit, H., T. Becker, R. Backofen, J. Calder, J. Capstick, L. Dini, J. Dörre, G. Erbach, D. Estival, S. Manandhar, A. M. Mineur, G. van Noord, and S. Oepen. 1996. *The EAGLES Formalisms Working Group. Final report (Technical Report).* Saarbrücken, Germany: German Research Center for Artificial Intelligence (DFKI).

Wu, L. 2002. On Le1 and Le2. *Studies in Language and Linguistics*, 1, 23-27.

Yang, C. 2013. Deep linguistic processing of pivotal construction: From linguistic design to implementation. *Journal of Foreign Languages*, 3, 69-78.

Yang, C, and D. Flickinger. 2014. Mango: Grammar engineering for deep linguistic processing. *New Technology of Library and Information Service*, 3, 57-64.

Zhang, Y., R. Wang, and Y. Chen. 2012. Joint grammar and treebank development for mandarin Chinese with HPSG. In *Proceedings of the 8th International Conference on Language Resources and Evaluation (LREC'2012).* 1868-1873. Istanbul, Turkey.